ROMANCING THE BARD

The Taming of the Shrew, 1962: Kate Reid as Katharine, John Colicos as Petruchio

STRATFORD
Romancing the Bard
AT FIFTY

Martin Hunter

DUNDURN PRESS
TORONTO • OXFORD

Editor: **Ramsay Derry**
Copy Editor: **Martin Boyne**
Design: **V. John Lee**
Printer: **Transcontinental**

National Library of Canada Cataloguing in Publication Data

Hunter, Martin, 1933-
    Romancing the bard: Stratford at fifty

ISBN 1-55002-363-2

1. Stratford Festival (Ont.)—History. I. Title.

PN2306.S7H85 2001   792'.09713'23   C2001-902253-0

1   2   3   4   5   05   04   03   02   01

THE CANADA COUNCIL | LE CONSEIL DES ARTS
FOR THE ARTS | DU CANADA
SINCE 1957 | DEPUIS 1957

Canada

ONTARIO ARTS COUNCIL
CONSEIL DES ARTS DE L'ONTARIO

We acknowledge the support of the **Canada Council for the Arts** and the **Ontario Arts Council** for our publishing program. We also acknowledge the financial support of the **Government of Canada** through the **Book Publishing Industry Development Program** and **The Association for the Export of Canadian Books,** and the **Government of Ontario** through the **Ontario Book Publishers Tax Credit** program.

Printed and bound in Canada.⊕
Printed on recycled paper.
www.dundurn.com

Dundurn Press   Dundurn Press   Dundurn Press
8 Market Street   73 Lime Walk   2250 Military Road
Suite 200   Headington, Oxford,   Tonawanda NY
Toronto, Ontario, Canada England   U.S.A. 14150
M5E 1M6   OX3 7AD

CONTENTS

*For Judith, who has
played opposite me
in the theatre of life
for a very long run.*

Colours in the Dark, 1967

The Stratford Festival's legendary tent theatre was
raised annually from 1953 to 1956

FOREWORD

Dan Needles

HAVING GROWN UP IN THE THEATRE, I am uncertain about the possibility of making sense of any theatre's past by talking to the participants themselves. The people who make theatres tick are supposed to be masters of illusion, not careful custodians of documented fact. Their business is to make things a bit larger than life, not to record it faithfully. But then again, we already have factual histories of the Stratford Festival and we pretty much know who did what play in what year and what people said about it in the papers. No one has yet attempted a journalistic history of the Festival based on conversations with the people who made it happen and drawing from a long personal association with the institution. At least, not until Martin Hunter's *Romancing the Bard.*

Martin Hunter is in a very good position to offer us such a history. He is a theatre professional, a journalist, a faithful patron of the Festival for the past forty-nine years, and he enjoys close friendships with many of the participants, past and present. One of those friendships is with the Needles family. We know Martin from the Toronto Children Players, Hart House Theatre, CBC, and life behind the scenes at Stratford, where my father, Bill Needles, has been on stage ever since he played Second Murderer in *Richard III* in 1953.

My earliest memories of Stratford date from those halcyon days of the mid-1950s, running around the corridors as a snotty-nosed child, watching actors throw cricket balls on the lawn in the morning, darts in the green-room in the afternoon, and drinks in each other's faces at the parties after the show. Most of all, I remember a parade of vivid personalities who make up the pantheon of early professional Canadian theatre.

Theatre in those days was still very much a fringe occupation in Canada, and almost all of the actors who didn't have a private income lived a hand-to-mouth existence. My father's working season always divided into two distinct phases: "When will this show be over?" and "Will I ever work again?" He was one of the few to actually own a house, which was in Toronto. He lived in a succession of apartments for the first 25 seasons at Stratford because he never thought he'd be asked back. Our house in the city became a hotel in the winter for unemployed Stratford actors trying to find work at the CBC.

Actors largely ignore children unless they can be drafted to do parts on stage. I rebelled from this calling early on and refused to perform professionally after age 12. As my father says, "He ran away from the circus and joined an insurance company." But I saw all the plays every year, usually watching from a seat in the back of the lighting booth or sitting on the top step of Aisle 6. I was an enthusiastic member of the children's underground festival of stage fighting which took place in Douglas Campbell's backyard every summer with wooden swords and garbage can lids. And I slept on couches and under tables through boisterous late-night debating sessions, long after the audiences and other normal people had gone to bed.

After cricket and darts, an actor's favorite recreation is storytelling. I have listened to stories about Stratford ever since I could walk. And one of the first big words my mother taught me was "apocryphal." I have listened to many completely different stories of the people and plays at Stratford, each one placing the storyteller squarely at the centre of the action. With so many conflicting versions of what happened, I often find it difficult to form a clear picture of life at Stratford. But then, I'm not so sure if one clear picture is really all that necessary. As a playwright, I have come to learn that the theatre is generally unkind to single visions.

Like E.B. White, Martin Hunter is torn between "the desire to enjoy the world (and not be de-railed by a mosquito wing) and the urge to set the world straight." In this book he does a lot of both, and we are the beneficiaries. No one enjoys the people and the stories more than he does, whether the moment is high comedy or whether he is guiding us through an issue of great seriousness. All of this helps us to understand better the history of a great institution.

THE INSUBSTANTIAL PAGEANT

"THE FACES OF THE CHILDREN WERE SPELLBOUND—their eyes, bright in the reflected light of the stage, were fixed; their jaws hung happily open as if they were hearing through their mouths. Next to them sat six elderly women. They were holding hands, sharing the romance." The words are Tyrone Guthrie's. He is describing the audience at a theatrical performance, not *Hamlet* or *Oedipus,* but a matinee of a Christmas pantomime. Guthrie believed the greatest theatre is the theatre seen in childhood, when the imagination is open to romance, to magic.

My own experience bears this out. My first live theatre was a production of *Cinderella*, given by the Toronto Children Players at Eaton Auditorium. I was five years old. I remember, as if it were yesterday, the Fairy Godmother touching Cinderella with her wand and instantly her rags vanished and she was wearing a beautiful ball gown. A gilded coach appeared. Cinderella got into it and drove away behind prancing horses. I am told that I started up the aisle, so eager was I to enter that enchanted world.

I did become part of this company a few years later, starting as an actor but soon becoming involved in backstage work as well. We revived *Cinderella.* The actress playing the role rushed behind a cupboard where we hastily stuffed her into her beautiful dress while her Fairy Godmother covered for her by twirling through a little dance downstage in a spotlight. I held the cardboard cut-out coach from behind a curtain. Cinderella opened its cardboard door, about to step inside, and the lights dimmed. No instant transformation, no prancing steeds. Never mind, I knew what I had seen at the age of five. I had felt the magic of the theatre. I still feel it from time to time.

I was lucky to discover the Toronto Children Players. It deeply influenced me and hundreds of other kids. It was run by a remarkably sensitive, imaginative, and rigorous woman, Dorothy Goulding, who inspired and challenged us, deepening our awareness through experiment in rehearsal and performance on stage of what the theatre could be. Because of her, Toronto in the 1940s was not a cultural wasteland for me but filled with exciting creative possibilities.

I spread my fragile wings, flapping them with various degrees of success at Hart House Theatre and in CBC Radio. Blossoming talent was all around me and I fell in love with talent. It was to prove to be a lifelong affair. Then suddenly Stratford burst into full bloom. It is hard to imagine what artistic phenomenon today could stir similar feelings of excitement. We were beguiled, dazzled, inspired.

I left the theatre to do other things, but somehow always came back to it. I worked at different times as actor, stage manager, director, producer, playwright. I was fascinated by the totality of theatre, how it works, its incredible complexity and unpredictability, the mystery of the elusive spark that suddenly ignites to bring a play to life, and why sometimes there is no spark, no enchantment. I went as often as I could manage to the theatre in Toronto and New York and later in London, Paris, Vienna, Mexico City, Buenos Aires, Beijing, Bali, Cochin. I became a compulsive audience member.

Guthrie believed that the audience was an essential and integral element in theatre. He even went so far as to suggest that the audience was a sort of co-creator with the actors. They must be invited to enter in and interact on many levels: identification with the characters as the story unfolds, awareness of the performers' skills and the playwright's and director's ideas and intentions. "Only in the theatre can there be established the spontaneous, personal relation between the artists and the audience, varying with scarcely perceptible technical, but quite considerable psychic variation, from performance to performance. For my part," he wrote, "I believe this reciprocity to be essential to the full enjoyment of comedy or pathos or the emotional side of tragedy."

More than once I have experienced as an actor the moment when a wave of feeling comes back from the audience to the performer. As an audience member I have frequently felt the actor speaking to me as though I were on stage and part of the action. It is a compelling moment of emotional connection. This has happened to me many times in many places, but perhaps more often at Stratford than anywhere else.

I have never been part of this remarkable theatre but I have experienced it from its beginnings through to the present. This book is a celebration of its first fifty years. It is not a detailed chronological history but a take on various aspects of its development and achievements. I have chosen to highlight about thirty productions that seem to me memorable, either for their excellence or because they marked a new direction.

Any theatre is an aggregation of individuals who come together and make it what it is by the exercise of their talents and dedication. I have been lucky to know a good many of the people of Stratford, some slightly, some well. Through them I have been able to explore many aspects of their art in the hope of enriching the experience of their large and growing audience, of which I count myself fortunate to be a member.

RICHARD III · 1953

Alec Guinness as Richard III

Director: *Tyrone Guthrie*

Designer: *Tanya Moiseiwitsch*

The Coronation Scene

Patrons and plebs, pooh-bahs and pundits converged upon a sleepy town in southwestern Ontario. Stratford greeted them with flying pennants, church bells, factory whistles, and a manufactured explosion as they strolled across the lawn outside the imposing tent erected beside the Avon.

A fanfare of trumpets that would soon come to symbolize the Festival rang out. The spectators entered the tent, filling all 1477 seats. "God Save the Queen" was sung, and a great bell clanged as the lights dimmed. A single spotlight came up on the twisted face of Alec Guinness.

Sitting astride the parapet of the balcony, which he hacked with his dagger, Guinness embarked on an intricately original delivery of his first great soliloquy, "Now is the winter of our discontent, made glorious summer…," and then lurched down onto the main stage, his body humped and contorted, his walk simultaneously halting and lascivious. The second scene, in which he seduced the Lady Anne, invested with vigorous outrage by Amelia Hall, was conducted over the gory corpse of her husband. When she spat in his face, he wiped the spittle off with his finger, then lecherously licked it.

This extravagantly repugnant detail was echoed throughout the evening when Guinness tossed the head of Hastings back and forth like a football or squashed the imaginary bodies of the Woodville family by stamping on them like bugs. William Needles and Eric House casually chewed on apples as they taunted Clarence before stuffing him into a barrel of malmsey. Richard's enemies were kicked in the head and the crotch before being thrown into a pit in the stage floor.

Guthrie's love of grotesque comedy was paralleled by his penchant for pageantry. Splendid banners unfurled in battle; choirboys swarmed down the aisles bearing huge crucifixes; at Richard's coronation his crimson robe flowed across the stage like a river of blood. The final battle was a welter of flashing swords and leaping warriors with the victorious Richmond hoisted up by his soldiers to dominate the scene from the balcony where Richard was first seen.

The applause went on and on. The members of the audience not only stood, but embraced each other in their excitement. Backstage, Guthrie told his cast, "All right, people, we just got away with it." The critics would cavil that the production was too clownish. But a great enterprise had begun. Actors and audience both felt the theatre work its magic. For fifty years they would keep coming back for more.

Richard on the battlefield

READY, AYE, READY

I T WAS A MOST UNLIKELY VENUE FOR A MAJOR ARTISTIC ENTERPRISE. The little city of Stratford in southwestern Ontario was a railway junction with a few major industries that packed meat, crafted furniture, and bottled soft drinks. The social life of its 18,000 residents revolved around a half dozen churches of different denominations; its recreational passion was hockey. It had been the scene of a major strike in the Great Depression and had acquired the reputation of being a centre for Communists. Otherwise it seemed unremarkable. And by the early 1950s it was seriously in decline.

Tom Patterson returned from Europe after the war and determined to do something to reverse the fortunes of his native town. Why not take a leaf from the English Stratford-upon-Avon and start a Shakespeare Festival? Many of his fellow townspeople thought him "a bit touched," including the editorial writer of the local newspaper, *The Beacon Herald,* but Patterson was undeterred and a handful of local businessmen rallied round to support him. In his lively memoir, *First Stage,* he recalls, "By 1951 I *knew* the Festival was going to happen. I was going to make it happen." His book recounts how he came to enlist the services of the eminent director Tyrone Guthrie, the acknowledged *enfant terrible* of British theatre.

Patterson's idea had several things going for it of which he himself was largely unaware. The mood of disillusion that prevailed between the wars had been replaced by optimism and confidence. Those who had fought in Europe or kept the home fires burning had learned to face and overcome challenges, to improvise in difficult conditions. Returning veterans were given the option of going to school on subsidy, thus empowering many who would not otherwise have been able to afford "higher learning." Those with an artistic bent injected new proletarian vigour into what remained of the rather narrow and snobbish cultural scene of the thirties.

Anglophilia was rampant. Five years of singing "There'll always be an England" must have reinforced the notion of British cultural dominance. After all, English Canada began as a reaction to the United States when it declared its independence. Despite the staggering depletion of her political influence, Britain's culture bloomed as soon as the hostilities ended in 1945. Donald Wolfit crossed Canada with the shabby but grandiose Shakespearean productions he had bravely played in London amid dropping bombs during the Battle of Britain. John Gielgud toured with a glittering cast in *The Importance of Being Earnest*. The Sadler's Wells Ballet took New York by storm and its first season at Toronto's Royal Alexandra was sold out before it opened. Light-hearted fare such as Terrence Rattigan's *O Mistress Mine* provided evidence that British humour was undimmed, while the verse plays of Christopher Fry and T.S. Eliot (a pseudo-Brit but thoroughly assimilated) were hailed as evidence of a renaissance of Elizabethan-style poetic drama. But more than anything it was British films that caught the imagination of the Canadian public. The stirring patriotism of Olivier's *Henry V* and the lush romanticism of *The Red Shoes* tugged at the heart-strings while the Ealing comedies had audiences in stitches. They crowded the newly built Odeon cinemas to chuckle at *Passport to Pimlico, The Belles of St. Trinian's* and *Kind Hearts and Coronets*. And the acknowledged king of British comedy was Alec Guinness. Guthrie's inspired notion that Guinness should star in Stratford's initial season was eagerly seized upon by both the theatrical community and the press.

Theatrical activity in Canada was already burgeoning. In mid-century the acknowledged metropolis, the centre of sophistication and wealth, was Montreal. A boldly adventurous repertory theatre soon appeared there, providing opportunities for young actors such as John Colicos, Richard Easton, John Gilbert, and Christopher Plummer, known locally as "The Four Horsemen of the Apocalypse." They played at the outdoor space beside Beaver Lake on Mount Royal, in Moyse Hall at McGill, and in summer at Brae Manor in the eastern townships. Many of them also appeared at the Canadian Repertory Theatre in Ottawa.

Meanwhile in Toronto, Robert Gill was training aspiring Thespians at Hart House Theatre: Donald Davis, Eric House, William Hutt, Charmion King, George McCowan, and Kate Reid were among his protégés. Donald Davis and his brother Murray extended their acting opportunities by establishing the Straw Hat Players at Bracebridge and Port Carling in Muskoka, giving ambitious young actors an opportunity to apply the techniques learned from Gill in more commercial summer fare.

William Hutt recalls playing Vershinin in *The Three Sisters* in Ottawa when he learned that Tyrone Guthrie would be in the audience one afternoon. He had heard that Guthrie was being shown around Canada by someone called Tom Patterson. In the green-room after the performance he was surprised to discover that Tom Patterson was one of his fellow classmates from Trinity College, and the two were catching up on college gossip when a stentorian voice boomed out, "Well, young man, are you interested in acting in my company?" Hutt accepted Guthrie's offer and that was that.

Timothy Findley had a similarly brief audition, but on the first day of rehearsal he realized that the assembled company was the cream of the available crop. He and the other actors sat in rows facing a low dais on which sat Guthrie, designer Tanya Moiseiwitsch, Alec Guinness, and his co-star from the London production of *The Cocktail Party*, Irene Worth. There was an electric moment when one of the Canadian actors came up with an extraordinarily vivid reading. Guinness turned to Worth and gave her a look that signalled, "These kids are going to be all right." A bond of confidence had been forged.

The assembled company began its journey toward opening night. Costumes and props were being built, music was being written, publicity was being prepared, tickets were being sold. But how many people would be willing to make the three-hour journey from Toronto, let alone Montreal, Buffalo, Detroit or New York? Would they want to see plays by Shakespeare, one of them utterly unknown? Would the critics come to this backwater? How were visitors to be fed? What accommodation was available for those who wished to stay overnight? Above all, would the theatre be ready in time? And how was all this to be financed when there was no government support of culture and virtually no history of private subsidy?

The whole enterprise was an enormous act of faith. Guthrie believed that the Festival was successful because the timing was right: Canada was ready, willing, and (just barely) able. Tom Patterson would later write, "I think one of the reasons it's been so successful is the fact that not only myself but the committee in Stratford that was formed knew nothing about the theatre. Had we known beforehand, we probably would have thrown up our hands in holy horror. As it was, we didn't know … so we just went ahead and did it."

ALL'S WELL THAT ENDS WELL · 1953

Director:
Tyrone Guthrie

Designer:
Tanya Moiseiwitsch

A play by William Shakespeare that almost no one in North America had ever seen performed. The production of *All's Well That Ends Well* in the first season of the Stratford Festival was a revelation and the epitome of all the qualities least associated with the work of the Bard of Avon. It was surprising, contemporary, funny. A fairy tale with the elegance and grace of Jean Anouilh, a problem play with the wit and paradox of George Bernard Shaw, a fantasy with the rich poetic colouring of Christopher Fry. A bright and fanciful romance grounded in gritty reality.

The play chronicled the story of a clever and ambitious girl of undistinguished parentage and her pursuit of a young but callow nobleman. Its characters included an unusual mix of distinctive individuals, complex but immediately recognizable: an older woman of mature beauty, accustomed to privilege but unfailingly gracious; an aging patriarch,

above left: Eleanor Stuart
as the Countess of Rousillion
above: Irene Worth as Helena

tetchy and capricious in his illness but quickly receptive to the charms of youth and beauty; a hot-headed, immature playboy unwillingly learning from his rash mistakes; his seedy sidekick, shameless in his deceptions but somehow still attractive for his vulnerable humanity; an officious do-gooder fussily running a bed-and-breakfast; her attractive daughter, a young woman with her wits about her; and at the centre of the story a radiant young woman, brave, vulnerable but implacably determined to win the man she loves.

Alec Guinness as the King of France, Lloyd Bochner as Longaville, Robert Goodier as Dumain

The Stratford performance grew out of a clever conception: a society of climbers and poseurs cunningly explored and developed in precise detail. (Can the model have been Toronto in the 1950s?) A series of vivid images lingers in the mind. Helena dancing like an eager débutante with a bevy of charming young officers. The Widow anxiously touching up her face with a giant powder puff before her appearance at court. Parolles, a blustering old blow-hard in an out-moded dress uniform, desperately clinging to the authority he would like to imagine he once enjoyed. The spark of quick, acknowledged kinship blossoming momentarily between the disillusioned Parolles and the worldly Lord Lafeu. The King's sudden attraction to Diana and then his swift, impatient flare-up when she declines to give a direct answer to his imperious questioning.

These key moments depended upon a felicity of invention and inspired casting: the skillful use of master comedian Alec Guinness as the capricious King of France, the ebullient and audacious Douglas Campbell chosen to portray the knave Parolles, the handsome and winning Donald Harron undercutting the arrogance of the callow Bertram, Eleanor Stuart's innate dignity as the Countess, the comic invention of Amelia Hall as the Widow, and above all the radiant charisma of Irene Worth, who brought to Helena the endurance of Patient Griselda coupled with the ingenuity of Becky Sharp. Even the minor roles were admirably sketched in by such skilled actors as Richard Easton and Timothy Findley as a pair of spirited subalterns, and Eric House, tellingly comic in the tiny role of the Interpreter.

The production was a spoken symphony, or perhaps rather a concerto in which the soloist was Helena, her every speech clear and thrilling, setting the tone in her splendid first-act aria on what a lover might expect of his mistress:

There shall your master have a thousand loves,

A mother, and a mistress, and a friend,

A phoenix, captain, and an enemy,

A guide, a goddess, and a sovereign,

A counsellor, a traitress, and a dear;

Even as the ear was enchanted, the stage picture unfolded as a constantly moving delight to the eye, the clothes composing a tone-poem of subtly graduated colour, relieved occasionally by an unexpected bright splash—Parolles' garish necktie or incredibly vulgar uniform or, in the final scene, the brilliant lemon-yellow gown that revealed Helena not as merely clever but as a great beauty with every right to claim the love and admiration of her chosen lord.

The ballroom scene: Irene Worth curtsies to Alec Guinness

THE GREAT WHITE HUNTER:
GUTHRIE STALKS TALENT IN CANADA

TYRONE GUTHRIE WAS LOOKING FOR NEW WORLDS TO CONQUER. He came to Canada as Livingstone went to Africa or Gordon to China in the nineteenth century. He possessed the instincts of both explorer and general, having been trained at Wellington, an English boarding school that specialized in turning out leaders for the British military establishment. There he learned the importance of dedication to a goal, the value of filling one's time with purposeful endeavour, and the adoption of a Spartan attitude toward obstacles and hardships. He brought these attributes to the pursuit of art, specifically the art of the theatre.

By 1952, at the age of 52, he had arrived at the height of his powers and was looking to use them without hindrance and confinement. He had established himself as the most adventurous and imaginative director in England. He had worked with the major stars of the British stage: Laurence Olivier, Ralph Richardson, Sybil Thorndike, Edith Evans, and Alec Guinness. They recognized his extraordinary abilities but were not necessarily willing to accept his unquestioned leadership. Indeed, Olivier and Richardson had out-manoeuvred him at the Old Vic and appropriated his campaign to set up a National Theatre, a dream that Olivier would realize in the 1960s. Guthrie had also grown impatient with the practice of Shakespearean production in the British theatre and developed some idiosyncratic theories about classical theatre, which he was eager and indeed determined to put to the test.

One of his notions was that Shakespeare could best be presented in a theatre that resembled the one the Elizabethan dramatist had written for, where the audience surrounded the stage on three sides. This concept of Shakespearean production had its genesis in a performance of *Hamlet* starring Laurence Olivier which Guthrie had produced and which took place in the ballroom of the Marienlist hotel at Elsinore in Denmark. The performance was to have been given outdoors on the battlements of the castle of Kronberg, but torrential rain necessitated moving the performance inside. Because members of the Danish and Swedish royal families had already set out from Copenhagen and Stockholm, it was unthinkable to cancel. The show had to go on.

Guthrie charged Olivier with the task of setting up the ballroom for the performance. Olivier placed the throne at one end, designated the centre of the floor as the playing area, and specified entrances for certain actors; meanwhile, Guthrie greeted the arriving royal guests and led them in setting up chairs around the acting area. He treated the whole event as a kind of picnic, his favourite form of social occasion, much preferred to a formal dinner party. The acting company rose to the occasion with extraordinary energy and spirit. At the end of the first act Guthrie told Olivier, "Thought this was going to be a joke. Thought we'd just do one act and apologize, give everybody a glass of champagne and send them home, but everybody's taking it *far* too seriously, we'll have to go through to the end." The actors continued to improvise brilliantly as the audience watched with fascination, and although Guthrie admitted that "The end was a bit of a shambles ... pleasure flowed through the hall like warm strawberry jam."

It is significant that, although the concept of playing to an audience on three sides may have originated with Olivier, it was Guthrie who saw its potential and ran with it. He appropriated the idea of a projecting stage and experimented with it in Edinburgh, where he produced a medieval Scottish drama, *The Three Estates*. One mark of a great director is to see the genius of others' discoveries and find ways to apply and extend them. With similar immediate and intuitive perception, Guthrie saw the possibilities inherent in Tom Patterson's largely unformulated notion of producing a Shakespeare Festival in Stratford, Ontario and helped him realize it in terms that no one in Stratford could possibly have anticipated.

Though almost nobody in Canada could have known why, Tyrone Guthrie was precisely the man for the job. The people he met in Stratford were drawn to him immediately. He embodied the idea of an artistic leader as envisioned by the colonial enthusiasts who peopled the emerging arts community in Ontario at the time. He was enormously tall, and his prominent beak and glittering blue eyes gave him the air of a slightly bedraggled but exceptionally sharp-eyed eagle. He was witty, commanding, endlessly curious, and confident in his ability to take on all comers.

At the same time he was utterly without pretensions. His dress was unpredictable; he might appear wearing pajama trousers or a transparent raincoat over striped underdrawers. But whatever his garb he remained an impressive figure, full of energy and quick humour. He completely fitted people's image of the eccentric aristocratic Englishman, although in fact he was not English but a Scot who lived in Ireland, and not an aristocrat but an unabashed bohemian.

Whatever his private misgivings, Guthrie seemed never for a moment to doubt that the Festival would go ahead. His enthusiasm quickly fired the Canadians with whom he came in contact: the established cultural pundits Robertson Davies and Dora Mavor Moore, both of whom had known him previously and had recommended him to the Stratford committee; aspiring actors whom he met briefly on his exploratory visit to Canada in 1952; the committee of optimistic but theatrically naive Stratford citizens who formed the Festival Committee rounded up by Tom Patterson, to whom he gave an inspiring three-hour address insisting that they must commit themselves to a fully professional operation involving the best available talent.

Guthrie charmed them but he also challenged them. He dismissed their notion that the actors could perform in the tiny band shell beside the Avon and demanded that they construct a new kind of theatre built to his specifications and housed in an enormous tent. He left it to them to raise the money. His own financial demands were modest but the sum required seemed astronomic to the bank-managers, contractors, and soft-drink manufacturers of Stratford. Finally, Guthrie insisted that Patterson go to England to convince Alec Guinness to come as the Festival's first star player.

Guthrie gambled that the Canadians would rise to the occasion, and his gamble proved to be justified. The thrust stage, which he demanded, gave the Festival a unique character, one that attracted attention and controversy from the beginning and set a stamp of originality on the Festival that has never completely dissipated. The thrust stage was to be widely imitated, first at Chichester and then in Minneapolis, and during the 1960s in a host of other regional theatres, but even after a painstakingly accurate reconstruction of Shakespeare's own theatre was erected near the original site of the Globe on the south bank of the Thames,

Stratford retains the cachet of being the first to build such a stage in the twentieth century and its design is arguably still the most workable.

Guthrie's financial challenge confronted and began to break down the deeply held Canadian conviction that art was a domain peopled by amateurs who worked for the love of it and need not be given serious monetary support. This notion has still not been completely eradicated, as is evidenced by the ongoing struggle to erect an opera house in Toronto. (As the Austrian-born impresario Franz Kramer once said with deadly accuracy, "Toronto vants the very best NO money vill buy.")

Guthrie apparently realized that Tom Patterson's naive and apologetic air, which, as Mavor Moore pointed out, would prove so effective on so many, fired Guinness's pioneering instincts in spite of previous experience with Guthrie which had left him wary of uncritical allegiance to the great director. Guinness knew only too well that Guthrie could be domineering, manipulative and, when crossed, vitriolic, even vindictive. But Guthrie had given Guinness his first chance at stardom when he offered him the leading role in a modern-dress *Hamlet* in 1938. The two men then went their separate ways and there is evidence Guthrie was jealous of Guinness' rising fame as a film actor, but Guinness responded to Patterson's enthusiasm. He was also attracted by the prospect of a summer holiday that would benefit his son Matthew's delicate health and allow him to indulge his own passion for fly-fishing.

There was genuine affection and respect between Guinness and Guthrie, but their work together at Stratford would be marked by occasional conflict, and on one occasion they did not speak for several days. Their dispute concerned the head of Hastings, one of Richard III's victims, played by Douglas Campbell. Guinness thought Guthrie had agreed that the head should be represented by a plain cloth bag. He had worked out a bit of business in which he could "do something rather horrid by just feeling the contours of the head within the bag," and was furious when he saw on the prop-table a realistic recreation of the head of Campbell dripping in gore. He confronted Guthrie, who grandly dismissed him with "More important things to think about." After days of silence, at the dress rehearsal Guthrie came to the edge of the stage with a paper bag of rather overripe cherries and offered them to Guinness. Guinness looked at the gooey mass and remarked,

27

"Squashy, but not as revolting as Hastings' head." During the performance on opening night Guinness was handed not the bloody head but a plain cloth bag. He recalled being so moved by this that he momentarily dried.

The story illustrates both Guthrie's arrogance and his sensitivity. He was, as all directors must be, acutely aware of the inner needs and intrinsic qualities of the people he was working with. He accepted his actors for what they were and made use of what they had to offer. He did not attempt to change their conception of a role but left them to their instincts and respected their abilities to work out their own individual ideas of characterization and development. But for all that, he was not uncritical.

Constantly on the look-out for hidden meanings, new connections, more interesting patterns, he frequently changed his blocking, even to the point of coming up behind an actor in dress rehearsal and whispering, "Run round to the other side, dear boy, and make your entrance from there," thus altering the whole configuration of the scene and challenging the actors to re-think it. He frequently told actors, "You can do better than that," but when someone was having difficulties, "Never mind, dear boy, go home and think about it and come back and astonish us in the morning." He was delighted with spontaneous invention and would grin with approval, "Interesting. Keep that." His criticisms were often pungent. "Don't you realize that you're pulling the chain before you've done the job?" He could be genial or suddenly severe, mischievous or inspiring and sometimes utterly deflating, especially to established stars whose pretensions irritated him, though he was unfailingly patient with beginners and old stagers.

Occasionally he demonstrated an idea, usually in a comically overblown manner (Guinness described his acting as "operatic and consequently often execrable – wild, meaningless gestures, his arms ... seemed to bend backwards at the elbows like broken wings"), but he never tried to give an actor his performance. Rather, he assumed the stance of a patriarch presiding over an extended family. He saw the work as a progression that would continue even after opening night. Once he caught an actor writing in his script:

"What in blazes are you doing?"

"Marking in the moves, Mr. Guthrie."

"Don't. If I give you a bad move, you won't remember it and we'll think of a better one. If I give you a good move, you *will* remember it."

His commitment was to the work, not his preconception.

Often he would pay scant attention to his leading players while he devised highly detailed and vivid bits of business with the minor actors to give crowd scenes liveliness and depth. Olivier recalled, "He was always inclined to mask the central important business with all sorts of extraneous rubbish. As a leading man, you had to keep an eye in the back of your head." Guthrie believed it was the responsibility of stars to figure out how to take the stage and that if they were any good they would do so. Obviously with actors like Guinness and Olivier this confidence was justified.

Formidable, but never grandly aloof, Guthrie made himself eminently available, spending time with his actors and the ordinary citizens of Stratford. He and his wife Judy were notoriously bad cooks but enthusiastic entertainers, perhaps partly because in Canada they had no other social commitments, but also because they genuinely enjoyed people. William Needles remembers that Guthrie would not tolerate actors talking shop at parties, but delighted in charades, quiz games, and reading aloud. The Guthries established an atmosphere of a country house party that pervaded the whole first summer. Alec Guinness was impressed by the way they brought together townspeople of different persuasions, "the Anglicans and the Presbyterians and this, that and the others—they had very little to do with each other. Suddenly they were unified. I think because he *liked* them very much."

In fact Guthrie liked the whole idea of Canada. Though Tom Patterson did not know this when he first phoned Guthrie, Canada was not a completely unknown territory to the famous director. He had spent part of a year in Montreal in 1929 in the very early days of radio, before the founding of the CBC. Guthrie was hired by the Canadian National Railway to work on a series of radio dramas called *The Romance of Canada*, with scripts by the now almost forgotten playwright Merrill Denison, a ribald raconteur and bon vivant and very much a man after Guthrie's own heart. His other comrade-in-arms was the producer Rupert Caplan, who introduced him to the small acting community in Montreal and helped him recruit likely talent: not only professional actors but bellhops, elevator operators, and even a criminal, who was allowed to remain in the studio until he finished his performance and was then taken away in handcuffs by a pair of Montreal's finest.

29

At the end of the series Guthrie was given a free trip right across the country by his employer, the CNR. He later reported that it gave him "a glimpse of Canada, of its immensity and diversity and the chance to meet many kind and congenial people who have become lifelong friends. I left Canada thrilled with what I had seen, eager to return and to be somehow, at some time and in some way, a participant in the development of this land and its vast possibilities, so many of them still dormant, still undreamed—the *romance* of Canada."

Deep down Guthrie was highly susceptible to romance, not the cheap clichés of women's fiction but the noble fantasies of a latter-day Quixote. The very improbability of the Stratford adventure was a large part of its appeal to him. (His most successful productions in Canada were to be *All's Well That Ends Well, The Merchant of Venice* and *Twelfth Night*, all comedies in which the element of romance is a potent part of the mix.) He envisioned a National Theatre of Canada, travelling with a tent from coast to coast on the CNR, a vision he first conceived when he spent Christmas 1945 with his friends and former protégés at the Old Vic in the 1930s, Robertson and Brenda Davies.

But for all his love of adventure, his bold, visionary projections, his delight in the unexpected, his penchant for sudden reversals and perplexing paradox, his soaring idealism, a large part of Guthrie's authority depended upon his decisive and no-nonsense approach to whatever immediate problems presented themselves. Guthrie tilted at the windmills of convention, but he also projected a strong aura of practicality. His directions were specific and concrete, his judgments clear, quick and vividly phrased, his speech punctuated by percussive handclaps and the brisk snapping of his fingers. These incisive tendencies were no doubt innate and were further honed by years of working in difficult and marginal situations in the early days of broadcasting at the BBC, establishing theatre companies in such artistic backwaters as Belfast and Glasgow and in touring during the war years. Even the illustrious Old Vic, when Guthrie first worked there in the 1930s, was run by the tough-minded, penny-pinching Lillian Baylis. She initially saw Guthrie as too freewheeling and extravagant, but before long she recognized him as her logical successor.

Strangely, for someone who worked creating illusions in the theatre, Guthrie disliked pretence and never succumbed to the glamour of the big time. He welcomed the challenge of sowing seed on stony ground, of making the desert bloom, partly perhaps because he saw himself as an outsider. He seemed able to realize himself most fully, not in the great metropolitan centres of civilization, but in the previously unexplored and uncultivated wilderness. He had successes in London's West End and on Broadway but never settled in either. He did maintain a rough and ready flat in Lincoln's Inn where he and Judy camped out when he was working in London. It was described by one visitor as having "all the comforts of a stable in Bethlehem."

Guthrie's sense of being of an outsider, his feelings of "otherness" could be traced to a number of causes. His extreme height made him very self-conscious as a young man and probably led him to emphasize his eccentricity. His identification with his Scots and Irish heritage initially separated him from English values and mores, a separation that he later valued and cultivated.

This "otherness" encouraged him to explore foreign lands and draw from theatrical cultures as far removed from each other as Finland and Israel in an era when the majority of the English still believed that their way of doing things was the right way. Guthrie felt freer to express himself in Canada than in London's West End, and he encouraged his actors to be similarly freewheeling and exploratory. He believed that actors have a sacred duty to realize their potential by expressing themselves as fully as possible and for all his facetiousness his strong sense of the religious nature of the work of the theatre was constant and sincere.

Another aspect of his work was his undeclared homosexuality. In spite of a long and devoted marriage, a certain homoerotic sensibility underlay many of his artistic choices. It surfaced in some of his productions, notably at the Old Vic when Olivier's Iago was supposed to be in love with Ralph Richardson's Othello, at least until Richardson refused to play along. And in *The Merchant of Venice* at Stratford in 1955, Antonio was openly in love with Bassanio, an interpretation which at the time was groundbreaking. Antonio's sense of loss at the end of the play provided a poignant and highly original finish to the production.

Though he may have sympathized with Antonio, Guthrie did not see himself as a victim, nor was he interested in using his productions to further a particular cause such as gay rights (had such a thing existed at the time) or even universal tolerance. He had convictions that no doubt attracted him to certain projects, but his

31

goal was always to explore the play, to discover the text, and in doing so to delight and stimulate the audience, not to convert them or in some way to better them or the state of the world at large.

Guthrie had less the mindset of a reformer than of a general dedicated to victory, even when the odds appeared insuperable. He therefore put up with impossible rehearsal conditions in the first year at Stratford, working in a long wooden shed where rain often beat on the corrugated tin roof, drowning out the actors, while on clear days even the tiniest whisper was magnified into a roar. "Giants and giantesses seemed to be shouting through the vaults of a cathedral jointly designed by Cecil B. De Mille and Orson Welles," he would later recall. But when actors complained of these adverse working conditions, Guthrie's customary advice was, "Rise above it, dear boy."

Guthrie did not shrink from dealing with difficult situations head on. When he backed a losing horse, as inevitably sometimes happened, he faced up to the task of replacing him. When he realized that Cecil Clarke, the Englishman whom he had brought out to be general manager and his chosen successor as artistic director, bungled the direction of the 1954 production of *Measure for Measure* and failed to gain the confidence of the company, Guthrie stepped in to redirect the opening and closing scenes. (In fairness to Clarke it must be said that the star, James Mason was extremely nervous; he had not acted on the stage for over a decade and made it clear that he had come to Stratford to be directed by Guthrie, not some inexperienced novice.) Guthrie made no attempt to persuade Clarke to stay on but instead drafted in his place Michael Langham, who would prove a more determined character. When Guthrie saw that Mavor Moore, whom he had cast as Petruchio in his 1954 production of *The Taming of the Shrew,* was not able to carry out his conception of Petruchio as a sort of spineless dupe, he made the peremptory decision to recast the role with William Needles, a less well-known actor, apparently because Donald Harron pointed out that Needles looked exactly like Harold Lloyd.

Guthrie was decisive but not inflexible. He realized he could not expect to have all the good ideas and made no apology for borrowing and making use of the inspiration of others. In the end he acknowledged a primary responsibility not

32

only to his actors but to his audience. He understood that in spite of his delight in devising hilarious bits of business or sweeping panoramas of stage movement, an overview was vital to the work. The show as a whole must cohere and express the intent of the author. As a director Guthrie was both instigator and facilitator, but he always remained above all an observer or, as he himself expressed it, "an audience of one."

The image is somewhat godlike, yet Guthrie was not a supreme egotist. For all his occasional imperiousness, wrath, and hyperbole, all those who worked with him agree that he possessed a strong sense of humility and an acute awareness of the divine underlying the immediate. He himself attributed this religious element in his work to the influence of those of his ancestors who were ministers of the Scottish Kirk and, above all, to the simple faith of his mother. From youth onward he abandoned her adherence to a simple notion of right and wrong as defined by the scriptures. He also gave up on his early conviction that art should provide uplift, but he continued to believe in the power of the spirit in the theatre, especially as it played out in the performance of ritual. In his final statement on theatre, Guthrie insisted that the theatre *is* ritual, completed by the interaction of players and audience, who in responding to what is put before them become co-creators of the event.

Guthrie's belief in ritual was not just a delight in processions and vivid pageantry, though he was a master of these. In his autobiography he stated, "The purpose of the theatre is to show mankind to himself, and thereby to show man God's image." It was surely this underlying belief that allowed him to bring together the good people of Stratford of various religious persuasions and unite them in the common cause of creating a unique theatre. It also had an unstated but persistent effect on the actors who would carry on the work of the company in the years that followed.

The most complete expression of Guthrie's belief that the theatre should be a ceremony that brought people together for a higher purpose was embodied in his production in 1954 and 1955 of Sophocles' *Oedipus Rex*, his favourite play and his most boldly ritualistic production up until that time. He wrote that he had been guided or inspired in his choice of this play "as all God's prophets have been, from

The Great White Hunter in Canada

Elijah down to the dottiest persons who have believed themselves to be guided or inspired. If this is not so, then for me the term *artist* is meaningless." In his production of *Oedipus*, Guthrie endeavoured to carry the audience beyond their everyday lives into a higher realm and to encourage his actors to "glorify their Creator by expressing themselves."

Director:
Tyrone Guthrie

Designer:
Tanya Moiseiwitsch

A spectacle unique in its splendour and stark inevitability, the ancient story unfolds before us as the mythical king discovers he has killed his father and married his mother. Oedipus comes to an understanding of the deepest currents in his dark psyche and painfully acquires a knowledge of the complexity of his own humanity.

Guthrie's re-invention of classical Greek staging challenges us to see beyond the petty concerns of our everyday existence. We are given figures larger than life whose human characteristics are artificially enhanced by elevated boots and expressively modelled masks but who are also made splendid by the richness of robes and regalia. Oedipus is not a recognizable individual like

King Oedipus

35

Hamlet, Peer Gynt or Estragon. He is a king, a man, all men, and yet no single man. His story is presented to us as the Passion of Oedipus, acting out his destiny for the benefit of us all as Christ did. He is a man associated with light, the light of the god Apollo, a man who, in blinding himself, is shut out forever from the light at the centre of life.

Thus Oedipus appears to us as a man of gold, masked, his expression proud and exalted, his spiky crown's golden rays suggesting the Sun in all its glory.

His consort Jocasta is clothed in silver like the moon. They are at all times covered: even their hands are encased in long-nailed gloves. Their gestures are heightened, regal, magnificent. Their speech is eloquent, formal, consciously public. The other characters are of a lower order, of lesser stature and more simply dressed. They too are masked. Their faces show greater individuality and their movement is less grandiose but their speech is more taut, more rhythmic, more fully reasoned and expressed.

Douglas Campbell as King Oedipus with the chorus

Everything is subordinated to the unfolding of the central story. We see these great personages act out their doom and accept their fate, not as we would, but as we wish to imagine heroes might behave, men and women of passion and intelligence who rise above the petty and the mean, the trivial and the transient. Our link to these godlike creatures as we try to understand the meaning of their story is the chorus, fifteen men who speak now in unison, then individually, who move with a common impulse and whose interconnection represents the bond of humanity that unites and ties us all.

And yet for all its attempted universality, this Oedipus was not for all time but of its age. Its inspiration was boldly contemporary, the symbolic interpretation of literature as propounded by critics like C.S. Lewis and Northrop Frye, the underlying psychological meaning of human behaviour to be found in the writings of Freud and Jung. It evoked a particular world view and provoked the audience to interpret their experience in the light of it. It would be revived forty years later when its intellectual underpinnings had been largely blown away, yet it would still impress with the magnificence of its concept and the skill of its execution.

Douglas Campbell (or James Mason) as Oedipus, Eleanor Stuart as Jocasta

MEDEA · 2000

A

vengeful witch or the first feminist? The story of Medea, the barbarian princess who befriends and runs away with the Greek hero Jason, only to be abandoned by him when he sees the possibility of marrying the daughter of a king and establishing himself in his homeland, is one of the great roles for an actress. It was memorably played by Judith Anderson on Broadway in the 1940s and by Maria Callas in Pier Paolo Pasolini's film in the 1960s. Seana Mckenna playing Medea at Stratford in 2000 matched their emotional power but achieved greater subtlety and intimacy.

Director: *Miles Potter*

Designer: *Peter Hartwell*

Scott Wentworth as Jason,
Seana McKenna as Medea

*E*uripides was the least ritualistic and most psychologically complex of the great Greek dramatists. His characters shift and twist, suddenly changing direction as their journeys accelerate toward the fatal resolution of their lives. The American poet Robinson Jeffers has rendered Euripides' text in monumental verse, a towering structure of massed word-clusters studded with scathing epithets and bleak imagery, a verbal mountain range washed by sweeping rhythms that suggest the tides of a great ocean.

Miles Potter's production is simple, allowing the rolling majesty of the words to dominate and at the same time bringing the drama close to us. The chorus of three women in plain white dresses wait, watch, comment, react. Slowly, irrevocably they are drawn into the drama as it

The Chorus: Michelle Giroux,
Patricia Collins, Kate Trotter

unfolds, like housewives fascinated, terrified, paralyzed by the scandalous doings of their neighbours. Like them we become caught up in what unfolds before us, shocked as we witness the inexorable fate this powerful, complicated, deeply wounded woman wills for herself and her children.

Seana McKenna inhabits not only the richly embroidered black and red caftan but the very skin of Medea. She is swift, witty, insightful, dangerous. She remembers past joys and triumphs, ponders present shame, schemes as she stalks the bare stage. With Jason she is wary, wily, seemingly submissive, then uncoils like a hissing snake. With the Athenian king she is offhand, then engaged; we see the temptress she must have been, sense the ruthless drive beneath the seductive smile. With her children she is playful as a kitten, protective as a panther. She kills them not because she does not love them enough, but because she hates Jason more. McKenna's triumph is that she takes us with her. We cannot condone what she does but we understand.

Stratford has mounted only one other Greek play (The Bacchae in 1993) other than Oedipus, and this Medea is a far cry from the high theatricality of Guthrie's conception in its pared-down modernity and simple immediacy, yet the power and majesty of this towering drama come through unimpaired. We experience the famous catharsis; gripped by pity and terror we leave the theatre moved, satisfied, and strangely exhilarated.

VISION OR VANITY?
DESIGN AT STRATFORD

"I DON'T CARE ABOUT THE PLAYS, I GO TO STRATFORD TO SEE ALL THOSE *FABULOUS* COSTUMES." The speaker was a professor of history and her comment was only partly in jest. Nor is it unique. One of the great attractions of Stratford has always been its superb production values. In the first seasons they were a revelation to audiences and theatre people alike. They had seen the glitter of Broadway musicals like the *Ziegfield Follies*, *The King and I*, and *Kiss Me, Kate*, and Hollywood spectaculars from Busby Berkeley to Esther Williams, but Shakespeare on tour usually involved tired and tatty outfits that were vaguely Elizabethan or medieval and looked as though they had been on the rack for decades (they probably had). I remember seeing Donald Wolfit in a performance of *Macbeth* in which he leaned against a rampart that fell over; shortly after that, the handle fell off his sword, giving Macduff a distinct advantage not intended by the author.

But although much of the audience continues to marvel at the splendour and ingenuity of Stratford's costumes and the theatrical magic they create, there are others who feel that the design element overpowers the plays, stealing attention from the actors and undermining the intention of the playwright. As early as 1958, the American critic Gerald Weales asked, "Is the best-dressed acting company in the hemisphere in danger of becoming simply a clothes-horse?" Less eminent spectators mutter darkly, "They spend more on suede boots than they do on the actors," or "*Alice Through the Looking Glass* is nothing but a chance for the prop department to show off." One man's magic is another man's vulgar opulence. Even allowing for the whims of fashion and individual differences of taste there is the more legitimate, or perhaps only more pretentious, question of what constitutes art in the theatre as opposed to mere spectacle. Was Soulpepper's 1999 Toronto production of Schiller's *Don Carlos,* with its total absence of a set and its bare-bones costuming superior to the recent Stratford *Hamlet* with its towering Gothic arches, acres of billowing artificial mist, and a change for virtually every actor for every scene? (The designer created five costumes for Ophelia although she only makes four appearances. But of course she had to wear something to her funeral.)

The fact is that Stratford has been a designer's theatre from the beginning. Tyrone Guthrie insisted on the highest production values, although in private life he cared nothing for smart clothes or chic decor. He was ably abetted by Tanya Moiseiwitsch, his favourite designer and long-time collaborator, and also by Jacqueline Cundall, one of the most experienced prop-makers in Britain, and the internationally recognized cutter Ray Diffen. They worked under the direction of Cecil Clarke to put together a production team of art students, craftsmen, and seamstresses and taught them the tricks of the trade. They even found a European shoemaker in Toronto's garment district who learned by trial and error to make period boots.

The importance of costumes and props was a vital element in selling Guthrie's idea of using a bare stage. Elaborately caparisoned actors set the scene: they became the court, the inn, the brothel, the teeming street, the battlefield, aided and abetted by one or two carefully chosen props: a throne, a two-wheeled chariot, a looming crucifix. These objects had to be mobile, to appear and disappear rapidly; otherwise the fluidity of staging which was one of the chief virtues of Guthrie's style and a primary reason why he wanted to use a thrust stage would be destroyed. The costumes and props created a world that could be mustered in seconds and vanish in a trice.

By starting from scratch at Stratford, Guthrie and Moiseiwitsch had a huge advantage. They could create their own design and production team from people with few if any preconceptions of what the work should look like or how it should be done, and they would be judged by an audience with similarly few expectations. Even the most experienced Canadian designers and directors such as Herbert Whittaker and Robert Gill were bowled over.

Central to the whole concept was the stage itself. Although Tanya Moiseiwitsch designed it, she was greatly influenced not only by Guthrie's ideas but also by his initial sketches, often made on the backs of envelopes or on table napkins. Indeed

Romancing the Bard

she has written that the stage was really designed by Guthrie, but the truth probably is that when two artists work so closely together it is impossible to know exactly who invented what. A further but vital contribution was made by Alec Guinness early in rehearsals when he told Guthrie that the playing space was too small and needed to be increased by another foot all round. Guthrie adopted his suggestion and always referred to it as "the Guinness foot."

One characteristic of the Stratford stage is that it is relatively small. The much-vaunted intimacy of players with the audience is matched by intimacy between the players themselves. This allows for great intensity in small-scale scenes but demands close co-operation. The need for teamwork is even greater in large scenes where blocking becomes vital if the audience is to see the principal players and have its attention focused on whatever the director decides is of primary importance. This is a vitally important aspect of direction that can be enhanced or encumbered by design. Above all it places the director in an extremely powerful position.

Guthrie's mastery of stage groupings stood him in good stead in the early years. Frequently he would re-block whole scenes even after several weeks of rehearsal, but he did so with an air of supreme confidence. If an actor complained, "I can't see anyone in the first row with those soldiers standing downstage, so I don't suppose they will be able to see me," Guthrie would plunk himself down in a seat in the first row. "Can see perfectly. On." Not all his successors were able to cope so successfully. Cecil Clarke did not master the stage's dynamics for *Measure for Measure* in 1954, and Michael Langham encountered problems with his first production, *Julius Caesar,* the next year. But Langham in time became the great master of thrust staging and no one has shown greater skill and flexibility in using the Stratford stage to maximum advantage.

It was Langham who fully explored the use of diagonal movement, the exploitation of the floor as an acting space, the employment of the balcony in various ways to gain intimacy, distance or a sense of public occasion or to allow one or more characters to observe the action below while remaining unseen. He experimented with a variety of groupings possible on the staircases leading to the balcony or to the exits at stage right and stage left and at the mouths of the vomitoria (the tunnels downstage right and left that provide actors an additional means of access to the stage) which, because of the pattern of the aisles, do not block the audience's view. Inevitably, work on a thrust stage demands that the director think in three-dimensional terms. He must learn to use space in quite a different way than on a proscenium stage, where the audience is always looking at an essentially two-dimensional picture.

Not every actor enjoys working on a thrust stage. Guinness gallantly played out his roles in the opening season but wrote in his autobiography, "The theatre where a performer cannot make a clean entrance or exit seen by the entire audience at the same time and is obliged to make artificial moves purely for the sake of movement, so that the audience, weary perhaps of a back, can get a glimpse of his face; where, when stillness is called for, the actor must rotate through 180 degrees to reach most spectators as well as other actors, is not so much a theatre as a circus."

It is perhaps not surprising that the stage has been modified several times in its fifty-year history. First to go was the central pillar under the balcony. It was a favourite element of Guthrie's design and certain actors enjoyed leaning against it, hiding behind it or swinging around it, but these effects became stale and its loss has not been much lamented. (It also meant that props and furniture could not be over a certain size, if they were to be got on and off the stage quickly, thus exercising a certain control on designers' extravagance.) No one objected to the pillar's loss, largely because Moiseiwitsch, as the theatre's acknowledged designer, was thought to possess the right to make modifications as she saw fit.

A further modification instigated by Moiseiwitsch and her colleague and protégé Brian Jackson, reconfiguring the exits at stage left and right to provide small platforms at the top of the flights of stairs, was primarily a safety measure and also drew little criticism. But when Robin Phillips had the central balcony motorized so that it could slide completely out of sight, some die-hards were outraged. Phillips also removed the step up to the space under the balcony, which Douglas Campbell pointed out "gave the actor a splendid entrance, something Guthrie understood better than some of his successors."

Guthrie made it clear that he did not consider the thrust suitable for plays written for a proscenium stage, in effect anything dating from 1660 onwards. But, by the time Phillips was running the Festival, its stage had already seen productions of the work of Molière, Sheridan, Shaw, Chekhov, and Ibsen. In the case of the eighteenth- and nineteenth-century plays, a good deal of furniture was required. It had to be got on and off stage efficiently and this required access from backstage as well as hours of rehearsal. Stratford's technicians and minor actors became masters of this particular art, the apotheosis of which occurred in Phillips' 1978 production of *Macbeth*, in which the entire banquet scene was set up in a 30-second blackout covered by the dying screams of the murdered Banquo, providing a truly memorable *coup de théâtre*.

In spite of Guthrie's lively and fertile intelligence he was not always consistent. It might seem that if his goal was to restore the Elizabethan stage he would also believe in using the kind of costumes the original actors wore. Not so. The clothes for *All's Well That Ends Well* were modern Ruritanian, *The Taming of the Shrew* was set in a sort of archetypal Old West, the design of *The Merchant of Venice* was inspired by Botticelli, and *Twelfth Night* by Van Dyck. Of his five mainstage Shakespearean productions, none was done in Elizabethan dress, and only *Richard III* was set in its actual historical period. Thus he laid the groundwork, or should one say set the stage, for an ongoing tradition of positioning classical plays in every period but the one in which they were written. We have been treated to a modern-dress *Comedy of Errors,* a Caribbean *Twelfth Night,* and even, from the Canadian Players, an Eskimo *King Lear,* though not as yet a 1950s doo-wop rendering of *School for Wives* or a science-fiction version of *The Three Musketeers.* (But, after all, why not?)

In the first decade of the Festival the design element was controlled by the guiding hand of Tanya Moiseiwitsch. She was not a diva, but quiet, reticent, flexible, and a good listener. Before coming to Canada she had worked extremely closely with Guthrie and understood her role as trying to realize his concepts and ideas, although all her work was obviously filtered through her own unique sensibility. She had a masterly command of colour and an understanding that theatrical effect did not depend on meticulous detail. At a recent lunch in her honour she spoke about the twenty-foot crimson cape that Alec Guinness wore for his coronation scene in *Richard III.* It was made from a remnant of the cheapest rayon velvet

45

trimmed with cotton batten: "Tony's idea was that it should be like a river of blood. It was a central image in his production concept but I couldn't spend a great deal of time and money. After all it was on stage for only ninety seconds."

Moiseiwitsch was able to build up a highly-skilled staff of local people who worked under her direction and to her specifications. She found and trained two brilliant protégés, Brian Jackson and Desmond Heeley. Both became fine designers and expert at producing wonders from limited resources. Desmond Heeley in particular worked in the shops creating magical props from discarded medicine bottles or old toilet floats or Christmas tree ornaments. On one occasion he arrived from New York with four tea chests full of end-of-line samples he had acquired from a draper who was going out of business. From these tag-ends he created 250 resplendent costumes for John Hirsch's 1968 production of *The Three Musketeers.*

The other prominent designer in the early years was the English painter Leslie Hurry, who made costumes out of yards of cheesecloth hand painted by himself and a collection of fledgling painters he recruited from art schools. These were ambitious young artists who wished to enhance their skills and their credibility by working for as prestigious an institution as Stratford. They worked long hours for meagre financial reward in conditions that would no longer be allowed by unions, even if the mentality of students had not been radically changed by the opportunities offered by television production. There is still at Stratford a considerable pride in craftsmanship, as evidenced by the embroidery lavished on Lady Bracknell's bum roll for her fourth-act costume in the recent production of *The Importance of Being Earnest,* a detail that the audience never had a chance to see.

Over the decades, different artistic directors have dealt with the technical aspects of production according to their differing temperaments. Jean Gascon introduced the established Montreal designers Mark Negin and Robert Prevost, who brought their own Gallic flair to bear as well as giving opportunities to other young hopefuls, notably Michael Annals; but Desmond Heeley, Leslie Hurry, and Brian Jackson continued to dominate the scene, and Tanya Moiseiwitsch returned occasionally. The staff they had built up continued to function effectively under their guidance.

Robin Phillips dealt with the design aspect of the Festival more directly than most of his predecessors. Like Guthrie he had strong visual concepts. He brought with him a designer, Daphne Dare, who was used to his ways and saw herself as an interpreter of his ideas. During the Phillips regime the production team worked very much under his supervision and he brooked no interference. Once, when working with a young designer, Phillips said,

"I'd like a clothesline in this scene with four sheets hanging on it."

"Or maybe some underwear."

"No, four sheets."

End of discussion. Although tales of Phillips' extravagance are legion, he often was able to cut costs by saying something like, "In this scene we'll use four dresses from the masquerade scene in *Much Ado.* They're in storage, I saw them last week." His fondness for the Edwardian era was at least partly motivated by the fact that wardrobe had a large supply of costumes from that era, including a great many uniforms that were frequently recycled with only the buttons and insignia changed.

As the Festival gained an international reputation for the excellence of its workmanship and the lavishness of its productions, more and more domestic and international designers wanted to work for it. They often arrived with highly extravagant expectations and this led to a complicated and sometimes acrimonious atmosphere in the production workshops. There have been bitter disputes behind the scenes that rival any conflicts seen onstage.

Actors often have very strong ideas about what their characters should wear. Some wear clothes well and are very shrewd about what flatters their assets and camouflages their defects. Others have little or no clothes sense and always look as though they had just got up out of a haystack unless they submit to the ministrations of a trained dresser. Of course a spear-carrier who complains about his costume is likely to get short shrift from a designer, but a star will demand and usually get quite different treatment.

Moiseiwitsch was particularly responsive to actors' ideas. For *All's Well That Ends Well* she acceded to Irene Worth's request that her final costume should be designed by Valentina, but Moiseiwitsch chose the colour that would allow her to dominate the stage in the last scene. When she was designing *Love's Labour's Lost,* Moiseiwitsch welcomed Paul Scofield's suggestions about his costume and let him devise his own preposterous disguise for the Hector scene and dress his own wig and beard.

However, her successors have not always had her tact and sensitivity to actors' wishes; nor have they had the unassuming but effective authority that her international reputation commanded. In 1978 Maggie Smith approved Daphne Dare's designs for her clothes, then set out for California to make a movie. She came back late for rehearsals and refused to wear any of the costumes that had been constructed in her absence. Her entire wardrobe was redesigned and made over from scratch.

Today there are at least ten or twelve shows mounted in three theatres in every Stratford season, all directed and designed by different people. The organizational challenge of co-ordinating all this work is staggering. Shows are often designed before they are cast. Directors who wish to make major changes in rehearsal are out of luck. Designers may be told by the production manager that there are exactly three days to make a certain major prop, and if it cannot be done in the allotted time it must be either simplified or eliminated. On the other hand elaborate props are sometimes constructed and then scrapped by the director at dress rehearsal. Although every effort is made to give directors the designers they choose, they are sometimes paired with designers whom they know only slightly. As neither directors nor designers are likely to be based in Stratford but are apt to be busy working on shows anywhere from San Francisco to Tel Aviv, just getting them together for consultation can be horrendously complicated.

And then there is the question of budget. Not only the unions but also the members of the Board insist that technicians and workmen be paid good wages. Union regulations insist they be paid time-and-a-half or double time if overtime work is required. The once relatively simple lighting equipment is now highly sophisticated, and long technical rehearsals are required to execute the complex plots devised by lighting and sound designers. A spectacle like the flamboyant *The Three Musketeers* has hundreds of cues. The technical rehearsals for the 2000 season on the Festival stage took nearly a week. A stage manager was hired whose last assignment was *The Lion King* in New York. All of this added to the costs of this production.

With its 300 costumes, *Musketeers* had to be built at the same time as the equally elaborate and complicated *Fiddler on the Roof* and *Hamlet*. The director of the latter play wanted to have four ladies of the court, but although actresses were available it was decided that it was too expensive to make costumes for them. Apparently it was considered unthinkable to pull costumes from stock. The director and designer complained that the Festival had not budgeted enough, although the allotment for costumes for this show was the highest in the Festival's history. The fact that the Festival had shown a record profit in the previous year was cited as a reason to up the budget. These wrangles are not so much about art as about power.

Stratford is proud of building all its productions in-house. Sets, costumes, and props have traditionally been made in the workshops and stored in warehouses belonging to the Festival. This provides the town and the surrounding area with jobs and subsidiary income. (Artistic Director Richard Monette remarked recently, "Sometimes I think the Festival exists to keep the dry-cleaners of Kitchener in business.") It also gives the Festival a high measure of control. Directors and designers can visit the shops and see how work on their shows is progressing, though propmaster Roy Brown reports that some designers "throw a hissy-fit" if they discover he is working not on their show but someone else's. Production managers learn quickly if work is behind schedule. These are significant advantages but the costs are becoming prohibitive, and not just in financial terms.

The theatre has become in a very real sense a factory that turns out art. As the productions proliferate and the demands on the technical staff become ever greater, the territorial bickering between the heads of the various departments—costumes, props, wigs, and lighting—increases as they battle for bigger budgets, more time on stage, and what in the end manifests itself as political supremacy. Ultimately this may well lead to the disbanding of these feudal fiefdoms. It is probably only a matter of time before Stratford begins to follow the example of such major production companies as the Metropolitan Opera where at least some of the work is farmed out, with Sheraton-style chairs being shipped from Grand Rapids and shirts being made in Hong Kong.

As artistic director Monette believes he cannot afford to give in to what he perceives as the exorbitant demands and irresponsibility of visiting designers and directors nor tolerate endless in-fighting from his technical staff. At the same time he appreciates that for all their grousing, many of these technicians have contributed years of devoted labour to the Festival and still have what they perceive to be its best interests at heart. Faced with this Gordian knot it is not surprising that he periodically mutters darkly about "Death by Design."

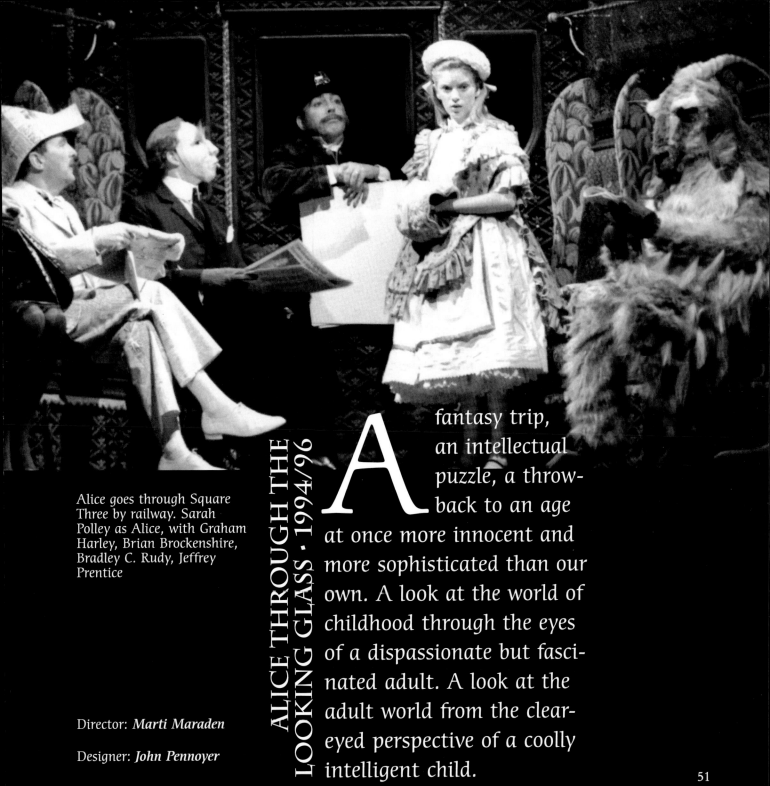

Alice goes through Square Three by railway. Sarah Polley as Alice, with Graham Harley, Brian Brockenshire, Bradley C. Rudy, Jeffrey Prentice

Director: *Marti Maraden*

Designer: *John Pennoyer*

ALICE THROUGH THE LOOKING GLASS · 1994/96

A fantasy trip, an intellectual puzzle, a throwback to an age at once more innocent and more sophisticated than our own. A look at the world of childhood through the eyes of a dispassionate but fascinated adult. A look at the adult world from the clear-eyed perspective of a coolly intelligent child.

Douglas Rain as Humpty Dumpty with Sarah Polley as Alice

A lice Through the Looking Glass *made use of all the formidable assets of the Stratford Festival, beginning with its ability to realize a uniquely original text. There is nothing quite like the imagination of Lewis Carroll, whose quixotic inversion of the mores and manners of nineteenth-century England is lovingly preserved in the sensitive re-shaping of his words by fellow satirist and observer of human foibles James Reaney. The Canadian poet matched the outrageous invention of this bold Victorian versifier and fantasist with respect, but also with a certain boldness.*

The Canadian actors picked up the cue from Reaney and inhabited this most English of books in completely Canadian terms. In the central role of

Sarah Polley as Alice with Keith Dinicol as Tweedledee,
Bernard Hopkins as Tweedledum, Mervyn Blake as the Red King

Alice, Sarah Polley was self-contained, curious but uncommitted, questioning
whatever she encountered with a sharply honed intellect. She was our fearless
guide through madness and misunderstandings and with her to lead us we
could not lose our way. She offered detachment and delight in equal measure
and we followed her willingly into the heart of the maze and out again.

And what fabulous creatures we met along the way: the delectably dotty
White King of William Needles; the soporific Red King of Mervyn Blake;
those mischievous schoolboy twins Tweedledum and Tweedledee, impishly

impersonated by Keith Dinicol and Bernard Hopkins battling with saucepans and coal-scuttles on their heads; the scatty White Queen of Barbara Bryne; the cantankerous Red Queen of Michelle Fiske; the romantically mournful White Knight of Tom Wood; and Douglas Chamberlain's wistful Carpenter.

Topping these wonderfully detailed portraits was the triple threat of Douglas Rain as a slyly greedy Walrus, the voice of the insufferably superior Gnat, and the preposterously self-satisfied Humpty Dumpty teetering on his wall. These bold, vigorous characterizations showed Stratford's stable of actors at their most idiosyncratically inventive. Liberated from considerations of plot, motivation, and the necessity to chart an emotional course, they were free to follow their imaginative bent to the hilt and they rose to the occasion with gusto.

And then there were the oysters, the glittering insects, the silly sheep, the chorus-girl flowers, and the Jabberwock, brilliant creations of the Stratford propmaster Roy Brown working closely with designer John Pennoyer, whose fantastical costumes provided the eye with constant surprises, while the playful score of Keith Thomas assailed the ear. Pennoyer's work was not mere decoration but an essential element that threatened to take over but never quite did so. Pennoyer's design was not slavishly derivative of either Tenniel or Disney, but it made a statement on its own imaginative terms, equating the wonders of Alice's adventure with the Victorian notion of the wonders of the modern world: pillars that suggested the engineering of a railway station like Waterloo or Victoria, animal costumes that emphasized the Darwinian structure of insects' wings and crustacean shells.

Everything was carefully orchestrated in this vivid and playful production presided over by Marti Maraden, who seemed to command a whole world of childish innocence and precocious knowingness, as if by divine right. We could only marvel at it, as we were meant to do.

Keith Dinicol as the Lion, William Needles as the White King,
Graham Harley as the Unicorn, Sarah Polley as Alice

THE INVENTION OF CANADIAN ACTING

"WE AIMED FOR A MID-ATLANTIC STYLE," Herbert Whittaker remembers, speaking of his theatre work in Montreal in the 1930s and 1940s. "We were influenced by the companies that visited from England but also from New York. They were our idols and so, of course, they became our models." It was an era when upper-class American speech in Boston and New York was almost indistinguishable from the accents of Mayfair, an era when theatre people looked and acted not like ordinary people but like a race apart. Their speech was clipped, the consonants clearly articulated, the vowels elongated and pear-shaped. They laughed musically, smoked suavely, and raised their eyebrows. In fact they did a lot of eyebrow and cigarette acting. They never went out without looking their best. They dressed up to go to rehearsal, the women wearing hats and gloves and if possible furs, the men with jackets and ties or casually knotted scarves. They wore elaborate make-up on stage, and frequently off.

All this was to change rapidly. The English actor Alec McCowen recalled seeing Marlon Brando on stage in *A Streetcar Named Desire*. "I didn't think he was acting. I thought, my God, they've cast an actual lorry-driver in the part." Brando mumbled, snarled, and sweated, and of course he exuded raw animal passion: in a word, sex. He would be much imitated, but not just yet in Canada. The Stratford Festival did not invite Elia Kazan to direct its first season, but rather Tyrone Guthrie.

At the time, theatre training in Canada was in the hands of energetic but largely self-trained enthusiasts. At Brae Manor in the eastern townships of Quebec, the husband-and-wife team of Filmore and Madge Sadler ran a summer operation that was part stock company, part drama school, part happy family. Students learned by participating in shows. They believed, as I do, that an actor needs to get in front of an audience and learns as much by experience and instinct as by formal instruction. Rising actors who worked at Brae Manor included Eric Donkin, Richard Easton, Robert Goodier, Joy Lafleur, and Christopher Plummer. In the winters many of these same actors appeared in Ottawa at the Canadian Repertory Theatre run jointly by

Amelia Hall, Sam Payne, and Bruce Raymond. The plays produced were ambitious but designed to entertain: Coward, Kaufmann and Hart and Rattigan were favoured playwrights. A spirit of light-hearted sophistication prevailed, as suggested by this fragment taking off a Cole Porter lyric of the day:

> I get no kick from Sam Payne,
> Amelia Hall doesn't thrill me at all
> But I get a goose out of Bruce.

Robertson Davies, who had not yet turned his attention to novel writing, directed summer shows at Brae Manor before he and his wife Brenda helped to establish a summer theatre in Peterborough. I remember visiting when I was still a teenager. My friend Jean Robb (later known professionally as Jean Templeton) was painting sets in her strapless "formal" because she had already dirtied all her other clothes. Her favourite expression: "My dear, I'm fainting." Quelle sophistication. One of her fellow apprentices was a young kid from the States who was sent home in disgrace after he polished a borrowed silver tea service with steel wool before returning it to its owner; his name was Anthony Perkins.

Among the actors seen at Peterborough that season were Kate Reid and Barbara Hamilton, who also appeared with the newly formed Straw Hat Players in Muskoka, presided over by Donald and Murray Davis. All four had trained with Robert Gill at Hart House Theatre at the University of Toronto. Like the Sadlers in Quebec, Gill believed in learning by performing. He was a sensitive artist who brought to his work a strong pictorial sense and an atmosphere of rigorous professionalism, working to a tight schedule of three-and-a-half weeks of evening rehearsal and brooking no insubordination in the ranks. Once, when I missed a photo call, Gill told me he wouldn't speak to me again for a year and didn't. When he auditioned William Hutt for his first season he was apparently put off by the young actor's flippancy, and when the cast list for the initial production of *Saint Joan* was posted, Hutt's name was not on it. He went to see Gill and explained it was his intention to become a professional actor. Gill gave him an icy stare: "You should have told me that in the first place. Very well, you can carry a spear. Then we'll see." Hutt must have redeemed himself; next year he played the lead in Gill's production of *Jason*.

Gill maintained a more or less friendly rivalry with another director who also worked at Hart House Theatre. Herbert Whittaker had been a director and designer in Montreal and at Brae Manor as well as writing criticism for *The Gazette*. Always alert to shifting trends, he sensed that Toronto was becoming a hotter theatre town, at least for Anglos, than Montreal, and in 1949 accepted a post as film critic for *The Globe and Mail*. He soon began to direct shows for the independent colleges, Trinity and Victoria, and the leading amateur group in town, The University Women's Alumnae. These productions introduced Montreal actors John Colicos and Richard Easton to Toronto and showcased a host of young talents from Kay Hawtrey in the 1940s through to Jackie Burroughs in the late 1950s.

Whittaker also directed productions for the New Play Society founded by Mavor Moore and his redoubtable mother Dora, and for the rival Jupiter Theatre at the Royal Ontario Museum. These two ambitious young companies offered imaginatively designed and cleverly cast productions of such new works as Bertolt Brecht's *Galileo* and Christopher Fry's *The Lady's Not for Burning*, as well as new plays by Ted Allan, Morley Callaghan, Lister Sinclair, and the formidable young critic Nathan Cohen.

"Herbie" Whittaker's style was very different from "Bob" Gill's. Gill's rehearsals began at seven and ended promptly at ten, when he went home to a solitary glass of whiskey; Whittaker's often started half an hour late and went on till nearly midnight, followed by rambling discussions at Diana Sweets. Later Gill recounted that one student, who had worked for both of them, remarked, "You're so organized, Mr. Gill. Mr. Whittaker never plans anything ahead. But of course Mr. Whittaker is a *genius*." Gill's ordinarily scarlet face turned fuchsia.

In the small acting community of those days amateurs and professionals mingled freely, but professionalism was what all the young actors sought to achieve. They worked for car-fare and cigarette money, but they worked hard. Often labouring for inexperienced or absentee directors, they had to improvise and solve their own problems. This bred a spirit of independence and indeed irreverence. Inevitably native humour bubbled up. The scripts penned by Robertson Davies and Mavor Moore depended heavily on satire and comic situations. Their flowering comic invention found a focus in *Spring Thaw*, the annual revue that sprang, like Athene from the forehead of Zeus, more or less fully formed from the ingenious brain of Mavor

Moore, and exploited the talents of a bevy of comics led by Jane Mallet and Donald Harron. What they established would later be extended by the performers of *Saturday Night Live*, *Codco*, and *The Kids in the Hall*.

The young actors' great ally in their climb toward professionalism was CBC Radio. The kings of radio drama were Rupert Caplan in Montreal and Andrew Allan in Toronto. The balance of power shifted when Caplan moved to New York and Allan's Sunday Night Stage Series began to achieve a significantly large listenership across the country. Allan employed the best actors available, veterans of the 1930s Robert Christie, Jane Mallet, and Tommy Tweed and a host of up-and-coming young talent: John Drainie, Judith Evelyn, Lorne Greene, Frank Peddie, and Aileen Seaton. These actors and a few fortunate others actually made a living from radio acting. Allan commissioned original scripts from Bernard Braden, John Bethune, Joseph Schull, and Lister Sinclair and music from Louis Applebaum and Lucio Agostini. He built up a court around him that assembled regularly at *Chez Paree* on Bloor Street where Allan pontificated on life, politics, and the arts to those fortunate enough to get a seat at his table.

Allan could be exceedingly grand but he was also endlessly curious and had a knack for drawing out young talent, particularly in young women. But most importantly he provided ongoing opportunities for experiment by casting actors in a wide range of roles. If they failed sometimes, no one was overly concerned. Next week they would be playing something else. Radio is a highly flexible medium, partly because it is relatively inexpensive to produce. There is no need for set or costumes or for the actors to learn their lines. Rehearsal can be and usually is fairly minimal. Actors learn to work on their feet. Allan made strong demands and gave his actors a healthy respect for the word, which in radio is all there is. Many of them seized the opportunity to expand and develop their vocal range and expressiveness, setting them apart from their American cousins who were already submerging themselves in The Method. More rooted in Freud than Stanislavsky in its emphasis on inner feeling and naturalistic expression, Lee Strasberg's technique (some would say anti-technique) laid the groundwork for modern film and television acting. But the concentration on vocal expressiveness that radio demanded bred both flexibility and dexterity, and this was one thing that most impressed Tyrone Guthrie about Canadian actors when he came scouting talent for Stratford in 1952.

For Guthrie, vocal expression was paramount. He had a keen ear for and appreciation of ordinary speech. He did not encourage or indeed allow his Canadian actors to ape British models, understanding that what London actors considered to be proper speech was governed by matters of class, geography, and fashion and that speech and accent vary not only from region to region but from one epoch to another. The correct speech of yesteryear, the once highly valued "Oxford" accent, would soon become a laughable affectation, even in Mayfair and Belgravia.

The inflections and pronunciation of Henry Irving were not the authentic accents of Shakespeare and would have been as inappropriate in Stratford in 1953 as the speech of an Irish bogtrotter or a Texas rancher. (Though in fact Guthrie might have employed either for comic effect.) Guthrie forced his Canadian actors to use their own speech, to find their own voices. Nothing earned his scorn more quickly than a "Rosedale" accent.

Guthrie heard any play, especially a Shakespearean play, as a musical composition. He relished its sounds, its rhythms and *tempi*, its *crescendos* and climaxes. He often gave directions using musical terminology: *allegro agitato, con rubato, molto vivace.* Michael Langham recalls that Guthrie's rehearsals had to have rhythm, "had to *pulse*; he saw the alternative as death preserved." Guthrie insisted on pace and demanded that his actors speak very quickly. He interpreted a script in terms of contrasts, scenes of quick repartee followed by more languorous lyrical passages, spoken *andante* to bring out the dynamic shape of the work. He believed the most important aspect of an actor's training was vocal; the actor must learn to control his breath, to use his full vocal range, to speak distinctly. Clarity was the primary objective: the audience must be able to understand what was said, no matter how rapidly it was delivered.

Guthrie auditioned over three hundred Canadian actors for his first Stratford company. That is to say he met them and chatted with them briefly; they were not required to trot out two pieces, one classical and one contemporary, as is the custom today, when many actors spend more time auditioning than they do performing. Nowadays actors take classes in how to audition, work with special coaches and spend long hours polishing their pieces; indeed it sometimes seems as if their actual performances are an extended audition for their next gig. Some actors give wonderful auditions but fail to live up to them, while others cannot audition at all. Having auditioned hundreds of actors in the last thirty years, I have come to the conclusion that a director learns a great deal about an actor in the first two minutes. He will not find out much more until he has worked with the actor for four weeks of rehearsal and seen him in performance.

Alec Guinness noted of Guthrie, "Whatever conclusions he came to on a first meeting, I doubt if he ever changed them." His snap judgments must have been shrewd; for the first season of Stratford Guthrie selected Lloyd Bochner, Robert Christie, Timothy Findley, Amelia Hall, Donald Harron, Eric House, William Hutt, William Needles, Douglas Rain and Eleanor Stuart, all of whom would make significant contributions to the Festival in the first decade and some of whom are still in evidence fifty years later. (He rejected Christopher Plummer as too difficult to handle on the advice of Rupert Caplan, who was at the time competing with Plummer for the favours of a certain Montreal actress.)

Actors like to believe they can play many different roles. They derive understandable satisfaction from appearing in a play and not being recognized by their fans for the first five minutes. But essentially every actor is what he is; not even a forest of crepe hair or a squeaking falsetto can fundamentally change his individual personality. He can alter his walk and the timbre of his voice, assume the infirmities of age or the manners of the nobility, but he cannot change his height or the colour of his eyes and he brings to any role certain physical tics, mental quirks, and qualities of temperament. Alec Guinness was a master of disguise, but whether he played Fagin, Lady Agatha D'Ascoigne or Obi-Wan Kenobi, he was always unmistakably Alec Guinness.

Wise actors accept their strengths and weaknesses and learn to make the most of them. An actress will sometimes assume an accent or wear the garments of another time or clime, but a Canadian actor playing a Russian or a Spaniard inevitably filters her impersonation through her own sensibility, which is comprised not only of her idiosyncratic personality but also of the circumstances of time and place, era and nationality, in which she is rooted. She deludes herself if she imagines that this is not apparent to her audience. And she is misplacing her energies if she dedicates them to the superficial delineation of an assumed age or ethnicity rather than devoting her concentrated attention to realizing the emotional drives and conflicts that constitute the heartbeat of the piece she is performing.

A lisp, a hump, a squint or flat feet, a Scottish brogue or a Southern twang may

61

help an actor find his character, but whether he works from the outside in or starts from an emotional centre of rage, frustration or jealousy and lets that lead him to outward expression, he must find his own individual solutions to the problems imposed by the role. Today he may watch videos to see how a certain role was played by Laurence Olivier, Orson Welles or Lawrence Fishburne. He may pick up interesting phrasing or bits of business but he must integrate them into his own interpretation, which will take shape as he interfaces with other actors. He cannot play Othello in a vacuum; his performance will be highly dependant on the vibrations he receives from the actors playing Iago and Desdemona and even Brabantio.

If the actors are old hands who have played the roles before and seen them played many times, as is often the case in England, they will probably be strongly influenced by the tradition that surrounds their craft. They will discuss what Garrick did in a certain scene. Or Kean or Irving. But at Stratford Guthrie assembled a company of actors who were young and had relatively slight theatrical backgrounds. They were no doubt awed by the stature of Alec Guinness and James Mason in the first seasons, but these were two of the least aggressive actors on the professional stage. The Canadian actors had to come up with something of their own, to evolve at least the beginnings of a style.

Initially this style might be said to be Guthrie's. It featured his flair for telling detail, his inventive orchestration of crowds to give them vitality and depth, his love of rapid speech and fluid movement, his restless energy and probing spirit. But Guthrie did not stay to impose his will on the Canadian company for long. He set the top spinning and went off to play other games elsewhere. The Canadian actors were forced to take what he had given them and work with it as best they could. They had been thrown in the water and had to swim or drown.

Almost immediately they unleashed their natural bent for outrageous humour, following the elegant comic invention of *All's Well that Ends Well* with the more extravagant Wild West production of *The Taming of the Shrew* in the second season. Donald Harron and Eric House had already demonstrated their facility as comics in Toronto and they extended and embellished these skills, taking Bruno Gerussi, William Hutt, Peter Mews, and William Needles along for the ride. The production was thought by many to be "too much of a romp" or, as we would say today, "over the top," but people laughed. Before Stratford, nobody in Canada expected

Shakespeare's comedies to be funny. But once opened, the comic vein continued to be richly mined. Indeed, the principal glory of Stratford's first decade was its realization of Shakespearean comedy.

Another distinctive characteristic quickly made itself evident. This might be characterized as grittiness, a mixture of sharp-edged, hard-earned wisdom and undemonstrative but persistent stubbornness. It was evident in the more serious work of such actors as Frances Hyland with her proud angularity as Isabella in *Measure for Measure*, her fragile earthiness as Ophelia and her awkward but cherished pride as Varya in *The Cherry Orchard*; in Kate Reid's forthright Emilia in *Othello* and salty humour as Juliet's Nurse; in Douglas Rain's deluded tenacity as Malvolio and level-headed clarity as Prince Hal; in William Hutt's pretentious but pithy Polonius, foolishly nostalgic Slender, and self-deprecatingly sardonic and slavering Pandarus. These performances blended comedy with down-to-earth reality and achieved a native wittiness, rough-edged, hardheaded, pungent.

As these actors worked together they gained confidence and fed off each other as good performers always do, spurring each other on, competing as well as cooperating. But they would likely not have achieved the clarity and command they soon displayed without leadership. Fortunately, Tyrone Guthrie's brief reign at Stratford was followed by the lengthier regime of an equally dominating if distinctly different personality. Michael Langham had neither Guthrie's experience nor his breezy confidence. They shared Scottish ancestry but the formative years of Langham's early twenties had been spent not at Oxford but in a German prisoner-of-war camp where he read constantly and put on plays with his fellow inmates to boost their morale and help them retain their sanity. His approach in working with actors was, like Guthrie's, deeply psychological but more severe and also more secretive.

Langham and Guthrie had met shortly after the war and immediately hit it off. Guthrie invited the aspiring young director to Stratford in the third season to direct *Julius Caesar*. The production lacked stars and was dominated by veterans of the first two seasons: Lloyd Bochner, Robert Christie, Donald Davis, and Donald Harron, and one of the CBC's heavy hitters, Lorne Greene. Langham had not cast the show and thought some of the actors inadequate. He was unsparing in his critical remarks, and the actors found his approach overly meticulous. Where Guthrie had been free-wheeling and exploratory Langham was precise and rigorous. He knew the play intimately, having directed it at England's Stratford-on-Avon with John Gielgud and Anthony Quayle. Nevertheless he kept making radical changes right up to opening night and indeed even beyond. The cast sensed his uneasiness and rebelled.

Far from retreating, Langham held his ground. His tenacity would prove to be justified; the next year he emerged as a strong and commanding artistic director, achieving a triumph with his groundbreaking production of *Henry V*. In the years that followed, Langham mastered the thrust stage as nobody else was to do for over a decade—some would say ever. He also kept a firm grip on the company and proved to be something of a martinet. Indeed, in the opinion of some actors he was a bully. Donald Harron left the company because he found Langham cold and forbidding. William Needles considered himself so insulted in rehearsal that he packed his bags and was heading out the door to the train station, when Langham arrived, ostensibly to say goodbye, and talked him into staying on.

Langham lost some of the actors from the first years but he recruited many other talented Canadians including James Blendick, John Colicos, Eric Donkin, George McCowan, Christopher Plummer, and Kate Reid, and later Mia Anderson, Jackie Burroughs, Martha Henry, Heath Lamberts, Roberta Maxwell, and Richard Monette. He worked closely with these young performers, counselling them intimately on specific points of interpretation. Kate Reid claimed that Langham taught her more about acting than any director she had ever worked with. Frances Hyland also learned from Langham and recalls particularly how he lambasted company members for "trying to sound English," pointing out that Canadian pronunciation was closer to what Shakespeare had in mind when he wrote.

Langham insisted on precise phrasing and forced his actors to analyse their speeches, often word by word. He taught them how to think their way through the text. His own preparation and intellectual exploration before he met with the actors were complex and probing, as the preparatory notes for his 1967 production of *Antony and Cleopatra* (published in *The Stratford Scene*) attest. He blocked and re-blocked until he had achieved the exact pictures that would express his understanding of the particular piece he was working on.

He could be lacerating but also wittily inventive. Joseph Shaw recalls standing centre stage as the doctor when Lear is carried on in a litter. Langham wanted a strong reaction that would throw focus to Lear, but Shaw felt his character would be

64

puzzled and uncertain. Langham jumped up on stage and said, "You are an old quack. You failed medical school, you are about to be fired from the clinic where you work. If you don't come up with something decisive at once, you'll be taken away and thrown in the clink. Is that enough background and motivation? Now react, damn you."

As the skills of his Canadian actors grew, Langham saw to it that they were given opportunities to play the big, demanding roles: Hamlet, Lear, Timon, Cyrano, Benedick, Richard II, Desdemona, Katherine of Aragon, Olivia, Cressida. But Langham also continued to import stars who would challenge and inspire his Canadian actors, bringing out their latent talents, egging them on to greater heights: from England Paul Scofield and his wife Joy Parker, the Scottish actress Eileen Herlie and Langham's own wife Helen Burns, as well as the Australian Zoe Caldwell and Americans Julie Harris, Jason Robards and Irene Worth.

These luminaries came for a season and lent their lustre to the Festival. Langham also strengthened the company with a brigade of young British players: Bernard Behrens, Mervyn Blake, Ann Casson, Peter Donat, Eric Christmas, Pat Galloway, Mary Savidge, Joseph Shaw, and Tony van Bridge. As the seasons unfolded they learned to work together, not to create a mid-Atlantic style but rather a fresh Canadian one, the natives strongly influenced by the newcomers but constantly evolving as the young country itself was evolving. Canada is still a country that attracts and absorbs talents from abroad, less a melting pot than a mixing bowl in which diverse skills, wills, and wishes season the pudding.

And all the while Canadian talent springs up in unlikely places: towns on the Prairies, villages on Cape Breton, the slums of Montreal's east end and the dreary wastes of Scarborough, as well as the more privileged purlieus of Oakville or Shaughnessy. What is most remarkable is how the Festival allows these talents to grow and develop. Here as nowhere else they have an opportunity to play many roles, large and small, working alongside some of the most accomplished actors of the age, backed by the highly sophisticated technical and visual support in front of large and increasingly discerning audiences and playing in repertory over a season that now extends from May to November. Nothing quite like it exists in North America.

The native-born and locally bred continue to be joined by outsiders from Britain or the United States. Many of these people come for a season and expect to go back again, but somehow Stratford becomes home and they stay on. With actors as with war brides, it seems often to take an extended stay back in the Old Country before they can fully appreciate what they have in the New Land. Not all actors take to it; there are bitter stories and recriminations. But there is hardly a major stage actor in the land who has not spent a season or two at Stratford.

It is perhaps ironic that two Scots, Guthrie and Langham, presided over the birth of a distinctive Canadian acting style, but this country owes its beginnings and much of its character to the vision of visitors whose stay was often brief: Cartier, Champlain, Simcoe, Vancouver, Durham. We seem to need to start with foreign models and then be prodded to abandon them and find in ourselves something less lofty, cut down to size but also tougher, more basic, more true to our essential nature. We continue to need the stimulus of outside influence both to keep us from becoming too turned in on ourselves and to convince us that what we are doing measures up. So we have continued to import visitors to challenge the work of the natives: Alan Bates, Uta Hagen, Maggie Smith, Jessica Tandy, Peter Ustinov.

Before any of these luminaries arrived it was Langham who introduced that glittering grain of sand—rigorous textual analysis—that provided the ongoing irritant that stimulated Stratford's raw and palpitating young oysters. Later, Robin Phillips' insistence on emotional truth provided a further provocation toward greatness. Yet the initial over-arching vision was Guthrie's. He once declared that what he expected from Stratford was theatre in which great protagonists pitted themselves against the universe; his bare stage was meant to provide an image of the cosmos. Guthrie's Stratford *Oedipus* was one realization of this idea; others were his *Tamburlaine the Great*, his earlier Old Vic *Peer Gynt*, and his later *Peter Grimes* at Covent Garden.

Guthrie's bare stage demands playing that emphasizes the word and calls for sharply etched, vivid physical characterization to complement it. Acting on a cosmic scale in which emotion is exposed that must be true but heightened: this vision, which permeated all his work, persists at Stratford to this day, whether the piece onstage is a contemporary take on Greek tragedy like *Medea*, the dark mix of prejudice and lyricism offered by *The Merchant of Venice* or the tough-minded musical evocation of a lost world found in *Fiddler on the Roof*. The best Canadian acting at Stratford is still articulate and gritty, balancing the claims of heart and mind, and possessing a certain scale, a quality less of innate and studied elegance than of reckless audacity and a sort of improvised grandeur.

Romancing the Bard

An unknown chapter of history bursts into unexpected flame. An ancient tale of forgotten feudal rivalries gains relevance and immediacy as we are transported into the world of a young English King, quick, vigorous, yet still uncertain of his powers as he tests himself and his peers. His swift reaction to the deliberate insult of the French Dauphin, who sends him a gift of tennis balls, underscoring his reputation as a playboy, is fierce, but shaped by a controlling wit.

[above] Christopher Plummer as Henry V
[right] Jean Gascon as the Constable of France

Director: **Michael Langham**

Designer: **Tanya Moiseiwitsch**

HENRY V · 1956

Guy Hoffman as Le Fer, Robin Gammell as the Boy, Douglas Campbell as Pistol

*C*hristopher Plummer's Henry has charm, a dash of danger, and great curiosity. Determined to conquer and rule, he carries us with him. For all his brashness, his confidence and energy are irresistible. We watch his growing self-awareness as he steers a path between his own vaulting ambition and a deepening appreciation of its price in terms of human suffering. In victory he retains his sense of humour and love of adventure as he savours the delight of conquering a decadent court and a fresh young beauty. The capitulation of the ingenuous high-bred Princess Katherine of France signals the inevitable dominance of his aggressive spirit, but we sense that the more cultivated French will be an ongoing influence. There is the promise of a tension that could be energizing and fruitful.

It is the chemistry of two opposing races

[above] The battle of Agincourt:
Christopher Plummer as Henry V
[left] Gratien Gelinas as the King
of France

69

that brings excitement to the clash of battle. The Québécois actors have been brought to Stratford by Gratien Gelinas and Jean Gascon. Their portrayals of the French court are rendered with exquisite detail. Gelinas, as the half-mad old King, desperately struggling against his sense of his own impotence, signals his weakness in a vain attempt to command a chessboard. Ginette Letondal's delicate skittishness as the Princess barely conceals her underlying willfulness.

The elegant French, caparisoned in a blaze of blue and silver, fantasize about their anticipated victory on the eve of battle. The saturnine, self-assured Constable of Jean Gascon shows his contempt for the petulant Dauphin of Roger Gascon, who envies his splendid armour, with a single dismissive gesture. All of them exude hauteur and self-satisfaction in contrast to the scruffy uncertainty of Douglas Campbell's brash overbearing Pistol, Eric House's cocky bantam of a Fluellen and their ill-assorted cohorts. The opposing armies are like oil and water, ale and champagne, roast beef and pheasant under glass.

The two-hundred-year-old conflict between the French and English in Canada is given focus, acted out upon a stage with all the vitality that both sides can bring to it. Under the guise of recreating an ancient historic battle, we sense and almost smell the raw confidence of the Anglos, the anger and pride of the defeated French. The emotions suppressed for two centuries bubble up.

The Québécois actors excite the curiosity of Anglo audiences who have not yet begun to tune into the new Quebec. This production piques their curiosity. And the exuberance and panache of these French players powerfully stimulates the acting company, providing an influence at once playful and passionate, onstage and off. Its effect will not soon dissipate but continue to permeate the work of the company for many a year.

LES TRÈS RICHES ANNÉES
DE JEAN GASCON

MICHAEL LANGHAM'S DECISION TO RECRUIT Québécois actors to play the French court in *Henry V* was more than a bright idea. It a decisive factor in providing Langham with his first unqualified success at the Festival and it introduced an element that would profoundly affect the work in the years that followed. William Hutt paid tribute when he declared, "The French Canadians and especially Jean Gascon had such an exuberant passion for life that it spilled over into everything they touched." William Needles recalls, "When I stepped out onto the balcony as the Chorus in *Henry V* my nostrils were assaulted by the unmistakable odour of Chanel No. 5. I realized we were entering another dimension." Passion and style: these were the contributions of the contingent from Montreal headed by Jean Gascon. Their influence was to be ongoing and irreversible.

Gascon, who directed half a dozen Stratford productions before he succeeded Michael Langham as artistic director in 1968, brought to Stratford a sensibility that was as mature and fully formed as Guthrie's, but attuned to very different influences. As a schoolboy in Montreal he had been given a rigorously classical education by the Jesuits. As a student of medicine he learned to use his intelligence like a scalpel, his psychological perceptions like a skilled diagnostician. As a young actor in France working with such accomplished artists as Charles Dullin, Louis Jouvet, Georges Pitoeff, and Gaston Baty and the innovative young directors Jean-Louis Barrault and Jean Vilar, he was exposed to both the tradition of intellectual comedy stretching back from Giraudoux and Anouilh to Molière and the most advanced experimental theatre in Europe.

Returning to Montreal in 1951, he helped to create *Le Théâtre du Nouveau Monde* (TNM), conceived as an ensemble of equals, in which his confrères, many of whom had been in France with him—Georges Groulx, Guy Hoffman, Denise Pelletier, and Jean-Louis Roux—reflected the influence of their Parisian models in work that was vigorous, inventive, boldly experimental but firmly rooted in the traditions of French classical theatre. The TNM quickly became the dominant force in Quebec theatre.

The ambience in Gascon's company was that of a large French-Canadian family: intimately linked, high-spirited, quarrelsome, affectionate. In this it reflected the spirit of Quebec itself, a society where all inhabitants were cousins, which said to the rest of Canada, "We know who we are; if you don't, that's your problem." At the TNM, Gascon soon emerged as father-figure, his irrepressible enthusiasm driving the company forward, his vision of theatre expressed in his pungent dictum, "Le théâtre est comme la merde, ça se sent."

Where Guthrie and Langham were autocratic and Spartan, Gascon was expansive, generous, and extravagant. Like them, he could on occasion be uncompromising and indeed scathing, but he depended primarily on his capacity for persuasion, his innate charm, and a willingness to explore that may have been partly motivated by his awareness of working in a language other than his mother tongue. His understanding that he was in some sense an outsider leading a company dedicated to the British tradition was perhaps one of his greatest assets in enlarging the horizons of Stratford and its actors.

At the same time he had a signal advantage that his British predecessors did not enjoy: he was a wonderful actor. In Montreal he had succeeded brilliantly in the Molièrian roles of Pancrace, Arnolphe, and especially Don Juan, in which he amply displayed his magnetism. His temperament seemed especially suited to comedy, where his personal blend of intelligence, warmth, and irreverent wit were allowed full play. He married the precision and theatricality of Jouvet and Barrault to the ribald energy of the Québécois *habitant* and the panache of his playing delighted audiences not only in Montreal but also in Europe and the United States, where his company toured extensively in the mid-1950s. Then he invaded Ontario.

In mid-century there was still in the former Upper Canada a kind of envious fascination, and even infatuation, with the more sophisticated and glamorous Lower Canada and particularly the city of Montreal with its fine restaurants, hot nightspots, and unabashed enjoyment of life. William Hutt recently recalled the easy-going good humour of his Québécois compatriots in the Canadian Army in the Second World War; my own memories of serving in a destroyer during the Korean War with a largely French-Canadian crew are similar. *Les gars du Québec* sang, drank, told dirty stories, and seemed to possess an innate instinct for having a roaring good time with only the slenderest resources. Sadly, the fifty-year-old love affair of us uptight Anglos with our Québécois cousins has been largely unrequited. It is with *une certaine tristesse* that we find the robust geniality we remember replaced by rancour and suspicion.

But in 1956, when Gascon led his TNM actors into the unknown territory of western Ontario, which must have seemed to them almost as alien as the jungles of Borneo or the wastes of Siberia, there was no politically motivated hostility on either side. Separatism was not yet even in a gleam in the eyes of Gascon's contemporary René Lévesque. Gascon took on the role of the Constable of France and encouraged his actors to learn their lines phonetically. One of the most brilliant moments in *Henry V* was provided by Guy Hoffman as a French foot soldier, revolving on his back like a round black bug in a circle of confused and frustrated bewilderment, an emotional state born of the fact that he simply could not master his English lines. The TNM actors may have lost the battle of Agincourt onstage, but they won a place in the hearts of their audience.

Langham was quick to perceive Gascon's leadership qualities and invite him to direct at Stratford. In 1958 the TNM played 16 performances of *Le Malade imaginaire* in French at the Avon to laudatory notices and small but highly enthusiastic audiences. The next year Gascon was asked to co-direct *Othello* with George McCowan, which proved to be not a very satisfying experience for either of them. Gascon went back to Montreal but he and Langham remained in touch. Then, in 1963, Gascon suffered a heart attack. He resigned from the leadership of *Le Théâtre du Nouveau Monde and* took time out to recover.

Gascon returned to Stratford in 1963 to direct a wildly slapstick *Comedy of Errors* in the manner of the *commedia dell'arte*, followed in 1964 by an exuberantly hilarious staging of *Le Bourgeois gentilhomme* with a cast that included the cream of the Stratford company: Douglas Rain as the deluded Jourdain surrounded by Helen Burns, Len Cariou, Eric Christmas, Eric House, William Hutt, Frances Hyland, William Needles, and two brilliant young actors Heath Lamberts and Martha Henry.

Both productions were marked by an extravagance of invention distinctive in its visual and rhythmic elements, echoing the work of Jouvet and Barrault but also foreshadowing the freewheeling imagination of Robert Lepage and Gilles Mathieu two

Les Très Riches Années de Jean Gascon

decades later. The infusion of Gallic energy seemed to liberate a sensibility shared by Canadian Anglos and Francos, the raw humour of country people, quick to spot the ridiculous and deflate pretension, a common thread linking the work of Roch Carrier, La Bolduc, and Michel Tremblay to Don Harron, Dan Needles, and Stuart Maclean.

The cast also included two bright young actors of Italian ancestry, Leo Ciceri and John Juliani. They shared with Gascon a Latin sensibility and joined the parade of Latinos following the impetuous and fiery lead of Bruno Gerussi, who over the years would bring their distinctive flavour to the Festival: Berthold Carrière, Gabriel Charpentier, Antoni Cimolino, Juan Chioran, Diane D'Aquila, Colombe Demers, Paul Essiembre, Diana Leblanc, Ginette Letondal, Monique Leyrac, Nick Mancuso, Louise Marleau, Diego Matamoros, Mark Negin, Albert Millaire, Robert Prevost, Maria Ricossa, Jean-Louis Roux, a bright thread of scarlet running through the motley of the Stratford company. And ultimately, holding the whole magic garment together, we have Richard Monette. It has to be significant that the only native-born artistic directors of Stratford have both been Quebeckers.

Gascon's arrival coincided with a growing conviction on Langham's part that the company could not survive and grow if it were only to play Shakespeare. Eventually they would run out of plays and also the actors needed the challenge of essaying other styles, sounding other notes. Together Langham and Gascon began to add new flavours, more exotic dishes to the banquet. But the theatrical fare served up was not all profiteroles and crêpes suzettes.

Gascon's innate musicality made him a natural choice to direct the first of a series of stunningly realized Mozart operas, *The Marriage of Figaro* in 1964. The next year he set alongside it the acrid modernity of Brecht and Weill's *The Rise and Fall of the City of Mahagonny.* Before long it became apparent to Langham that Gascon with his wide range, keen intelligence, and ability to handle people was a logical successor, and in 1968 Gascon became executive artistic director with John Hirsch as his associate.

Gascon's signature production was Molière's darkest comedy *Tartuffe,* soon followed by Ben Jonson's *The Alchemist.* Gascon showed a real affinity for the sombre, savage creations of the Jacobean dramatists Jonson and Webster, who portrayed a world of corruption and cupidity that paralleled the hypocrisies and delusions portrayed in Molière's darker comedies (and perhaps echoed the chicaneries of the

Romancing the Bard

Quebec of Maurice Duplessis). Gascon's realizations of these works and of *Tartuffe* and *The Imaginary Invalid* were given body and dimension by the extraordinary comic talents of William Hutt. His portrayals of the lustful, sanctimonious Tartuffe and the obsessively fearful Argan, the preposterously grandiloquent Sir Epicure Mammon and the beguilingly deceitful miser Volpone were starkly outlined, brilliantly detailed, and utterly hilarious. Working together, Gascon and Hutt created a gallery of sharply original comic portraits that remains unsurpassed in the Festival's subsequent history.

To these Gascon added productions of hypnotic and unworldly beauty and power: Shakespeare's mythic parables of deception and redemption *Pericles* and *Cymbeline* and John Webster's coruscating depiction of madness and depravity, *The Duchess of Malfi*, revealed Gascon's uniquely fluid and poetic vision and his capacity for the inventive use of music to underscore and amplify his visual concepts.

At Stratford as in Montreal, Gascon acted roles both large and small, notable being his riotously foolish Dr. Caius in *The Merry Wives of Windsor* and his intensely tortured Edgar in Strindberg's *The Dance of Death* opposite Denise Pelletier. Gascon was always an actor among actors and this gave him a special claim on the company's affections. Pat Galloway affirms that no one before or since was more loved and certainly no one is more missed by the actors who worked closely with him. No one who speaks of Gascon has a harsh word for him; they remember his vivacity, his generosity, his loyalty, also his immediacy, his frankness, his boldness in taking risks, both in casting actors and choosing plays. He exuded confidence; he believed in his actors and encouraged them to believe in themselves.

During Gascon's tenure the company also toured extensively, playing in Ottawa, Montreal, Minneapolis, and Chicago. In the winter of 1973 they visited Europe with their productions of *King Lear* and *The Taming of the Shrew*, and in the following year took *The Imaginary Invalid* to Australia. On the company's return Gascon was awarded the $50,000 Royal Bank Award for his contribution to Canadian theatre. It was a fitting tribute and climax to his work at Stratford. No other director of the Festival has demonstrated as great a range or as wide a scope or has created a working environment so dominated by an unabashed love of the actor's art.

By 1974 the stress of keeping all these balls in the air was obviously telling on him; Gascon's health was precarious and he was drinking heavily. Although he was hailed

Les Très Riches Années de Jean Gascon

as a major theatre artist, Gascon had burned his bridges in Quebec, where the theatre was dominated by playwrights writing in *joual*, the language of the streets. He scolded his actress daughters for not speaking their own language properly on stage. He was considered *vieux jeux* and *vendu aux anglais*. He had abandoned his *nation* and married an Anglo, Marilyn Gardner, a Stratford actress whose warmth and charm complemented his own. He fretted and chafed but refused to retire into the shadows. In 1977 he was appointed Director-General of the National Arts Centre, where he directed notable productions of John Coulter's *Riel* and Molière's *Le Médecin malgré lui.* He also gave passionate performances in Strindberg's *The Father* and O'Neill's *Long Day's Journey Into Night.*

Then, in 1983, came another heart attack. Gascon left Ottawa and returned to Montreal where he worked sporadically in the theatre. He and Marilyn received old friends and, as ever, the wine flowed. In 1988 John Neville wooed him to come back to Stratford, where he undertook the direction of *My Fair Lady* on the Festival stage starring Neville, Douglas Campbell, and the young Lucy Peacock, a bright new star shining between two splendid actors of the old school.

The undertaking proved too much for Gascon and he was not able to complete his work, but the production was an enormous hit. He died in Stratford before it opened. "Of course he should never have taken it on," said Pat Galloway during a recent interview. But it seems likely that Jean Gascon would have been content to die while working in the theatre he had done so much to shape and nourish, like his adored Molière before him.

1968: William Hutt as Tartuffe

Above the stage a luminous cross appears, at once stark and mysterious. It hovers above our world, an unattainable and menacing image, promising salvation, threatening damnation.

TARTUFFE

TARTUFFE · 1968

Director: **_Jean Gascon_**

Designer: **_Tanya Moiseiwitsch_**

TARTUFFE · 2000

Director: **_Richard Monette_**

Designers: **_Tanya Moiseiwitsch,_**
Ann Curtis

*S*uddenly the stage bursts into vigorous life as a razor-tongued old woman gives her family a piece of her mind. We are in the comfortable house of a wealthy bourgeois, a scene familiar yet foreign. The speech is sharpened, the emotions heightened, as we are drawn into this drama of the effects of religious hypocrisy on a bourgeois household. As Grandma sounds off, we realize her comments are pointed by the precision of rhyming couplets.

[far left] 1968: Leo Ciceri as Cleante, Jane Casson as Flipote, Barbara Bryne as Mme. Pernelle, Pat Galloway as Dorine, Martha Henry as Elmire

[left] 2000: Brian Bedford as Tartuffe, Lucy Peacock as Elmire, James Blendick as Orgon, Seana McKenna as Dorine

The members of the family respond with spirit but are rebuffed, as a world takes shape: ordered, rational, witty, passionate.

This is the world of Molière, the master French dramatist, as realized in English by the elegant, meticulous metrical invention of the American poet Richard Wilbur and the exuberant and audacious invention of the Québécois director Jean Gascon, provoking his actors into giving free, flamboyant *expression to the bubbling emotions underlying the cool precision of the words.*

Molière pits reason against passion but he doesn't take sides. The conflict between these two opposing powers gives life and dimension to his characters. Some are enslaved by the confining strictures of the head; others are unduly swayed by the unruly urgings of the heart.

Orgon is betrayed by his obsessive desire to win the approval of Tartuffe, while Tartuffe is undone by his compulsive lust for Elmire. Cleante is too dully rational to prevail with either of them, Damis is too impetuous to be taken seriously, and the young lovers are too much smitten with each other to comprehend anything clearly.

Molière, like Pascal, knows the heart has its reasons, but he also understands these reasons can create chaos.

So the domestic drama unfolds and it seems everybody will lose—except the audience, whose hilarity mounts as the characters play out their follies. In the end, two women find a balance between heart and head, affection and ingenuity. Elmire, the wise and resourceful wife, and Dorine, the perceptive and outspoken maid, prove to have the clearest vision. But they are not able to save their master from the consequences of his own foolishness. Only the intervention of a higher power can do that.

The pleasures of this play have their culmination in the ridiculous but irresistible seduction scene as Tartuffe chases Elmire around the table beneath which her husband is hiding. She expects him to rush out as soon as Tartuffe's intended assault upon her becomes evident, but in fact it is only when Tartuffe expresses his contempt for Orgon that Orgon can no longer contain his anger and reveals himself.

In Tartuffe we see the hypocrite writ large, but Orgon is equally dishonest. The difference is that he is deceiving himself. Is this more reprehensible than deceiving others? Molière poses the question but doesn't presume to give us the answer.

His play provides extraordinary opportunities for actors to embody the

1968: Douglas Rain as Orgon, Pat Galloway as Dorine

vanities and ambitions of the human animal. As Tartuffe, William Hutt was a monster so self-satisfied in his sliminess, so unabashed in his audacity, so bold and facile in his rapidly shifting mendacity, so full of enjoyment of his seemingly infinite capacity for deception that he was irresistible. He would play the role twice at Stratford before passing it on to another master of comic invention, Brian Bedford, whose hypocrite would be scruffier, cruder but equally a man at once repulsive and charming, a creature we love to hate.

Tartuffe is matched by Orgon's willing submission to his own unacknowledged need to be overmastered and seduced. This masochistic quality has been caught in splendidly individual performances by Douglas Rain, Donald Davis, Douglas Campbell, and James Blendick.

Martha Henry's Elmire was at once warm and cool, innocent and knowing, Domini Blythe in the same role was provocative and mocking, Lucy Peacock serene but subtly scheming. The maid Dorine is more knowing and also more detached. Pat Galloway and Seana McKenna both brought edge and intelligence to the role. Skeptical, practical, and fuelled by curiosity, Dorine is smarter than her masters, more aloof than Tartuffe: she is a virtual Molière in skirts.

A Russian play with a Canadian soul. The first production at Stratford of a very special Canadian director, a Hungarian Jew who survived the Holocaust before settling in Winnipeg as a teenager. John Hirsch, the outsider, seemed to understand the Canadian sensibility intuitively and draw it out of his actors as few native directors have managed to do. There was no attempt to emulate the wild volatility of Slavs or the pale nostalgia of British aristocrats that we had come to associate with Chekhovian productions. This *Cherry Orchard* might have taken place in the Ottawa Valley in 1905.

Director: **John Hirsh**

Designer: **Brian Jackson**

Kate Reid as Mme. Ranevskaya

Frances Hyland as Varya, Kate Reid as Mme. Ranevskaya

*T*he stage is filled with sofas and oil lamps, the colours subdued, the lighting soft and shadowy. The rhythm is subtle, endlessly shifting. Each character is allowed the time he needs for his dreams, his longings, his frustrations as this extended family drink tea and chatter, frittering away the days that lead inexorably to the loss of their beloved home. These people are complex: impulsive and at the same time inhibited, sad and silly, lovable and infuriating. They embrace their folly and glory in it. They love and forgive each other but cannot come to terms with their own impracticalities.

At the centre is Kate Reid's Ranevskaya: frank, generous, sharp-tongued,

Mary Savidge as Charlotta does card tricks for the family

and pleasure-loving. Her rapport with her foolish brother Gaev, played by William Hutt, bespeaks an intensely shared fondness in which both are deeply aware of the other's faults, powerless to protect but utterly, unswervingly loyal. The underlying pain and determined gallantry of Reid's Ranevskaya are echoed on a smaller scale by Frances Hyland's angular, buttoned-up adopted daughter Varya and the whimsical bravado of Mary Savidge's displaced governess Charlotta. These women are hopelessly caught in the web of their own sensibilities. They sympathize with each other's predicaments but cannot bring themselves to compromise their standards or change their ways. Like Alice Munro's rural Ontario spinsters, they choose to decline.

They thread their way through their lives not wishing to see where they are headed, their fate unheeded and therefore inevitable. Ranevskaya's realization in the last act that Varya will never marry Lopakhin combines pity and rage in equal measure, directed at the intractability not only of others but also of life itself. These women have learned to accept life with its unrealized promise and inevitable decay and to keep moving on.

*More optimistic and therefore more ridiculous are the men. William Hutt's
Gaev clinging to his faded fantasy of himself as a young man-about-town;
the persistently hopeful but hopelessly accident-prone Yepihodov of William
Needles; the high-minded but emotionally unaware middle-aged student
Trofimov of Hugh Webster; the dignified but creakily decrepit valet Firs of
Powys Thomas; and, most of all, the beaming, enthusiastic peasant-turned-
entrepreneur Lopakhin of Douglas Campbell, a clown who takes himself seriously, failing to see why others cannot accept his simple-minded solutions,
yet unable to find ways to express his own simplest feelings.*

*In Hirsch's hands the interplay of these people is now comic, now pathetic,
one moment melodramatic, the next subdued, always intensely human. He has
shaped the work of these actors to show us a family who share a sense of time
and place, bound to each other by needs and circumstances yet each alone, isolated, unable to empty out an overburdened heart. They create a world that
touches us with its aching familiarity. We share their joys and sorrows because
they are our own.*

Hugh Webster as Trofimov, Douglas Campbell as Lopakhin, Susan Ringwood
as Anya, Kate Reid as Mme. Ranevskaya, Frances Hyland as Varya

MASSAGING THE MANDATE

WHAT IS STRATFORD'S MANDATE? This currently fashionable concept was unknown to the Festival's founders, who were trying to get a theatre going and did not have the time or inclination to concern themselves with critical commandments graven on granite. Tom Patterson's idea was to do the plays of Shakespeare in Stratford simply because of the name. By his own admission he had read few of the plays and had no innate feeling for their literary or dramatic value. Guthrie chose to believe that Patterson had drunk at the wells of European culture during his experience in the Second World War (some soldiers did) but Patterson has revealed that, as far as he was concerned, this was Guthrie's romantic fantasy. Patterson was at heart an idealistic huckster who wanted to bring prosperity to his home town. He succeeded beyond his wildest dreams, but those who berate the Festival for its subsequent commerciality might remember that promotion and peddling were as much a part of the original vision as any high-minded literary ideals.

Guthrie believed the thrust stage was suitable only for plays written before about 1660. In the second year he broadened the idea of the Festival going beyond the work of the Bard to tap into the Greeks. Guthrie also believed the Festival should feature other attractions and from the very beginning encouraged a musical component. His notion of a national theatre encompassed opera and dance and when he was running the Old Vic his seasons included these elements. But Guthrie did not remain artistic director long enough either at the Old Vic or at Stratford to establish a fully developed policy for those theatres. All of his successors—Langham, Gascon, Phillips, Hirsch, Neville, William, and Monette—have struggled with the question of exactly what the Stratford Festival should be attempting to do.

In the early years, the Festival offered a season of two or three plays by Shakespeare, a pattern that persisted until 1962 when the Festival offered up *Cyrano de Bergerac,* a play which, although it was written in the nineteenth century, had many affinities with Renaissance drama: high rhetorical and poetic speech, splendid period costumes and sweeping changes of locale that could be facilitated by the fluid style of staging that Guthrie and Langham had developed on the thrust stage. This innovation was soon followed by further incursions into the classical repertoire: Molière's *Le Bourgeois gentilhomme* and Wycherley's *The Country Wife* in 1964, Chekhov's *The Cherry Orchard* in 1965, Gogol's *The Government Inspector* in 1967.

Meanwhile the Festival began playing in a second house in Stratford, the Avon, a proscenium theatre that had been built for live performances but reverted to a cinema in the 30s. It came into regular use during the 1960 season with Guthrie's rollicking production of Gilbert and Sullivan's *H.M.S. Pinafore*. The success of this operetta was followed by other musical shows at the Avon: works by G&S, Benjamin Britten, Mozart and Kurt Weill. The balance of the Festival had shifted away from the purely Shakespearean to a richer and more varied sampling of classical works.

This began in Langham's time. He may well have been influenced in broadening the scope of the repertoire by the fact that Guthrie himself was staging Chekhov and Molière on the thrust stage he had caused to be constructed at the theatre named for him in Minneapolis. But the main impetus toward a more varied program undoubtedly came from Jean Gascon, whose production of *The Comedy of Errors* in 1963 won plaudits from its viewers if not from the critics. It established him as a lively and innovative director with a vision of his own and a knack for knowing what would please an audience.

Gascon was every bit as committed to classical theatre as Guthrie and Langham but he didn't see Shakespeare as the only peak in the range of dramatic master-pieces. Gascon's idea of classical theatre included Chekhov, Turgenev, Strindberg, Ibsen, Feydeau, and of course Molière. He made Molière the second playwright of the Stratford company, and he probably did more than anyone else to revive interest in Molière in North America (with the exception of the American poet Richard Wilbur, whose witty and elegant rhyming verse translations have captured and encapsulated the spirit of the great French playwright for contemporary English-speaking audiences).

Gascon was concerned not only with broadening the range of the Festival's dramatic repertoire but also with stimulating and surprising the audience. From the beginning, Guthrie and Langham understood that audiences do not want to see *King Lear* followed by *Hamlet* and then *Medea*, so every year they programmed a comedy. In the early years this meant the discovery by the audience of the joys of a series of rarely performed works of Shakespeare: *All's Well That Ends Well*, *The Merry Wives of Windsor*, *The Winter's Tale*, *Love's Labour's Lost*, *The Comedy of Errors*. These little-known plays were brought to life and provoked unexpected laughter and delight. But Gascon felt the need to find other plays that would be fun for the audience.

Gascon also encouraged the creation of new works that would connect with a contemporary public following up the success of James Reaney's rural Ontario fantasy *Colours in the Dark.* He mounted Tom Hendry and Stanley Silverman's provocatively outrageous musical take on Petronius' *Satyricon*; Peter Luke's suave adaptation of Baron Corvo's highly-coloured novel about a gay Pope *Hadrian VII*; Roch Carrier's *La Guerre, Yes Sir*, a politically charged piece about wartime life in a Gaspé village; and finally a whole season of new plays by leading European avant-gardistes Arabal, Mrozek, and Wesker. The critics were intrigued but the public wasn't. This was not what they expected from Stratford and they stayed away in droves. Gascon, always audience-sensitive, abandoned the absurdists and returned to comedy from Goldsmith to Labiche and Offenbach as well as bringing to life two late Shakesperean romances, *Pericles* and *Cymbeline*. In retrospect, the audacity and range of Gascon's experimentation are astonishing.

Any serious theatre has an obligation not only to respond to the aspirations of its artists but also to understand and develop the taste of its public. Nowadays the Festival spends a good deal of time and money analysing the demographics of its audience to ascertain age, socio-economic status, geographical location, and the like. Thus it has determined that 25 per cent of its customers are under twenty-five, 60 per cent are in the $50,000 to $100,000 income bracket, and 40 per cent are American. Like all statistics, these can be and are manipulated to argue for and against certain kinds of programming.

And of course the statistics keep changing. The nature of any audience is bound to change. In the beginning there was a preponderance of curious if somewhat uninformed enthusiasts. Guthrie pointed out that Stratford's earliest audiences were unsophisticated but not unintelligent. They included a number of people who knew little of theatre but a good deal about literature, typified by Toronto's bluestocking matron Mrs. Iliffe-Dean, who was heard to remark as she left a performance of Guthrie's "Wild West" *Taming of the Shrew,* leaning heavily on the arms of her two forty-something bachelor sons, "I think it's perfectly dreadful, but if it sends people back to *reading* their Shakespeare, it may be accounted a good thing." Her spiritual descendants are still with us.

On the whole, however, Stratford's earliest audiences were open-minded and adventurous. Some of them were young people who had discovered Shakespeare at university and were getting their first taste of live theatre, but even the middle-aged were fired with enthusiasm when they saw the plays realized on stage. They were unashamedly elitist and as they picked up on the positive buzz from the first season they prided themselves on being discerning. They quickly formed the habit of making an annual expedition to see what the Festival would come up with next and were the foundation upon which the initially fragile finances of the Festival could begin to build a more solidly based institution. (I am still asked every season when the Stratford brochure comes out, "What's going to be good this year?" I can't tell any more than the people who ask me, but I make recommendations anyway, based on my own prejudices.)

The elements that constitute today's theatre audience have probably not changed fundamentally. Guthrie believed that theatre offers its viewers a ritual experience essentially spiritual in nature. The theatre is like a sort of secular religion, with passionate devotees, less committed well-wishers, and those who go to the temple primarily to be seen by others. There are the theatre professionals who are in the know and have a sense of obligation, rather like nuns and monks. There are the critics, who roughly correspond to theologians. These include among their ranks the professionals who earn their living by pronouncing for the benefit of the less perceptive, but also a knowledgeable clutch of amateur critics who derive enormous pleasure from passionately debating the merits and defects of a production with their peers. There are students, skeptical but curious, willing to be won but withholding ultimate commitment, and finally tourists, who have been told this is something they should experience, like the Eiffel Tower or the Coliseum.

Today's audience still contains all these elements, although with time the balance has shifted somewhat, away from the original zealots who saw themselves partaking of "caviare for the general" and toward a more middlebrow crowd whose idea of art has inevitably been affected by Disney, Andrew Lloyd Webber, and *Star Wars*. (It seems there's no escaping Alec Guinness.) There are a certain number of people who

Massaging the Mandate

feel they've seen it all, or that the Festival has been dumbed down and who stay away. Of course this was true thirty years ago. I remember a comment when Robin Phillips took over the reins, "Thank goodness they've got rid of that decadent Frenchman and given the stage back to a real *English* director."

Robin Phillips did not in fact betray the legacy of Gascon. By the time Phillips arrived, the Board had already made the decision to abandon opera on financial grounds: musical productions were more costly than "straight" plays and invariably lost money. But Phillips was interested in musical theatre and would offer shows with a musical element beginning in his first season with *Trumpets and Drums*, Brecht's adaptation of Farquhar's *The Recruiting Officer*, which featured songs with music specially composed by Alan Laing. In later years there would be productions of Leonard Bernstein's *Candide* and John Gay's *The Beggar's Opera*, but the main thrust of Phillips' innovation in programming was concerned with extending the scope of the organization.

Phillips talked about the Festival in business terms, comparing it to General Motors, which increased its share of the market by making an increasing number of different models of cars to appeal to the growing variety of tastes of the North American middle class as it expanded and attained greater wealth and sophistication. Phillips' approach was to increase the number of productions and the length of the season. Whereas during Gascon's regime a typical season included four mainstage and three Avon productions, a typical Phillips season had six shows on the Festival stage, four or five at the Avon and another three at the new Third Stage, which opened in a temporarily converted badminton court in 1978.

Phillips expanded on Gascon's programming, adding modern British plays: Noel Coward's *Hay Fever* and *Private Lives* but also more challenging dramas such as Shaw's *Saint Joan*, John Whiting's *The Devils*, and Edward Bond's *The Woman*. American plays included Arthur Miller's *The Crucible*, Robert Patrick's *Kennedy's Children*, John Guare's *Bosoms and Neglect*, and D.L. Coburn's *The Gin Game*. Phillips was obviously inspired to some extent by the example of Britain's National Theatre in his effort to combine the classical with the contemporary. For the most part this mix of shows proved popular with audiences who were ready to see the best in theatre, ancient and modern, side by side. Far from abandoning the Bard, in most seasons Phillips offered six Shakespearean productions, balancing comedies, tragedies,

90

and histories. Phillips' tenure did not last long enough for him to run through the entire canon but his voracious consumption of the available masterpieces would eventually pose problems. How often is the public prepared to see *Twelfth Night* or *Hamlet*? The question continues to perplex Stratford's programmers.

Phillips also took up the challenge of producing new work, aided and egged on by his dramaturge Urjo Kareda. The majority of these offerings were disliked by critics and audiences alike. The most notable exception was Larry Fineberg's *Eve*, which was conceived as a vehicle for visiting star Jessica Tandy. Her celebrity as an actress and her luminous and richly detailed performance ensured that the production was seriously reviewed and well attended. This was not lost on Phillips and Kareda, who began to option scripts designed to show off the talents of stars: *Virginia*, in which Maggie Smith portrayed the Bloomsbury novelist, went on to a run in London while *Foxfire*, devised by Hume Cronyn and Susan Cooper for himself and his wife Jessica Tandy, was later a success on Broadway. Both scripts brought reflected lustre to the Festival but of course neither was particularly Canadian.

Phillips' experiments with new work would have ongoing repercussions, but his immediate successor John Hirsch believed that Stratford had no business doing new work and that he should return to the original vision of a classical theatre. He reduced the number of productions, although he allowed modern classics such as works by Shaw, Durrenmatt, and Tennessee Williams alongside the works of Shakespeare, Molière and Sheridan.

In the 1980s most new scripts seen at the Festival tended to be compilations of material from respectable literary sources, usually Shakespeare: Nicholas Pennell's *A Variable Passion*, Irene Worth's *Letters of Love and Affection*, David William's *In Other Words Shakespeare*, Brian Bedford's *The Lunatic, the Lover and the Poet*. Others were plays about established literary figures: Chekhov and his wife in *Intimate Admiration*, a vehicle for Neville and Lucy Peacock; and *Blake*, a piece about the visionary English poet designed around the splendidly rumbustious performance of Douglas Campbell.

Hirsch, Neville, and William retreated from the heady, full-out programming of Phillips' heyday and established what Urjo Kareda would later describe as "a mix of comedies and tragedies spinning around in a permanent rinse cycle," the five best-known comedies and three most accessible tragedies appearing at least once every five

Massaging the Mandate

years. Although Kareda's formula is a bit of an over-simplification, this pattern persists to this day. It is argued that because of Stratford's growing dependence on and obligation to student audiences, these plays find a new crop of young people who come to the plays with fresh expectations every five years.

In his first year John Neville experimented with the notion of a thematic grouping of plays, electing to do Shakespeare's three late romances and to couple *Hamlet* with Tom Stoppard's *Rosencrantz and Guildenstern Are Dead*. This intrigued the critics but not the audience; they did not want thematic consistency, but rather craved variety. An idea dear to many academics bit the dust when confronted with popular taste and economic reality. And not for the last time. Financial imperatives would loom ever larger in the last two decades of the century.

Neville also courted his public with a mainstage musical. The original idea was to do musicals grounded in Shakespeare, and as the rights to *Kiss Me, Kate* were not available, Neville led off with a production of Rogers and Hart's *The Boys From Syracuse*, loosely based on *The Comedy of Errors*. The show proved popular with audiences but it was the huge box office success of *My Fair Lady* in 1988 that would establish a precedent that rapidly became as devoutly sanctified in the unwritten traditions guiding Stratford's programmers as the primacy of Shakespeare. A new orthodoxy was taking shape.

Neville and William continued to program modern classics: Brecht's *Mother Courage* and *Arturo Ui*, Tennessee Williams' *The Glass Menagerie* and *Cat on a Hot Tin Roof*, T.S. Eliot's *Murder in the Cathedral*. (Reaction to this title indicated that a shift in audience perception of Stratford was already underway. One ticket-buyer complimented Stratford on being hip enough to do a play by the author of *Cats*; another commented, "It's great that you've finally followed the lead of the Shaw Festival and included a murder mystery in your line-up.")

David William was committed to the idea of producing Canadian classics. He had considerable success with revivals of Michel Tremblay's early plays: *Les Belles-Soeurs*, *Forever Yours, Marie-Lou*, and *Bonjour, là, Bonjour*. He also programmed previously produced works by Sharon Pollock and John Murrell and adaptations of works by Robertson Davies and Lewis Carroll.

By the time Richard Monette succeeded David William as artistic director of the

Festival in 1994, it had been losing about a million dollars a season for several years and its reserves were exhausted. It was made clear that Monette's first duty was to turn the place around. In a recent interview he stated, "When I took over, my 'artistic vision' was to keep the place from closing." In his early years he clearly focused on making the Festival financially viable.

Monette accepted the "rinse cycle" pattern of rotating the popular comedies and tragedies, the Shakespeare texts that had proven to be good box office, no matter who played in them or how well or less well they were done. He also accepted the inevitability of the annual musical. He felt strongly that the Festival needed to build young audiences, holding to a theory enunciated by Guthrie that "the only great theatre you see is the theatre you experience when you are young and impressionable." Stratford's audiences were visibly aging, although the company did play to students in the spring and fall. Monette wanted to find shows that young people would enjoy and attend even in the middle of the summer.

This led him to develop what he called "The Family Experience." This idea was encouraged by the success of Reaney's adaptation of *Alice Through the Looking Glass*. Other family shows followed: *The Miracle Worker*, *The Prime of Miss Jean Brodie*, *The Diary of Anne Frank*, as well as adaptations of literary masterworks: *Pride and Prejudice*, *Little Women*, and *The Three Musketeers*. The fact that these productions reflected a sensibility apparently owing a good deal to classic comics proved to be part of their appeal. The musicals began to exhibit a similar character: *Man of la Mancha*, *Camelot*, *Dracula*, *Fiddler on the Roof*, *The Sound of Music*. These productions reached and pleased a wider audience. Sales mounted; so did profits.

Monette also added to the repertoire modern works that were crowd-pleasers in their day and that he believed would still please his audience if they were sufficiently well acted and produced. These were mainly Broadway or West End hits of yesteryear: *Sweet Bird of Youth*, *The Little Foxes*, *Amadeus*, *Death of a Salesman*, *A Man for All Seasons*, *Who's Afraid of Virginia Woolf?*, *Equus*, *Inherit the Wind*, shows chosen to display the talents of the best and best-known actors in the Stratford company. Actors rose to the challenge and audiences rose to the bait. These productions changed the financial picture and the character of the season.

Mindful of the poor showing of such new scripts as *In the Ring* and *Victoria*, Monette was cautious about programming similar material. Not that he was unsympathetic to new work: his early experience as an actor included new plays like *The Drummer Boy* in the 1960s at Theatre Toronto and a stint with Charles Marowitz in London, followed by a lengthy appearance in *Oh Calcutta*. Back in Canada, Monette appeared in a number of new Canadian plays in the early 1970s, most notably Michel Tremblay's *Hosanna*, which effectively put him on the map as a leading actor and gained him entrée into Phillips' Stratford company.

In the early years of his tenure, Monette took the position that Stratford's mandate should be to do the best plays available, "and that doesn't necessarily include many Canadian works. Most Canadian playwrights don't know how to write a second act." Nevertheless, under his leadership new scripts were workshopped. Some, such as Lee MacDougall's *High Life*, have had successful subsequent productions. And he programmed Canadian works that had succeeded elsewhere, most notably Timothy Findley's *The Stillborn Lover* and David Young's *Glenn*, based on the life of the eminent Canadian pianist Glenn Gould. Then suddenly the extraordinary critical and box office success of Timothy Findley's *Elizabeth Rex*, in 2000, turned the tide. As a result, the 2001 season contained four new Canadian scripts and Monette's longtime but buried dream of a small space devoted entirely to new work seemed about to be realized.

Today the Stratford mandate states that the Festival's aim is to do great plays with special emphasis on the works of William Shakespeare. This is grand, sweeping, and open to a variety of interpretations. What is meant by "great" and who defines it? The company, the critics or the audience? Monette is highly sensitive to all three and they will continue to influence his judgment. Unlike Guthrie he does not make up his mind in the first two minutes. He listens and ponders. His ideas and his gut feelings are in constant intercourse and are constantly evolving. This ongoing process guarantees only one thing: the face of the Festival will continue to change as long as Monette is in charge.

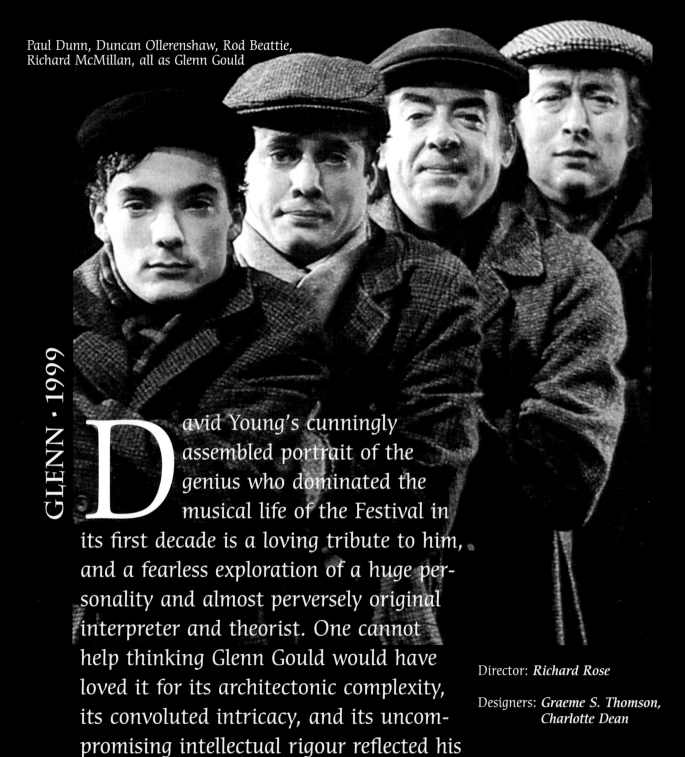

Paul Dunn, Duncan Ollerenshaw, Rod Beattie,
Richard McMillan, all as Glenn Gould

GLENN · 1999

David Young's cunningly
assembled portrait of the
genius who dominated the
musical life of the Festival in
its first decade is a loving tribute to him,
and a fearless exploration of a huge personality and almost perversely original
interpreter and theorist. One cannot
help thinking Glenn Gould would have
loved it for its architectonic complexity,
its convoluted intricacy, and its uncompromising intellectual rigour reflected his
own artistic personality

Director: *Richard Rose*

Designers: *Graeme S. Thomson,*
Charlotte Dean

The four Glenns making music

*G*ould the man is split in four like a figure in a David Hockney collage, not just chronolgically but psychologically. Four different actors play Gould as The Prodigy, The Performer, The Perfectionist, The Puritan. They interact, throwing and catching the baton like athletes, tossing it back and forth like voices in a well-tempered fugue.

The actors playing these roles have not been encouraged to stay within a unifying stylistic straitjacket. They move from deadpan drollery to overblown oratory, fresh chopped logic to low comedy, classical rhetoric to colloquial quips. Rod Beattie, Paul Dunn, Richard McMillan, and Duncan Ollerenshaw look like different aspects of Gould at different ages, but they don't look much like each other. They give the man many facets, deepening his complexity rather than suggesting an essential homogeneity in his nature. Young, the practised wordsmith, gloats over his verbal dexterity very much as Gould relished and exploited his pianistic virtuosity. Like his hero, Young sticks his

*neck out, risking obscurity, courting the condemnation of purists and idola-
tors. This is elitist theatre, if you like, uncompromisingly cerebral and committed to aesthetic values of pattern, precision, and paradox.*

*Like many great artists, Gould was in many ways his own greatest cre-
ation. He played games with his personality, his unpredictable style, his growing eccentricity. In Young's script, modelled on the thirty Goldberg variations,
we see Gould run the gamut of moods and attitudes, now fiercely arrogant,
now coolly rational, then childishly vulnerable. He can be scathing, charming,
extroverted, withdrawn.*

*The pleasure derived from this performance lies not in a rush of emotion
but in a picture almost pointillist, hundreds of tiny details put together with
consummate skill until the whole is finally assembled, the big picture revealed.
Rose stages the work with bold imagistic strokes: a hundred roses dropping on
the stage; Gould in earphones locked in an inner musical universe or buried in
enveloping overcoat and trailing scarf, his hands muffled in woollen gloves,
his head topped by a preposterous cap with outsize ear-lugs, armour against
an alien, uncomprehending world.*

*Is this a play? Does it matter? It is an engrossing experience, a glimpse of
a unique artist who opened our ears and our minds to a world of shifting
tonalities, sudden dissonances, and unforeseen harmonies, an evocation of a
great spirit who once dwelt among us and still inspires and invigorates our
consciousness.*

A DYING FALL:
MUSIC AT STRATFORD

As a young man, Tyrone Guthrie had ambitions to be a singer. He studied with an ancient singing coach, Gustave Garcia, who eventually told him, "The voice is very *large*. You can sing at parties. People will ask you out. You will get into nice society. But you will not be much of a singer. You can make a good listener, a good audience. Stick to that." Guthrie did not set his jaw and determine to prove the maestro wrong, but accepted his judgment. However, Guthrie's musical sense became an important part of his equipment as a director. To him, a play was like a musical composition. And he never lost his interest in music. At home at Annagh-ma-Kerrig in Ireland's County Monaghan, Guthrie played and sang hymns for his guests or conducted concerts of Verdi's *Requiem*, singing along with the gramophone while his wife complained, "Can't we just listen, Tony?", to which he would answer, "No, must be *involved*."

So it is not surprising that from the very beginning Guthrie wanted the Stratford Festival to have a musical component. He believed it would add another dimension to the enjoyment of his audiences and possibly would induce some of them to stay overnight, to make an outing of it and see both plays as well as a concert or two. This would indeed become a pattern for many Stratford patrons as the Festival grew in size and scope.

Guthrie was fortunate to connect with Canadian composer Louis Applebaum in the very first season. Applebaum was a sensitive and inventive musician but realistic about the nature of composing for the theatre. He had been musical director of the National Film Board before going to New York and Hollywood to work in television, and he had already composed some 300 film scores. He quickly recognized Guthrie's musical sophistication and the need for collaboration. As he wrote in 1977, "music is there to underline the drama and set the mood....You must establish one mind about the music, not two. So what has to happen, is that the composer and the director must establish a very clear plan."

Applebaum wrote the music for both *Richard III* and *All's Well That Ends Well*.

At Guthrie's suggestion, he also composed two fanfares to be played before the curtain rises and at intermission to summon the audience into the theatre. This manifestation of Guthrie's fondness for pageantry would become a potent symbol of the Festival. When Richard Monette became artistic director forty years later and was charged with ways of economizing, he learned that the cost of having five musicians play these fanfares live for every performance was $100,000 a season. But such was the emotive value of these brazen flourishes in reinforcing the Festival's identity for the audience that the Board considered their elimination unthinkable.

In that first year Applebaum discovered that there was an accomplished group of singers in Stratford and Guthrie was delighted to integrate them into performances of both plays. Bruce Swerdfager recalled that the first time the singers rehearsed with the cast of *All's Well That Ends Well* he was directed to give them a signal to retire at the approach of Alec Guinness as the King of France. He did so, but the ladies remained rooted to the spot, whereupon Guthrie roared, "No, no, no. When Bruce waves at you women, fuck off." When Bruce asked one of the choristers, who happened to be his landlady, if she was upset, she replied, "Well, after that, I don't think we're likely to forget our cue."

Guthrie was keen to integrate the musical enthusiasts of Stratford into his shows but he wanted something more: concerts by the best artists Canada had to offer. Applebaum therefore set up programs to be given on Tanya Moiseiwitsch's stage under Skip Manley's tent. A series of 16 afternoon concerts featured a number of rising Canadian musicians, among them Lois Marshall, Ed McCurdy, James Milligan, Albert Praz, Jan Rubes, and a youngster named Glenn Gould. He played Beethoven to a house of perhaps sixty people in a crashing thunderstorm that completely drowned out the notes. The concerts were excellent but inadequately publicized and poorly attended. When Governor-General Vincent Massey arrived with his entourage to hear violinist Gerhard Kander, his party of thirty outnumbered the rest of the audience. But the critics were wildly enthusiastic.

In 1954 there were no official concerts; Applebaum was getting ready for a proper musical season in 1955. It featured Glenn Gould, by now beginning to receive international attention for his Columbia recording of the Goldberg Variations. Gould would become a major figure in the Stratford music program for the next ten years. He played solo concerts and chamber works, utilizing his growing celebrity to introduce the work of modern composers such as Hindemith, Kodaly, Krenek, Prokofiev, Schoenberg, Richard Strauss, and Stravinsky to an unfamiliar public. At one recital of 1920s music he made a notorious entrance through the trapdoor of the stage wearing a coonskin coat. He continued to play Beethoven, Brahms and, of course, Bach, introducing his controversial harpsi-piano, created by putting thumbtacks under the strings of a Steinway grand. Gould became a familiar figure walking Stratford's streets in the middle of summer in heavy overcoat, woolen gloves and romantically trailing muffler. He was nothing if not a consummate showman.

Gould appreciated and exploited the freedom that Applebaum, in building his program around Gould, allowed him. Gould was notoriously difficult to deal with but Applebaum found two first-rate musicians who were able to accommodate themselves to his demands and hold their own as artists. Cellist Leonard Rose and violinist Oscar Shumsky gave many concerts with Gould and the three functioned as a triumvirate heading up a program that soon included intensive workshops as well as performances, first on weekday afternoons and then, when the Lord's Day Act was finally relaxed, on Sunday afternoons in the newly erected Festival Theatre.

Gould gave his final public performance in Canada at the Festival Theatre. Pale and stooped, he came out on the stage and insisted that there be no applause. He then sat at his harpsi-piano in a narrow shaft of light and worked his way through Bach's Art of the Fugue, hunching his shoulders, grimacing and humming, mannerisms familiar to the many admirers who packed the house. When he came to the end of this great, uncompleted masterwork the lights dimmed. When they came up, Gould was gone and the audience poured out into the afternoon sunshine to ponder the mysteries of Bach's (and Gould's) extraordinary art.

Every summer in the 1950s and early 1960s, for six weeks a carefully selected group of some of the best musicians in Canada were selected from major orchestras across the land. Together they explored repertory and attended master classes by some of the greats of the musical world who came to give concerts: Claudio Arrau, Daniel Barenboim, Alfred Brendel, Van Cliburn, Jaqueline du Pré, Jose Iturbi, Zara Nelsova, Itzak Perlman, Roberta Peters, Jean-Pierre Rampal, Aksel Schiotz, Elizabeth Schwarzkopf, Rudolf Serkin, Ravi Shankar, and Isaac Stern.

Stratford had become, at least for the summer, the major musical centre in Canada and this was marked in 1960 when the city hosted the International Conference of

100

Composers arranged by Applebaum. Composers came from 22 countries to exchange views and hear each other's music. The CBC Symphony and a variety of *ad hoc* ensembles and soloists played compositions by everyone from Varèse to Tacktackishvili to Murray Schafer. Applebaum noted, "Canadian composers learned to their surprise that their output was on a par with that from other, long-established cultures—sound justification for the new self-confidence felt thereafter in Canada's musical life."

Applebaum also inaugurated a tradition of musical theatre, kicked off in 1955 with a production of Stravinsky's *A Soldier's Tale,* newly translated into English by Laure Riese, directed by Douglas Campbell with William Needles and Douglas Rain, dancer Lillian Jarvis, and introducing the French mime Marcel Marceau, who also did a solo program introducing his signature character Bip. The four performances were sold out and had a phenomenally enthusiastic response from the public, launching Marceau's career in North America and supporting Applebaum's conviction that Stratford was the perfect place to launch a program of "lyric theatre."

The next year saw a production of Benjamin Britten's *The Rape of Lucretia* with a cast that included Regina Reznik, Jan Rubes, Jennie Tourel, and an unknown young tenor, Jon Vickers. Five years later Vickers was an international star and offered to return to the Festival for half his usual fee. Unfortunately the figure he named was considerably more than the amount of Stratford's annual music budget. Applebaum continued to write music for the mainstage plays along with composer John Cook, and later Gabriel Charpentier and Alan Laing. He was by now too busy with other projects to give his full attention to administration but he managed to hire Gordon Jocelyn as administrative director of the music program. Jocelyn, a capable musician, was a Stratford native. His qualities of tact and low-key persuasiveness proved invaluable. He used them to convince Benjamin Britten to bring his English Opera Group production of *The Turn of the Screw*, with Peter Pears playing Quint, to Stratford for six performances. Britten and Pears also performed some of the composer's arrangements of folk-songs and made themselves generally available to the Festival musicians.

Jocelyn recalls that the good people of Stratford were often disturbed by the antics of Stratford's actors but even more uptight at the prospect of bringing in musicians with their reputation for promiscuity and drug addiction. To avoid scandal he discreetly arranged for Britten and his partner Pears to stay not in a hotel but in the apartment of his former music teacher. Even more sensitive was the task of finding accommodation for Billie Holiday, whose fondness for cocaine was no secret even in small-town Stratford.

The great blues singer was just one of the many jazz musicians who would visit the Festival in this period, along with Duke Ellington, who wrote a score for Langham's production of *Timon of Athens*, Count Basie, Dave Brubeck, Wilbur de Paris, Dizzie Gillespie, Benny Goodman, Cleo Laine and John Dankworth, Carmen McRae, Jimmy Rushing, George Shearing, and Canadians Moe Koffman, Phil Nimmons, Oscar Peterson, and Norman Symonds. In addition the Festival featured a series of concerts by folksingers, among them Richard Dyer Bennett, and Odetta and Pete Seeger, and showcased the talents of up-and-coming Canadians Bruce Cochrane, Dan Hill, Gordon Lightfoot, Kate and Anna McGarrigle, Loreena McKennitt, Murray McLauchlan, Joni Mitchell, Anne Murray, and Ian and Sylvia Tyson.

These formidable names attracted the attention of major American critics and they played to very good houses, but the musical offerings of the Festival consistently lost money. Wilf Gregory, the president of the Board, told Jocelyn, "I only took this job so I could shut down the music program. It's a continual drain on the Festival's resources." In presenting his budget Jocelyn reported, "I have two plans, A and B. Plan A will lose this much money, Plan B this much." Publicist Mary Jolliffe commented, "I admire your guts, Baby, but you're going to do yourself out of a job."

In an attempt to reinforce his program and put it in the black, Louis Applebaum wooed Guthrie to come back and direct a musical show. Guthrie, who had staged operas at the Met, surprised everyone by opting to direct Gilbert and Sullivan's *H.M.S Pinafore*, which he described as "just my cup of very sweet tea." His radically untraditional staging was a huge success. He followed it up with an equally inventive *Pirates of Penzance* and both productions played to ecstatic houses in Stratford before touring triumphantly in the United States and Britain. The musical nay-sayers were forestalled.

Then came Gascon's brilliantly inventive stagings of Mozart operas conducted by Richard Bonynge and then Mario Bernardi. They established a standard of work hitherto unseen in Canada, and Gascon would go on to commission new operas by Canada's leading composers, encouraged by the newly empowered and affluent provincial and federal arts councils. But once Guthrie departed, the red ink began flowing again, and soon government grants would stop growing. Gascon fought the inevitable dismantling of the music program, but Phillips accepted it as a necessary condition of his ambitions to expand the dramatic scope of the Festival.

By the mid 1970s the pioneering work of Applebaum and his cohorts had resulted in the establishment of a much more sophisticated and diverse musical scene in Canada. Ensembles who had been given early exposure at Stratford, such as the Orford String Quartet and the Canadian Brass, were in constant demand. Mario Bernardi was exploiting the affinity for Mozart he had discovered at the Avon in a series of acclaimed productions at the National Arts Centre in Ottawa. Singers who had achieved early success, from Maureen Forrester to Robert Goulet, were enjoying international careers. But the demands made by visiting artists, waiting limousines for Duke Ellington, daily bottles of Meursault for Jean-Pierre Rampal and more controversial perks for certain other artists, had become impossible to justify. Single concerts by popular musicians would continue culminating in the gala benefit when Liza Minelli would descend on the Festival in her own plane with a staff of fourteen, having kept the sold-out house waiting for forty minutes. And in 2001 the appearance of John Miller's Stratford New Summer Misic, inaugurated by a musical barge floating down the Avon serenading champagne-drinking guests on Tom Patterson Island while fireworks burst overhead heralds a renaissance of musical events: the Vancouver Choir performing Schubert and Murray Schafer at the City Hall, John Alcorn's late night stylings of Cole Porter, Irving Berlin and George Gershwin at The Church.

Writing prophetically as early as 1968, Louis Applebaum stated, "It is doubtful that the patterns and positions of the past can be sustained much longer.... Perhaps the necessary changes can be made in an evolutionary way but it is also possible that a sudden and dramatic revolution in purpose and presentation is required." The revolution came quickly with the Board and Robin Phillips manning the guillotine. The glory days of music at Stratford, the days of whole-hearted commitment to bold experiment, of sweat and shirtsleeves in humid halls, of transcendent performances by young musicians forging their musical destiny, passed away. Sic transit gloria musicae.

It is not that Phillips was unsympathetic to the charms of music. But the future he envisaged for Stratford was bound up in his determination to lead it to new heights of dramatic interpretation. And he wanted complete control of every aspect of the festival, including music. Phillips installed the eager young Berthold Carrière as his music director and the two enjoyed a close professional rapport, with Carrière often improvising in Phillips' rehearsals as well as composing music for many productions and conducting the festival orchestras.

Perky, shrewd, and energetic, a hard worker and also a bit of a *bon vivant*, Carrière has proved to be a survivor. Four regimes and twenty-five years later he is still music director of the Festival. As musicals began to feature more importantly in the Festival's programming, Carrière's responsibilities expanded and he now auditions singers, vets musical projects, and has worked closely with various choreographers, most notably Brian Macdonald. Macdonald's restaging of Gilbert and Sullivan operas at the Avon in the 1980s and his subsequent work on mainstage musicals from *Cabaret* in 1987 to his triumphant rendering of *The Pirates of Penzance* as a 1930s Hollywood movie in 1994 have made an enormous contribution toward expanding the Festival audience. The opening up of the Festival Theatre to popular musicals put Stratford back in the black. It is deeply ironic that the Festival abandoned musical production as a money-loser only to discover, a decade later, that long runs of large-scale musicals in the big house would turn out to be the very thing that could save its financial bacon. Applebaum must be grinning like the Cheshire Cat as he strums his celestial harp.

Three Classic Musicals

THE THREEPENNY OPERA·1972

Bertolt Brecht is the twentieth-century playwright most like Shakespeare in his use of highly idiomatic poetic language; his facility in fashioning a unique blend of the elements of comedy, romance, fable, tragedy, and farce; his ability to tell a complex story in a series of sharp, dramatic scenes of wildly contrasting tone; and his sharp nose for smelling out stories of universal significance. In spite of this, Brecht's work has been little seen at Stratford.

Director: *Jean Gascon*

Designer: *Robert Prevost*

Lila Kedrova as Mrs. Peachum   105

*B*recht wrote half a dozen masterpieces as a mature artist, but his most enduring and popular work came at the outset of his career when he collaborated with another German of genius, Kurt Weill. Weill would write memorable tunes for a lifetime, but his work would never top the extraordinary score he composed when he was in his twenties for The Threepenny Opera. His ability to take honky-tonk rhythms and overlay them with memorable tunes remains unparalleled and nothing he wrote surpasses the stark vigour of his boldly dissonant "Ballad of Mack the Knife."

Its insinuating rhythms and the starkly vivid images of its lyrics kicked audiences in the teeth right off the top at Stratford, as it had in Berlin in the 1920s and Manhattan in the late 1940s. Jean Gascon's lusty production opened with the gangster hero revelling in his dirty deeds, a man danger-ous, deceitful, utterly unremorseful, and therefore irresistible to women and audiences alike. Anton Rodgers was an elegant Macheath, capable of sudden moments of gentleness and fatal-ly susceptible to the charms of a lady.

And what a bevy of ladies were on display: the sweet-voiced and open-natured Polly of Monique Leyrac giving soaring voice to her imaginative fan-tasies in "Pirate Jenny"; the steamy, sinuous whores portrayed by Marilyn Gardner, Anne Linden, Iris Macgregor, Elsie Sawchuk, and Anni Lee Taylor, led by the irrepressibly slutty and wildly dishevelled virago Jenny Diver of Denise Fergusson. Her rendition of "The Solomon Song" was fiery and at the same time chilling, filled with the rage of a caged panther.

And then there was Lila Kedrova as Mrs. Peachum: vivacious, scatty,

Anton Rodgers as Macheath

lag-mag, smirking, guzzling, gesticulating wildly, a once dazzling creature reduced to rags and ridicule, but still vigorous and full of gusto as she faced down the vicissitudes of a life of petty crime. She was matched by the comic rascality of Jack Creley's Peachum, a rogue among rogues, and his low-life cronies played with unrestrained relish by Lewis Gordon, Jeff Jones, Robin Marshall, Henry Ramer, and Kenneth Wickes.

Gascon's love of outrageous theatricality was never more evident than in this sharply detailed and vigorous parade of the follies of greed and desire. It was a kick in the pants, a smack in the gobs, and a call to wake up and cele brate the sheer delight of being alive.

Anton Rodgers as Macheath, Denise Fergusson as Jenny Diver,
Anne Linden, Iris MacGregor, Elsie Sawchuk, Anni Lee Taylor

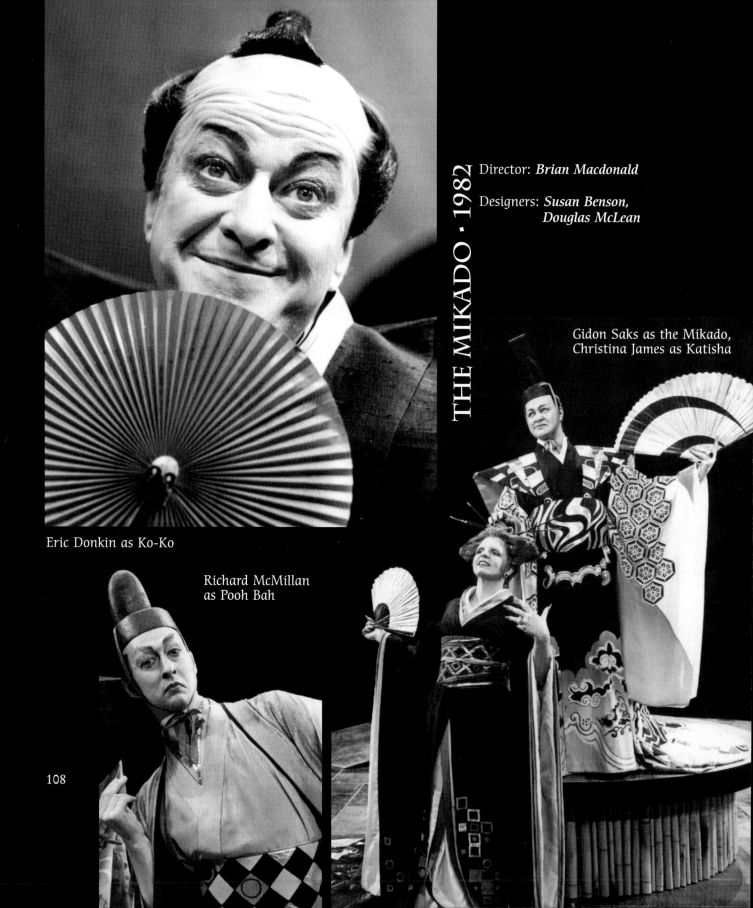

Eric Donkin as Ko-Ko

Richard McMillan
as Pooh Bah

THE MIKADO · 1982

Director: **Brian Macdonald**

Designers: **Susan Benson,
Douglas McLean**

Gidon Saks as the Mikado,
Christina James as Katisha

Thistice greatest of Gilbert and Sullivan collaborations takes the most absurd aspects of Victorian middle-class convention and views them through the exotic prism of Japanese social ritual. Etiquette is mocked and at the same time celebrated. No one could hold fast to traditional social values in the face of such hilarity (except the English and the Japanese). To bring this home to modern North American audiences requires both boldness and delicacy. Stratford's 1982 production achieved this rare combination.

Brian Macdonald's eclectic invention in staging perfectly matched the original material, a thing of shreds and patches cunningly stitched together by the magpie mind of W.S. Gilbert, who relished the juxtaposition of improbable verbal and social details just as Macdonald's directorial style drew on a wide range of artfully combined visual techniques drawn from many eras and traditions: the grandest of opera, old movies, Broadway musicals, Kabuki, the Diaghilev ballet, and circus clowning. His city of Titipu was inhabited by figures who knowingly echoed such comic figures as Charlie Chaplin, John Cleese, Bugs Bunny, and Dame Edna (not to mention Margaret Thatcher).

Macdonald's audacious originality nevertheless fully respected the spirit of the original. The characters were true to themselves, however outrageous their behaviour. They spoke Gilbert's lines (with a few topical insertions) and sang Sullivan's tunes with musicality, clarity, and charm. Berthold Carrière's musical direction sparkled like crystal and the extra flourishes provided by his orchestration added zing without vulgarity.

There was great visual exuberance in the finely detailed and imaginative design of Susan Benson's stunningly simple setting. A bonsai tree suggested the angular eccentricity of both ancient Japan and Gilbert's idiosyncratic world; an immense fan that opened during the musical numbers accentuated the elegance and richness of Sullivan's score. The use of bold colours and contrasting patterns made each character highly individual while painting a complex overall picture.

Carrière and Macdonald cast with precision. The voices of the three little maids—Marie Baron as Yum-Yum, Karen Skidmore as Peep-Bo, and Karen Young as Pitti-Sing—blended happily together. Henry Ingram's ringing tenor as Nanki-Poo provided a fine counterpoint to the full growling bass of Gidon Saks as the Mikado. But it was the contrast between Richard McMillan's towering, outrageous Pooh-Bah and Eric Donkin's gentle, worried, understated Ko-Ko that gave the show its comic drive. The interplay of their impeccable comic timing and their seemingly effortless ability to work within the framework of the songs and musical numbers set up a rhythm that moved the piece irresistibly along.

This was a show that ran, skipped, and danced. We no sooner got one outrageous allusion than some unexpected trick exploded in our faces. Macdonald has said that his favourite pace is allegro, the tempo that allows the most improbable things to come together. This production wonderfully illustrated the power of speed.

This Mikado toured more widely and received more attention internationally than any other show Stratford has ever initiated. It prompted one critic to comment that the Festival should forget about Shakespeare and concentrate on the works of Gilbert and Sullivan. But it might be argued that Stratford actually began to bring to bear some of the elements that worked so well in this production on the interpretation of Shakespeare.

The most pleasurable of all American musicals based on the most satisfying of George Bernard Shaw's plays. A wry comedy of two outspoken but deeply inhibited individuals sparring as they work together, discovering a psychological and emotional affinity that will bridge the deep divide of social class and personal prejudice that separates them. A story that is ultimately romantic under a crisp crust of caustic wordplay. The lyrics of Alan Jay Lerner extend and amplify Shaw's wit without diluting or vulgarizing it; Frederick Loewe's music provides an expression of sentiment that Shaw's story implies but never quite delivers. This as much as any American musical could be called a classic, yet the inspiration is British to the core.

Lucy Peacock as Eliza Doolittle, John Neville as Henry Higgins

Director: **Jean Gascon,**

Designers: **Richard Seger, Lewis Brown**

111

*T*he most pleasurable of all American musicals based on the most satisfying of George Bernard Shaw's plays. A wry comedy of two outspoken but deeply inhibited individuals sparring as they work together, discovering a psychological and emotional affinity that will bridge the deep divide of social class and personal prejudice that separates them. A story that is ultimately romantic under a crisp crust of caustic wordplay. The lyrics of Alan Jay Lerner extend and amplify Shaw's wit without diluting or vulgarizing it; Frederick Loewe's music provides an expression of sentiment that Shaw's story implies but never quite delivers. This as much as any American musical could be called a classic, yet the inspiration is British to the core.

This was Jean Gascon's last work for the Festival. Indeed, he did not live to attend the opening night but his stamp was on the production, extending the musical style he explored in staging such works as Don Giovanni, The Threepenny Opera, La Vie Parisienne, and indeed Pericles, which in his highly original version, was quasi-operatic. Like all Gascon stagings it was fluid but precise, inventive but always sensitive to the values and rhythms of the music.

The cast assembled in 1988 was felicitous. Lucy Peacock was a stunningly fresh and penetratingly honest Eliza. The sardonic reserve of Higgins aptly matched the talents of John Neville, who delivered every sparkling epithet with practised nuance and understated relish. Douglas Campbell's Alfred P. Doolittle was a brash buffoon delighting in his own rascality. He sang and danced with gusto and the unexpected grace reserved for large men.

These fine players were backed by a supporting cast that included Ann Casson as a warmly concerned Mrs. Higgins, Richard Curnock as an amiable if somewhat obtuse Colonel Pickering, and a skilled ensemble of excellent actors in the smaller roles, including Eric Donkin, Richard March, Joseph Shaw, and Susan Wright.

When everything falls into place and a great musical really works, it offers a unique and deeply gratifying pleasure, less lofty than tragedy, less immediate than comedy but, in a word appropriated from Robertson Davies, more "heart-lifting" than either. The world of the musical is the world of romance, and those who undervalue the genre might remember that Shakespeare turned his attention to this form in the final years of his work as a playwright. The musical has definitely earned a place on the Festival stage, at least if the audience is any judge.

Douglas Campbell as Alfred P. Doolittle, with Susan Wright and Kate Hennig

BEAUTY AND THE BEAN COUNTERS

THE STORY OF THE BEGINNINGS OF THE FESTIVAL has been eloquently told by Tom Patterson himself in his book *First Stage*. Though he was naive and disorganized, Patterson's optimism, persistence, and formidable powers of persuasion kept the project moving forward. There were plenty of sharp-tongued nay-sayers in Stratford and across the land but Patterson's vision attracted strong supporters: Harry Showalter, the fervently eloquent and implacably determined chairman of the Advisory Committee set up by the Stratford Rotary Club, a committee that would evolve into the Festival Board of Governors; Oliver Gaffney, the contractor who kept his men working round the clock even though he was not being paid and came close to bankruptcy; Mary Jolliffe, the vivacious school-teacher hired to do publicity who paid for office expenses out of her own pocket. These and many others went all out to make the Festival work. Their knowledge of theatre was virtually non-existent and their fundraising methods were amateurish, but when they consulted a professional he advised them to abandon the project. By opening night they had reached and even slightly surpassed their target of $150,000, a substantial portion of which consisted of small donations from ordinary Stratford citizens.

What professional expertise there was came from the Brits that Guthrie recruited. Chief among these were Cecil Clarke, who arrived in the winter of 1953, and his wife Jacqueline Cundall, a highly experienced property-maker who had worked with Tanya Moiseiwitsch and could assist her husband in sussing out seamstresses, milliners, and boot makers. She set up a workshop in Stratford (in an unused corner of a mop factory) and found infatuated young art students to work long hours without pay painting fabrics, fashioning jewellery from bits of wire and papier mâché, and making armour from felt dipped in glue.

Meanwhile Clarke handled the details of casting and contracting and consulted with Robert Fairfield, the young architect Guthrie had chosen the previous year. Together they worked out the details of the tent that was to provide cover for audience and actors working on the revolutionary stage that Moiseiwitsch designed.

Romancing the Bard

Fairfield would praise Clarke as the "pivotal guy around whom other people ran in circles. If there'd been any fluidity at the centre, the whole thing would have fallen apart." An unexpected donation of $10,000 from Vincent Massey allowed the planners to proceed, just when they were contemplating postponement. Guthrie and his actors arrived and began to rehearse. The tent arrived from Chicago and was erected by the colourful roustabout Skip Manley, as flamboyant a showman as Guthrie himself. And a clutch of Stratford people signed on to help in any way they could: Norman Freeman, Florence Patterson, Barbara Reid.

The whole enterprise had the miraculous aura of the building of the cathedral of Chartres in the twelfth century, when people spontaneously came from all over France to assist in its construction, not just stonemasons and glaziers, but knights and burgesses, merchants and squires. Writing of the opening night, July 13, 1953, when wealthy well-wishers converged on Stratford from Toronto, Ottawa, and even New York, the sober scholar John Pettigrew, in his excellent history of the first thirty years of the Festival, enthused, "A miracle was about to occur—the miracle of the Stratford Festival." The miracle involved rave reviews not just in Canada but in the major New York papers, the adding of an extra 150 seats to the theatre, long queues to buy tickets, 98% attendance and a loss of only $4,137.58. The Festival was to become an annual event, a major feature of the Canadian cultural landscape.

Tom Patterson has written, "One of the mistakes a lot of people make in promoting a thing like this, I think, is to get people who aren't the best. And the difference in the cost between the best and the not-so-good is a relatively minor thing." The spirit of this final sentence, echoing Guthrie's insistence on the highest quality, would reverberate over the years. But it was rapidly realized that, in the future, the fervour of the first year could not be relied upon to carry the enterprise. A stronger organizational structure would be required. One of the first casualties was Tom Patterson himself. Dreamer and salesman though he might be, his administrative skills were wanting. On this Guthrie, Harrison Showalter, and Cecil Clarke were agreed, and Clarke threatened to quit if Patterson insisted in staying on as general manager. Patterson resisted but eventually agreed to become director of planning, which he recognized was a rather hollow title.

Clarke became artistic director, a position that he would not long enjoy. His rehearsals of *Measure for Measure* in 1954 went badly. He had no previous experience

115

directing professionals and his style was soft-spoken and meticulous in contrast to Guthrie's roaring, free-wheeling brio. The actors went to Guthrie a week before opening and asked him to come in and save the show. He re-directed key scenes, particularly the opening and closing, but the experience was traumatic for Clarke, who informed the Board he would not be returning to Canada in 1955.

The second season was not the artistic bombshell that had exploded in 1953, but it consolidated the Festival's position. It racked up a profit of $30,000 on sales of $390,000 and, thanks to better organized fund-raising that brought in larger Canadian donations and a $40,000 contribution from the Rockefeller Foundation, there was a working capital surplus of $150,000.

Two people hired for the first year became key management figures. John Hayes was the son of an English actor and had been an assistant director to the celebrated scholar Wilson Knight at Hart House Theatre, an aide-de-camp to General Crerar, an actor in Manhattan, Dublin, and Stratford-on-Avon, and a rancher in Texas before he joined the Festival. There he began in stage management and eventually became effectively in-house producer. He would exert a strong, stabilizing influence. Hayes' skill as an organizer was legendary. For two decades he would handle contracting and salary negotiations with tact and ingenuity. He also worked out extremely complicated rehearsal schedules in his head. When he retired, no one in the organization could figure out a workable schedule and Hayes had to be called back to solve the problem.

Bruce Swerdfager, a successful typewriter salesman before he joined the acting company in the first season, became front-of-house and company manager in the third, and proved to be not only efficient in running the overworked box office but adroit in recruiting local people to act as ushers and dressers, all unpaid volunteers in the early years. He was tactful but firm in handling money matters for the actors, some of whom were inveterately profligate and would, if allowed, go through their whole season's salary in a matter of a week or two. Working with Swerdfager was Stratford accountant Vic Polley, who as office manager supervised the budget and the day-to-day running of a staff that slowly escalated in size as the scope of the Festival grew by the addition of several weeks to the season, a music program, and a film festival.

The great event of the first decade was the building of the permanent theatre in

1957. The Stratford Board set a fund-raising target of $1.5 million. The Board recruited some skilled canvassers, chief among them Floyd Chalmers of Maclean-Hunter. Chalmers had been Tom Patterson's boss and he quickly came on board as a fund-raiser and onto the Board as a representative of big business. He was a cigar-chomping tycoon, who would rock back in his chair and demand, "Well now, what do you fellas think you need?" He became a leading contributor and winkled major donations from such captains of industry as J.W. McConnell and R.S. McLaughlin, both of whom ponyed up $25,000. He also went after the federal government. Prime Minister Louis St. Laurent was just about to set up the Canada Council and, seeing an opportunity to show the kind of support for the arts he envisioned, announced a grant of $250,000. Chalmers then successfully challenged Ontario Premier Leslie Frost to add another $150,000. Chalmers' energy was matched by the imagination of publicist Mary Jolliffe, who had the bright idea of mailing a small piece of the old tent to all former subscribers. This gimmick caught their fancy and donations rolled in until, by the end of the season, the goal had been reached. The remaining cost of the theatre ($2.1 million in total) was financed by a $650,000 bond issue that was quickly subscribed.

The addition of business magnates like Chalmers gave the Board greater clout in the outside world but it set up tensions within the Board. The worthies of Stratford who made up the original Advisory Committee took an understandably territorial approach to *their* Festival; they were not about to turn its direction over to outsiders, much as they might welcome the financial support they engendered. Conflict would become apparent in the future when such issues as touring and a projected winter home for the company were discussed. Initially, however, the Board members pulled together and their financial sophistication increased

During the Langham years the Festival sometimes showed a modest profit, sometimes a small shortfall. Mounting government grants began to be a significant factor. When in 1960 the Festival had a good year with newly added school performances sold out, drama sales at 92% capacity and music at 91%, the Festival declared a profit of $64,000. The Canada Council responded to this fiscal success by cutting the Festival's grant from $75,000 to $25,000. The lesson was not lost. Thereafter the books were, if not exactly cooked, often gently simmered. Such elements as

117

depreciation could be manipulated. The Festival learned to present itself as a not-for-profit organization.

On the whole things ran smoothly. Vic Polley would comment nearly a decade later, "People are dedicated to making the Festival a success ... we really have no departments—everybody just pitches in. We never had an organizational chart until a couple of years ago when I was asked to lecture at another drama organization about stage management. I felt that no self-respecting theatre could be without an organizational chart so I drew one up. I doubt if anyone has seen it since." The Festival absorbed the loss of Mary Jolliffe, who was lured by Guthrie to Minneapolis, and production manager Tom Brown, who returned to his native Australia. His place was filled by John Hayes. Langham was general manager as well as artistic director and reported directly to the Board on all aspects of the Festival. His departure would bring a change that signalled trouble in paradise.

The decision was made in 1967 that the Stratford company should make the newly built National Arts Centre in Ottawa its winter home. This would give the actors more work and assure the federal government's new palace of culture, built to celebrate the nation's centenary, a high standard of dramatic performance. It marked a recognition of the Festival's pre-eminence in the Canadian theatre world and seemed a natural and happy extension of its mandate. However, the move would greatly complicate the administrative and production structures. Vic Polley was offered the position of general manager with the responsibility of supervising and integrating the winter and summer seasons. He turned the job down and the Board hired William Wylie, an experienced theatre administrator from Winnipeg's Manitoba Theatre Centre.

Wylie's style was very different from Polley's. He was brusque, hands-on, and highly systematic. His efficiency was recognized but his manner was not always appreciated. The staff respected Wylie, but they loved Polley; he was one of them. Inevitably there was a clash: Wylie made it clear he could not work with Polley, who resigned. The town was outraged. The Festival had earlier pushed out Patterson; now they'd dumped Polley. At the annual meeting in 1970, Patterson took the floor and denounced the Festival, demanding the resignation of Wylie and Board Chairman Dr. Ian Lindsay. "The people of Stratford have been treated ... like peasants," Patterson shouted. At this point Patterson was not yet seen as the Grand Old Man and Official Founder of the Festival but rather as a cranky idealist who was constantly promoting wild schemes, none of which seemed likely to enjoy the same success as the Festival. The Board stood behind Wylie but the animosity between townies and theatre that had existed from the beginning had obviously not disappeared.

Wylie continued to report to the Board, and because Gascon did not particularly enjoy the administrative aspect of his job and was increasingly busy directing productions, arranging tours, and trying to communicate with Ottawa, he was happy to let Wylie shoulder this responsibility. But the Ottawa connection would prove increasingly unworkable. The National Arts Centre had its own administrative staff with their own political and artistic agendas. The euphoric centennial year was over and the government that had so lavishly fostered the arts was having second thoughts. Grants were cut back just as arts organizations were getting used to the idea of ever-increasing subsidies. This wreaked havoc with budgetary planning and made board members distinctly uneasy.

In the last two years of Langham's tenure, and throughout Gascon's leadership, the Festival usually lost money. Production costs were rising, the music program never paid its way, and touring was expensive. By 1970 Stratford had an accumulated deficit of $600,000. But it was not alone: the Festival joined forces with other performing arts organizations and approached the Ontario Arts Council, pointing out that in Europe major companies were subsidized to the tune of as much as 85 per cent of their budget. The OAC didn't buy this line but they did agree to retire half the accumulated deficits. The Canada Council stepped in to cover the balance. But conditions were laid down: no more deficit budgeting.

Wylie was delighted: "This one move has done more ... than anything since the formation of both councils by wiping the record clean and taking measures to ensure it stays clean." Had it not been for his untimely death, he might have been able to make good on the council's conditions and balance the books. But in 1973 he choked at the dinner table and suffocated. His place was taken by Bruce Swerdfager, who proved a popular and capable manager, but the finances of the company remained erratic. Large grants such as the $100,000 from the Kresge Foundation in Michigan in 1971 to help finance a new lighting system and a $200,000 touring grant from the

Department of External Affairs in 1973 helped, but grants from the arts councils continued to fluctuate making accurate budgeting almost impossible.

The arrival of Robin Phillips signalled another shift in relations between the Board, the administration, and the artistic director. Phillips wanted complete control over all aspects of the Festival. His first season resulted in increased sales and a box-office gross of $2,638,000, up more than 10 per cent from the previous year, reducing the accumulated deficit to $86,000. The 1976 season was even more impressive with a gross of $3.7 million. In spite of escalating production costs, the profit of over $200,000 wiped out the deficit and left a surplus of over $100,000.

Despite this success, Bruce Swerdfager saw Phillips heading down a path that he believed would lead to financial ruin. But Phillips' charm and eloquence, backed up by success at the box office, prevailed. He knew exactly how to handle his Board, where the power seat in the room was, who were his supporters and who were the nay-sayers. He could produce facts to bolster his demands and omit negative details. Yes, designer Daphne Dare had ordered 50 pairs of boots at $800 apiece, but they would be worn by the principal actors in the company for five years in an average of three shows a year. Thus the real cost was less than six dollars per show. His grasp of the big picture threw the comparative ignorance of many Board members into sharp relief. Yet, unconvinced by Phillips' free-wheeling eloquence, Swerdfager resigned as general manager and was not replaced; henceforth only Phillips would report to the Board. In 1977, Phillips would chalk up a profit of nearly half a million dollars. Then the tide turned.

Phillips began to have health problems. He took on Secretary of State John Roberts and challenged the government's cultural policy. He wanted a training school, a film studio, a winter season in Toronto. The Board argued that he was already overextended. Exhausted and discouraged, he resigned and took off for England, saying that he might not be back. Was he looking to extend his power by blackmailing the Board with the threat of leaving? Was he serious in suggesting the appointment of an artistic director who didn't stage plays but merely ran the theatre? Would a sabbatical for Phillips solve the problem? Was he even capable of taking a sabbatical? This question would be put to the test in 1979.

Meanwhile, the 1978 season had the highest gross ever ($4,636,500), but lost

$200,000. The next year would show a loss of $647,000. The numbers were climbing. But in 1980, Phillips' final year, there was a surplus of $319,668, which effectively wiped out the deficit and left about $75,000 in the kitty. Phillips has acquired a reputation for extravagance and financial irresponsibility, but in fact he paid his way at Stratford, leaving the Festival in better financial shape than he found it. He had unquestionably increased the size of its audiences and its artistic renown, but the increased scale of operations would have profound consequences in the future.

Vienna, 1919. A sumptuous, sensual world on the edge of extinction. Long silences, long shadows, shaded lamps reflected in the polished surfaces of dimly lit offices, the clang of barred doors swinging shut in prisons and nunneries, people lurking in corners, whispering or laughing lewdly behind gloved hands.

Robin Phillips' first production on the Festival stage was electrifying in its simplicity, its carefully calibrated detail, its sense of brooding quiet and festering evil. Gone were high-vaulting rhetoric and fluting oratory. In their place were uncertain people struggling to survive and make sense of a disintegrating world, desperately trying to gauge each other's motives and intentions.

Martha Henry as Isabella

Director: **Robin Phillips**

Sheena Larkin as Mistress Overdone, Lewis Gordon as Pompey

At the centre was Martha Henry's Isabella, drawn unwillingly by family loyalty from a life of spiritual contemplation in a cloistered order. She has discovered the rapaciousness and duplicity of men: the lascivious hypocrite Angelo who wants to bed her, the brother who urges her to yield to this violation in order to save his skin; the slippery Duke who offers her his hand after a life of caprice and philandering.

Isabella is drawn into life as Eve was drawn by the serpent's worldly whisper. We go with her on her journey of discovery, we sense the pain and pressure when she cools her brow with water from a pitcher on Angelo's desk as she waits alone in his office, weighing her alternatives with the horror of someone who never dreamt the world could be so twisted and perverse. And at the end we watch in wonder as, again alone, she takes off her coif and spectacles and prepares to enter the imperfect world. This charged theatrical moment to which everything leads is pure Phillips, a coup de théâtre that caps and encapsulates the entire production.

Henry's rigorous innocence was set against the William Hutt's subtle, devious, mischievous Duke, the oily unction of Brian Bedford as Angelo in the first year and the dry, calculating lust of Douglas Rain in the second. Contrast was provided by the sneering vulgarity and knowing leers of Richard Monette's seedy Lucio and Kathleen Widdowes' flighty, lascivious Mariana. In the second year Jackie Burroughs' equally sensuous Mariana contrasted with Maggie Smith's painted Cockney bawd Mistress Overdone.

The production, designed by Daphne Dare, had what was to become the Phillips/Dare signature look: subdued and stark, employing a restrained palette of hues that threw the weight of interpretation onto the actors. No colour was allowed to be more intense than the performers' faces. And it was the acting style that marked the essential difference in tone. Phillips expressed it like this:

"I believe earth-shattering emotions are tiny: one of our most devastating weapons is the Bomb, yet it results from the tiniest splitting of the atom. Measure has huge emotions but it's ridiculous to feel you have to rant and roar and spew emotions all over the stage."

The marvel was that Phillips was able to carry his actors with him away from high theatricality into a territory of intimate interchange, shared conversation, savoured nuance, intense examination of both the text and the emotions it evokes. As William Hutt expressed it, "[Phillips] can recognize something that the actor is trying to say but is afraid to say. An almost insignificant gesture can achieve enormous significance in his mind." After this production, acting at Stratford would never be quite the same again.

Brian Bedford as Angelo, Geoffrey Bowes as Varrius,
Richard Monette as Lucio, Martha Henry as Isabella

STARS AND GARTERS

"FOR SEVERAL MORE YEARS IT WILL BE NECESSARY, FOR BUSINESS REASONS, to import 'stars', if suitable stars are available," wrote Tyrone Guthrie at the end of the second season in 1954. The first two years of the Festival had starred first Alec Guinness and then James Mason. And of course there was Guthrie himself, but the great director was itching to move on. In the next year, although negotiations were initiated with both Montgomery Clift and Stewart Granger, the Festival did not feature an imported star of international magnitude. The visiting Czech actor Frederick Valk gave a forceful performance as Shylock, while in 1956 the advent of the Quebec actors led by Jean Gascon and Gratien Gelinas and the emergence of Christopher Plummer as a recognizable Canadian star evoked a strong audience response. It seemed, at least for the moment, that the Festival did not need to import luminaries from abroad, and Guthrie's initial vision of a wholly Canadian company was about to be realized.

After Guthrie's departure, Michael Langham continued to give splendid opportunities to his Canadian actors. He admired their boldness but deplored their uneven execution, characterizing their work as "perhaps too energetic, for it tends to lack depth of realization." He challenged them by bringing in major players from both Britain and the United States. These visitors gave vivid, distinctive performances that opened up new possibilities to the Canadian actors, extending and enriching their understanding of classical texts. Siobhan McKenna's ruefully self-aware Viola ignited a bittersweet sympathy in Frances Hyland's Olivia in Guthrie's final Shakespearean production for the Festival. Bruno Gerussi's raw passion as Romeo drew fire and inspiration from the fragile delicacy and untrammelled emotion of Julie Harris's Juliet. Christopher Plummer's Benedick found greater humanity when matched with the warmth and wit of Eileen Herlie's Beatrice. Douglas Rain's Prince Hal gained stature by being pitted against the unflinching force of Jason Robards' Hotspur. Imaginations were sparked as the Canadians tested themselves against some of the best, and audiences were impressed by their ability to hold their own.

Langham was beginning to create Canadian stars by providing them with a stimulating, demanding environment, which he continued to manipulate with shrewdness and unsparing rigour. At the same time his Canadian actors had the opportunity to make valuable contacts in the wider world of theatre. And thus began the exodus. Success took the actors away from Stratford as they tried their luck on Broadway and in the West End. By the mid-1960s, John Colicos, Christopher Plummer, and Kate Reid became stars in their own right, playing leading roles on stage and screen. William Hutt played in premieres of works by Noel Coward and Edward Albee. Frances Hyland starred opposite Anthony Perkins on Broadway.

Back at Stratford, the company had gained in confidence, community spirit, and a sense of self-reliance. They had learned to produce a reliable product, but also one that began to seem somewhat predictable. Initially it was interesting to see an actor like Douglas Rain, William Needles or Robin Gammell stretch himself by tackling an unlikely role, but inevitably the day arrived when the audience felt it was seeing something not merely familiar, but warmed over. The lack of visiting luminaries did not greatly trouble Langham or Gascon in the later years of their tenure but it did begin to have an effect on the audience. Absence of star power was increasingly cited as a principal reason for flagging ticket sales. The initial glamour of Stratford seemed to have faded; the glory years had passed. But the arrival of Robin Phillips changed all that.

Phillips' appointment was greeted with equal parts elation and outrage. Critics like Ronald Bryden, who had brought Phillips' name forward and would become one of his most supportive Board members; Urjo Kareda, who quickly fell under Phillips' spell and was snapped up by him to be Stratford's dramaturge; and Gina Mallet, who replaced Kareda at the *Toronto Star* and immediately attempted to don the outsized mantle of the late Nathan Cohen—all of them hailed Phillips as a saviour who would reinvigorate and reinvent the Festival. At the same time a group of major Canadian theatre directors under the fiery leadership of John Hirsch protested Phillips' appointment. Equity expressed indignation, playwrights across the land protested, and actor John Juliani flamboyantly challenged Phillips to a duel. All of this made good copy, and from the moment of his arrival Phillips was a controversial figure whose every move was eagerly reported. There was a new star at Stratford, and his name was Robin Phillips.

Phillips had been a film actor and he knew about playing to the camera. He had the appearance of one of Caravaggio's boy saints: intense, sexy, dangerous. He was a passionate speaker who combined messianic fervour with a liberal use of four-letter words. (In his teens he had contemplated a career as a preacher.) He was extremely sensitive to the emotional currents around him, a relentless listener, and a resourceful diplomat. Before taking over as artistic director, Phillips criss-crossed the country viewing productions, interviewing actors, and meeting directors and designers.

He rapidly recruited a bevy of young talents: quirky comedienne Jackie Burroughs; sultry young earth-mothers Barbara Budd, Gail Garnett, and Donna Goodhand; bright, sympathetic ingenues Margot Dionne and Marti Maraden; comic character actors Rod Beattie, Peter Donaldson, Frank Maraden, Richard McMillan, and Tom Wood, and a parade of handsome young "fellahs," to use a favourite Phillipian term. Some, like Brent Carver, Richard Monette, and Alan Scarfe, were highly talented and imaginative; others were perhaps more beautiful than expressive. Not all of them were new to Stratford, but together they represented a massive infusion of young native blood and they formed the nucleus for the reinforced company Phillips launched in 1975.

Phillips demanded and obtained from his actors total commitment. He held out for nothing less than "absolute truth." In one barn-burning oration he insisted, "There is no greater pleasure than watching an actor achieve something he had no idea he was able to achieve…. It may be absolute hell for three days or three weeks, but the day arrives when you can look him straight in the eye and say, 'That was *wonderful acting.'*" Phillips set the example not only through his outspoken and ruthless insistence on the highest standards but also through his endless probing of every detail of the Festival's operation. He personally supervised not only programming, casting, and scheduling but also construction, financing, publicity, and promotion. The standard remark of his henchmen, "Of course Robin is a genius," became a joke to outsiders but an affirmation of faith to the elect. As Sheila McCarthy expressed it, "There's a tremendous pressure to be one's best for Robin, because he gives you so much."

Phillips was often said to be a workaholic. He put in eighteen-hour days as a matter of course. He was energetic, ubiquitous, unpredictable; sometimes open and friendly, other times preoccupied and covered. Like Guthrie and Langham before him, Phillips emphasized Canadian speech and deplored pretension and mannerisms, stripping them away with a brutality that seemed at odds with his own soft-spoken manner. He had a feel for period detail and the niceties of social codes but probed into hidden emotional areas and opened up sexual tensions below polite and polished surfaces. Jackie Burroughs commented, "The Edwardian era was a perfect fit to Robin's sensibility: everyone in whalebone and starched shirts but underneath they've all got a hard-on."

He played games with his actors: physical games with volleyballs and skipping ropes, word-association games in which the actors were called upon to spill out their emotional secrets, unexpected psychological challenges. Richard Monette recalled that when he was cast, much to his surprise, as Caliban, Phillips, who had always insisted on absolute clarity of speech, at the first rehearsal produced two ping-pong balls and insisted that Richard read the lines with the balls in his mouth. The other actors started to laugh but as Monette struggled with the pain of trying to express himself under this handicap their laughter turned to tears. He acquired a gut under-standing of the character's frustration and rage.

Phillips became more and more the guru, clad all in white like a cricketer or a novitiate. He was the White Rabbit, the Pied Piper, Peter Pan, leading his actors into the magical world of theatre. He was also the Duke of Dark Corners, seeming to know everything about every department and every actor. There were rumours he sometimes watched other directors' rehearsals from the catwalk high above the Festival Theatre, that he roamed the deserted streets of Stratford at three o'clock in the morning, cruising for fresh talent. Another fantasy was that the dressing rooms were bugged, so Robin could overhear the actors gossiping as they put on their make-up. His persona had entered the realm of mythology.

To inspire and lead his stable of fresh Canadian talent, Robin revived the practice of bringing in well-known foreign players: from London Keith Baxter, Jeremy Brett, and Margaret Tyzack, from New York Stephen McHattie, Kathleen Widdowes, Jessica Tandy and her Canadian husband Hume Cronyn, and of course most notably Maggie Smith and Peter Ustinov. Not all these choices were happy ones, but Smith and Ustinov gave extraordinary performances that brought lustre and réclame to the Festival. Despite their eminence they lived on comfortable terms with the company, entering into the spirit of the place with grace. Ustinov commented, "The Stratford of Robin Phillips produced the ideal climate for physical and spiritual enjoyment of hard work.... While the discipline was rigid, it was also strangely voluntary. It had all the advantages of drama school, luxury of time and the possibilities of profound research, without the disadvantages—puppy love and acne."

There was a strong sense of family, but it was not exactly a family of equals. The celebrated visitors were accorded certain privileges in terms of housing and transportation and in the way they were treated socially. Phillips wanted them to feel valued and also at ease in his bright theatrical realm. He also bestowed on certain Canadian actors a kind of special status: Martha Henry, William Hutt, Richard Monette, and Douglas Rain. Enjoying similar standing were British actors Brian Bedford, Domini Blythe, and Nicholas Pennell. Phillips professed belief in equality but tacitly encouraged certain players to think of themselves as stars. He himself displayed a certain dichotomy, proudly aware of his working-class origins but nostalgic for the vanished glamour and intrigue of Edwardian society. This ambiguity permeated Phillips' Stratford both onstage and off.

Suppressed sexuality and a battle for advantage became the twin hallmarks of Phillips' best work, both in serious drama and comedy. His signature production of *Measure for Measure* in 1975 was a sensation that bowled over critics and the public alike. A deceptively simple style enhanced the high outrage of Wildean paradox in *The Importance of Being Earnest*, which featured William Hutt in deadpan drag as Lady Bracknell. Hutt played the role with intense seriousness, but still managed to find a hilarious alternative to Edith Evans's famous intonation on the line "A handbag?" by preceding it with a six-part take. In the years that followed, Phillips unveiled the devious charm of Brian Bedford in *Richard III*, manuoeuvring Martha Henry's hypnotized Lady Anne, Mary Savidge's resigned, knowing Duchess of York, Maggie Smith's trapped Queen Elizabeth, and Margaret Tyzack's trenchantly scathing Queen Margaret. This dark vision was offset by the brilliant sparring of Brian Bedford and Maggie Smith in *The Guardsman* and *Private Lives*. An autumnal sheen surrounded the luminous performance of Maggie Smith's Rosalind as she courted with rueful self-awareness the impetuously callow Orlando of Jack Wetherall in *As You Like It*. An orgy of cruelty fuelled by lust coloured Patricia Conolly's Regan,

Martha Henry's Goneril, Richard McMillan's Oswald, and Richard Monette's Edmund, offsetting the bafflement of Peter Ustinov's Lear as he made his voyage of self-discovery in parallel with William Hutt's Fool and Douglas Rain's Gloucester in Phillips' final 1980 version of *King Lear*.

Phillips' productions were intricately plotted, with a cunningly calculated use of stage space, filled with lovingly explored detail, punctuated by moments of revelation as the characters discovered new and startling truths. They offered a vision of life as an on-going dance full of surprising turns and shifts of tempo, driven by a deep underlying need for emotional release. In part this drive was aesthetic, in part sexual. In Phillips work the two elements were intertwined and inseparable. He responded to his actors both emotionally and physically. As he once said, "I don't have to sleep with an actor to be able to work with him, but I have to *want* to." But beneath the surface, there was always a search for emotional truth and intensity of feeling.

Phillips developed a highly skilled ensemble but the idea of star presence was central to his work, just as sexual magnetism was an essential part of his concept of stardom. He needed stars to realize this concept, and at the centre was always the brightest star of all: Robin himself. The Festival revolved around what Phillips put on the stage and what he did or didn't do offstage. Tyrone Guthrie was fond of downplaying the myth of theatre people as temperamental divas, claiming he had experienced more tantrums and high-handed ultimatums among the staff of a small boys' private school than in any theatre company he had ever encountered. But the years of Robin Phillips' tenure bubbled and bristled with temperament and trauma, much of it emanating from Phillips himself. His recurring illnesses and frequent resignations kept his staff and his Board always teetering on the edge of uncertainty. And it was this behaviour that underlay and precipitated the much-publicized crisis of 1980.

Once Phillips was gone his successors seemed either unwilling or unable to attract foreign stars of the first magnitude. Hirsch showcased well-known Canadian actors Len Cariou, Barbara Chilcott, Fiona Reid, and R.H. Thomson and continued to feature actors who had a longstanding Festival connection: Brian Bedford, Douglas Campbell, and Nicholas Pennell. He managed to attract Nehemiah Persoff and Sada Thompson for single roles in relatively short runs and brought along younger actors who would become stars or near-stars: Brent Carver, Colm Feore, Seana McKenna,

Susan Wright, and Joseph Zeigler. And he showed off the talents of the star actor who would take over from him, John Neville.

As artistic directors, Neville and his successor David William continued the casting policy Hirsch established but found it increasingly difficult to attract stars. Stratford could not offer salaries large enough to tie up name actors for nine or ten months of the year when they could make much larger sums in film or television. As television and film production has proliferated in Canada even local actors have became less available.

Monette for his part continues to pursue big names from Alan Bates to Liza Minelli but with diminishing vigour: "It takes an enormous amount of time and in the end, they usually let you down. You don't know whether it's other commitments or cold feet. For a major movie star to be out there exposed on a stage for three hours when they haven't done it for years is a huge risk." Monette has had some success attracting names. The legendary Uta Hagen played for two months in 2000 to rave reviews (though less than packed houses). But the name actors Monette has attracted have been from the world of television: Cynthia Dale, Paul Gross, Al Waxman. All three have brightened the Stratford seasons, delivering vividly articulate performances and pleasing large audiences.

As television increasingly dominates the world of entertainment, it seems likely that this is where stars of the future will be born and nurtured. In the twenty-first century there probably won't be major actors operating in the style of Alec Guinness, Maggie Smith or even Christopher Plummer, pursuing their art on stage while reinforcing their reputation by work in up-market films. Television means series and establishing a personality accessible to a large audience. It offers one good role to be milked, rather than a variety of roles to show off sharply contrasting individual characterizations. Television stars who appear on stage are expected to offer their idiosyncrasies and familiar quirks. If they can act, and many of them can, so much the better. They bring glamour to the stage but a glamour based not on enigmatic charm but on familiarity. Today no T.V. star has the mystery of Garbo, Dietrich or even Cary Grant. Instead we are offered the reassuring ordinariness of Mary Tyler Moore or Jackie Gleason, Calista Flockhart or Seinfeld: people much like us, a little quicker with the smart remark, a little better groomed, and yes, though we may not want to admit it, a little sexier.

1978: Brian Bedford as Elyot, Maggie Smith as Amanda

PRIVATE LIVES

Even in his own lifetime, Noel Coward was acknowledged as the heir of Sheridan and Wilde, the great modern exponent of the comedy of manners. Yes, his emotional range was narrower, his moral and social concern virtually non-existent, but he reflected something quintessential to his era. Thirty years after his death his comedies still inspire hilarious laughter and a delightful stab of recognition as his reckless, high-spirited women and vain, urbane, self-absorbed men bicker and banter over glasses of brandy, roll on couches and strum the piano before succumbing to fleeting bouts of rampant sentimentality.

PRIVATE LIVES · 1978
Directors:
Robin Phillips, Keith Batten

Designers:
Daphne Dare, Barbara Materia,
John Pennoyer

PRIVATE LIVES · 2001
Director:
Brian Bedford

Designers:
John Lee Beatty, Jane Greenwood   133

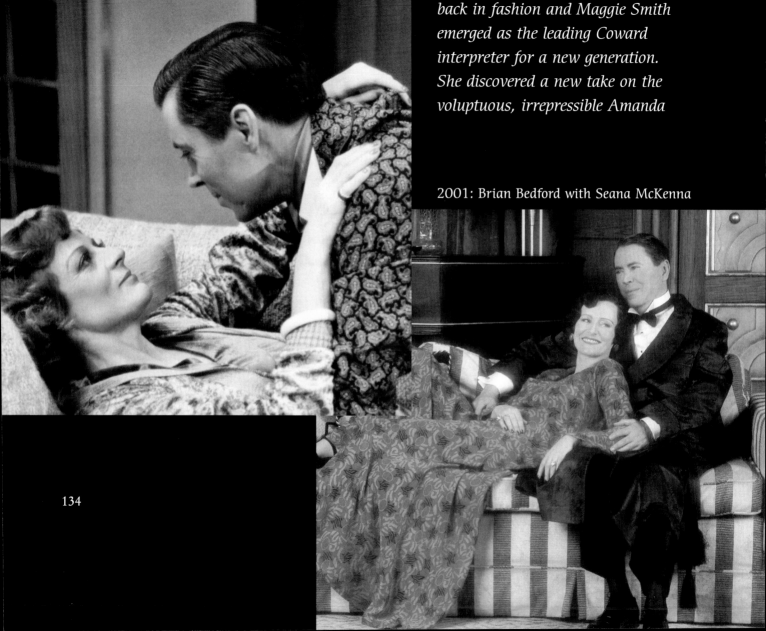

*back in fashion and Maggie Smith
emerged as the leading Coward
interpreter for a new generation.
She discovered a new take on the
voluptuous, irrepressible Amanda*

2001: Brian Bedford with Seana McKenna

134

us a woman so unconvinced of her own capacities that she bravely over-played the role of femme fatale, hoping she might just get away with it. This underlying vulnerability made her irresistible to the audience and also to her sparring partner Brian Bedford, who could not help but try to rescue her from the tedious Victor of Nicholas Pennell.

Coward's work embodied everything Guthrie was reacting against when he established his new theatre at Stratford, but this glittering production of *Private Lives* in the twenty-fifth season marked a recognition and coming home of one of the strongest influences underlying Canadian theatre: the British notion of triumphant style that inspired the indomitable amateurs from whose ranks emerged the first generation of Stratford actors.

The 2001 production, with Bedford again playing Elyot opposite Seana

2001: Wayne Best, Seana McKenna, Brian Bedford, Sarah Dodd

McKenna, attests to the remarkable sparkle this play still gives off. Although both actors are well past the age the script seems to call for, this improbability is forgotten mere moments after the curtain rises. McKenna exudes volatility, audacity, and a rueful self-awareness that once again make Amanda intensely human and appealing. Bedford is once more caught by this damnable woman's sheer outrageousness, and his enjoyment of his predicament makes him equally sympathetic.

The finely tuned mechanism of the play performs in a thoroughly satisfying way for today's audience, just as it did 70 years ago. Coward's grasp of sexual psychology is unerring and his impudent wit proves as potent as - well, as cheap music.

THE GREAT DIVIDE

"**Y**OU PIG!"

"What is your name, sir?"

"I've been acting here for twelve years and you don't even know who I am? We have spent our lives in this theatre. We have given of our time and art. You talk about money all the time. You have no morals. I don't know how you can sleep. I care deeply and passionately about this place, and you must address yourselves to your consciences and to your hearts."

This famous exchange between Richard Monette and Board President Robert V. Hicks on the snowy Saturday morning of December 6, 1980 memorably dramatized the conflict between artists and administrators that is inherent in any large arts organization. Toronto lawyer and politician Julian Porter recalls that this was his introduction to the Festival. He had just been invited to be a member of the Board by Hicks and at this, his first meeting, all hell broke loose. Hicks was called not only a pig but a liar who had offered a Brit, John Dexter, the artistic directorship of Stratford without the knowledge of the four-person directorate (the so-called Gang of Four: Pam Brighton, Martha Henry, Urjo Kareda, and Peter Moss) who had been appointed by the Board several months earlier.

By the end of the day Porter found himself appointed head of the newly-struck search committee: "My first question was, what does an artistic director do? Nobody gave me an answer. The one thing that was clear was it had to be a Canadian." In his first day on the Board, Porter was in the thick of a political jungle as dense as anything he had encountered in the backrooms of the Progressive Conservative party.

Behind Hicks loomed Peter Stevens, the recently appointed British executive director who had been hired the previous summer on the understanding that Robin Phillips would continue as artistic head of the Festival, assisted by a group of associates, and that part of the mandate would be to develop a winter season for the company in Toronto, engage in film production, and produce more contemporary plays.

These grandiose ideas appealed to Stevens but he arrived in Stratford in October to learn that Phillips was gone, his umpteenth resignation finally accepted by a reluctant and frustrated Board. The Gang of Four had put together a bold season involving Maggie Smith as well as a strong group of Canadian actors including Brent Carver, Clare Coulter, Martha Henry, William Hutt, Stephen Ouimette, Douglas Rain, Fiona Reid, Kate Reid, Gary Reineke, and R.H. Thomson and directors Pam Brighton, John Hirsch, John Neville and, it was hoped, Britain's Michael Bogdanov and Colin Graham. This was a stellar line-up that impressed the Board until Stevens predicted that it would lose a million dollars. The Board went into shock.

Stevens offered a solution: hire his friend John Dexter, who was available and interested. But he would not be willing to work with a group of associates; he would have to have absolute control of casting and choice of plays. Stevens no doubt honestly believed that Dexter could run a better show than any of the Canadians. But he hadn't counted on the repressed fury of the nationalists, captained by Mavor Moore as head of the Canada Council, who persuaded the Minister of Citizenship and Immigration, Lloyd Axworthy, that a proper search for a Canadian artistic director had not been carried out. Axworthy refused to grant Dexter a work permit. The Board argued that he had put the 1981 season in jeopardy, but Axworthy hung tough.

This situation illuminates the triangular power pattern of any large public performing arts institution. In one corner (presumably at the top) is the Board, a group of well-meaning and well-heeled citizens who often have a very limited knowledge of the art-form; in another are the administrators, whose job is to keep the organization running; in the third are the artists, whose job is to produce art of the highest calibre. The pattern is much the same the world over: the Metropolitan Opera, the Royal Shakespeare Company, and the Bolshoi Ballet all conform to it, with, in the case of the Russians, commissars standing in for bank presidents.

In the 1980 version of this drama, the three principal players were Porter, Stevens, and John Hirsch. Porter realized at a press conference held after the meeting that the Board he had just joined looked terrible and that the Festival was in real danger of going out of business. While spending the evening of December 6 at a party at the house of Dr. Ian Lindsay, a former Board president who briefed him on the Festival, Porter spoke at length with Hope Abelson, an experienced Board member from Chicago who came out strongly in support of John Hirsch as a first-rate director. Hirsch's name was on the short list of candidates the Board had drawn up.

Porter, who was staying at Stratford in Peter Stevens's house, phoned Hirsch the

138

next morning and set up a meeting for that afternoon. "If he's available, that's it."
"That's not it at all," Stevens retorted. "Your job is to make a search and report back to the Board. If you start making offers, you're going way beyond your brief."
"Look, you think I'm an asshole, and that's all right. You and I are going to wind up having a brawl over this and that's okay, too. Let's just both be sure we understand clearly what we're doing here." As a litigator, a tennis player and a former footballer, Porter appreciated a strong opponent; it put him on his mettle.

Both Porter and Stevens went to the meeting with Hirsch. Porter led off with "I've come here to offer you the job. Are you available?" Hirsch hedged; he had commitments in Seattle and Los Angeles. Stevens grinned:"So you're not available. That's all we need to know." But Porter was not about to leave. He spent the afternoon with Hirsch and left deeply impressed by him. He liked not only his expansiveness but also his wariness. He saw in Hirsch the kind of cat who could keep his footing on the slippery slopes and perilous crags of the Stratford landscape as Porter was starting to perceive it. The arch-WASP was captivated by this wily and passionate Jewish survivor.

Porter allowed Hirsch a little time to consider. Hirsch consulted advisors, among them Arthur Gelber, a Toronto philanthropist who had earlier suggested that Hirsch make a statement to the press when Gina Mallet, the drama critic of the *Toronto Star*, mentioned him as a potential candidate for the top job at Stratford. Hirsch leaked the story of his offer: "I have said yes, depending on certain negotiations." Although he and Hirsch had agreed not to go public, Porter confirmed the offer. The cat was out of the bag.

Stevens spoke to Mallet, who wrote an article saying the offer had not been authorized by the Board. Stevens also prepared a document for the Board, emphasizing they still had an obligation to Dexter and warning that the 1981 season, without Dexter's expert and experienced management, could lose up to a million dollars. Porter went to the Board and made them realize that the most important thing now was to show that they were acting in good faith. They had promised to have a search and they must be seen to have done so. They owed that to Axworthy, Hirsch, and Porter himself. They voted to accept Hirsch.

A season was put together with the help of Muriel Sherrin, an experienced CBC producer and longtime associate of Hirsch. Jean Gascon returned to direct Brian

139

Bedford and newcomer Sharry Flett in *The Misanthrope*; Bedford directed Len Cariou and Barbara Chilcott in *Coriolanus* and Colin Fox, Pat Galloway, Mary Haney, and Richard Monette in *The Rivals*; the Australian Derek Golby directed the resurrected nineteenth-century farce *Wild Oats* with Scott Hylands, Nicholas Pennell, and Fiona Reid; *H.M.S. Pinafore* was revived with Eric Donkin as Sir Joseph Porter; William Hutt appeared opposite Alexis Smith in *The Visit*. (The story is told, though it's a bit implausible, that Hirsch said to his underlings, "Get me Smith at any cost." He was appalled when they signed not Maggie but the aging Hollywood star Alexis.)

A host of Stratford veterans had rallied round and some promising new talent was introduced. The Festival was saved but the season did lose a million dollars. Stevens' prediction had come true, but by the time the tally was added up he was back home in England. Porter gives credit to Sherrin for making it work as well as it did: "She could have run the place better than anyone." But she didn't want the job. She retired back to Toronto as soon as Hirsch was able to be in Stratford full-time, though she would function as an extremely influential member of the Board until her sudden death from an aneurysm in 1994.

The whole debacle was a kind of watershed for Stratford in terms of the way the organization would be run in the future. Veteran stage manager Ann Stuart recalls Robertson Davies saying at the time, "For twenty-five years Stratford has been run in a gentlemanly way, deals sealed with a handshake. Now we're entering the cutthroat world of Broadway and Hollywood. Once you head down that road, there's no turning back." His words would prove prophetic.

Underlying all this backstage drama was a larger issue. Before coming to Canada, Robin Phillips had once remarked to Ronald Bryden, "The leadership of the English-speaking theatre is up for grabs. Why not go for it?" Bryden believes that Phillips saw the possibility of turning Stratford into "the Metropolitan Opera for theatre in North America." And, indeed, Phillips did greatly increase the Festival's scope and profile during his five-year reign. He saw this as a first step to be followed by incursions into the territory of Broadway and London's West End. *Foxfire* on Broadway and *Virginia* in London were the advance troops; the Ustinov *King Lear* was to be, as it were, the Normandy invasion. Douglas Rain's unwillingness to go to London to play Gloucester proved to be the horse-shoe nail for want of which the battle was lost. Phillips felt he could not replace Rain in time and the project foundered. This, as much as anything, triggered Phillips' final resignation.

Peter Stevens was hired, on the advice of Hume Cronyn, then a member of the Board, to help bring to fruition Phillips' ambitious plans to build for Stratford greater recognition abroad and to give it international clout. Stevens came to Canada with this goal firmly fixed in his mind. He saw Stratford as a potential rival to the great institutions of Britain, the National Theatre and the Royal Shakespeare Company. When Phillips decamped, Stevens saw John Dexter as the man most likely to take up this high-flown dream and run with it. Bryden, who was also on the Board, tried to explain to Stevens that the Canadian Festival was "a chariot, pulled by several horses, of which nationalism was one," but Steven was impervious to his advice. The Stratford Festival rejected Stevens' vaulting ambitions in favour of a smaller, more parochial model anchored to national interests. Stevens left Canada, a bit like Guthrie before him, because it was not ready or willing to embrace his larger vision. Guthrie had seen Canada as an immensely wealthy and enterprising country which could well afford to finance his grandiose notion of players with a tent traveling from city to city and eventually beyond its borders. He loved and admired the people of Stratford but was not content to settle for the kind of support they were able to offer: Presbyterian housewives serving homemade pies in a church basement did not quite match up with his romantic dream.

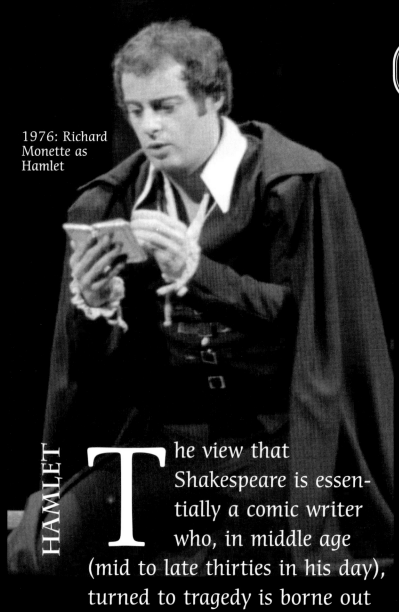

1976: Richard
Monette as
Hamlet

Twin Peaks

HAMLET & LEAR

Hamlet · **1957**

Director: *Michael Langham*

Designer: *Desmond Heeley*

Hamlet · **1976**

Directors: *Robin Phillips and William Hutt*

Designer: *John Pennoyer*

Hamlet · **1986**

Director: *John Neville*

Designer: *Sue LePage*

Hamlet · **2000**

Director: *Joseph Ziegler*

Designer: *Christina Poddubiuk*

HAMLET

The view that Shakespeare is essentially a comic writer who, in middle age (mid to late thirties in his day), turned to tragedy is borne out by Hamlet. Although it ends with a great heap of dead bodies, it contains some of the wittiest lines the poet wrote, and every production I have seen has evoked gusts of laughter among the clashes of steel and clatter of bones.

142

The character of Hamlet contains more facets than the most elaborately cut diamond, and this accounts for much of its brilliance. It means that almost any actor can use all the contrasting moods, emotional colours, and temperamental shifts he can summon up to play it and still not realize the text completely.

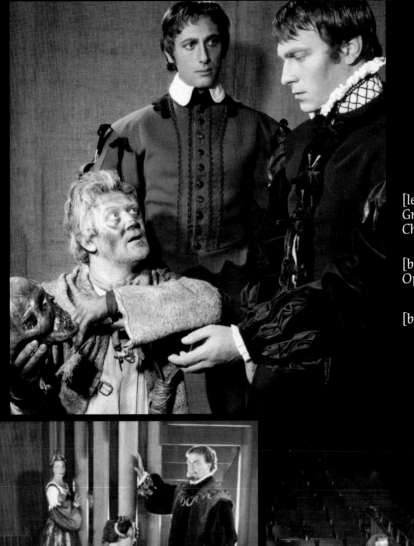

[left] 1957: Tony van Bridge as the Gravedigger, Lloyd Bochner as Horatio, Christopher Plummer as Hamlet

[below left] 1957 Frances Hyland as Ophelia, John Horton as Laertes

[below]: 1957 Ophelia's funeral

1976: Richard Monette as Hamlet with the Players:
Eric Donkin as Polonius, Graeme Campbell as First Player

1986: Scott Wentworth as Laertes,
Brent Carver as Hamlet

144

2000: Paul Gross as Hamlet, Juan Chioran as First Player, Jerry Franken as Polonius

Hamlet has been memorably portrayed in 1957 at Stratford, first by the young Christopher Plummer, who embraced the sardonic wit and the coruscating anger and made them his own. His pain was masked, his nobility violated and set aside. Early in the run he broke his ankle, and the need to use a cane gave his performance a special energy born of frustration and a need to rise above his situation. His trauma was counter-pointed by the fragile instability of Frances Hyland, hailed by critics as "the Ophelia of her generation."

The next memorable Hamlet was Richard Monette in 1976, giving a visceral performance that came from the gut, his agile mind a captive of his deep pain. He proved to be not only passion's slave but Time's fool, playing out whatever hand providence dealt him, knowing that indeed the readiness is all.

Brent Carver's 1986 Hamlet possessed a heart-breaking vulnerability; he was a man too sensitive for this or any world, swept along in a black current

he could not resist. His exchange with Eric House's wise, withdrawn Gravedigger caught the essential understanding of mortal frailty that lies at the heart of this play.

Paul Gross was a Hamlet for the twenty-first century. Agile and wily with a spirit that questioned everything, he employed his wit as a probe and included his audience in his jokes almost like a stand-up comic. He never came to rest, save perhaps for a moment when confronted with the haughty sensuality of Domini Blythe's Gertrude and in the end he accepted his fate with an amused appreciation of life's overarching irony.

　　　　2000: Paul Gross as Hamlet

1979: Peter Ustinov as King Lear with Jim McQueen as Kent and William Hutt as the Fool

KING LEAR

Where *Hamlet* is sharp complex, and unpredictable, *King Lear* is craggy, elemental, yet monumentally simple. It too is shot

[above and right]
1964: John Colicos as
King Lear, with
Martha Henry as
Cordelia

148

1979: Peter Ustinov as King Lear, Ingrid Blekys as Cordelia, Douglas Rain as Gloucester

As Stratford's first Lear in 1974, John Colicos was relentless in his early rigidity, cruelly commanding, unflinching in his determination to realize his will. This was a man no one could love, which made Martha Henry's headstrong Cordelia, the fallen apple of his eye, all the more believable as her father's daughter. This Lear had a long way to go, and we followed his journey stunned by its terrible progression. Hugh Webster's Fool provided a delicate counterpoint, his sanity perfectly offsetting his master's madness.

The next memorable Stratford Lear was Peter Ustinov in 1979 and 1980, a shrewd jokester, slightly ponderous, too fond of his own way. He brought the old king down close to our level. We understood his petulance and perversity and followed his outbursts as if we were watching our own geriatric parents. William Hutt's Fool was a wry companion. Their relationship was central in a world of lust, ambition, and greed vividly realized in the second year by Patricia Conolly as Regan, Martha Henry as Goneril, Richard McMillan as Oswald, and Richard Monette as Edmund.

William Hutt has played Lear at Stratford three times. His performance has grown in stature and humanity with each new incarnation until finally, in 1996, he gave a performance that was multi-layered and, suddenly, surprisingly witty. Wise one moment,

14

foolish the next, warm and self-deprecating, then icily arrogant, it was a remarkable portrait of a fascinating, fond old man, one that, for all his foibles, in the end no one could help loving.

1996: Jordan Pettle as the Fool,
William Hutt as King Lear

INSPIRED INTERPRETER OR TYRANNOSAURUS REX?
THE ROLE OF THE DIRECTOR

DURING THE TEN YEARS I WAS ASSOCIATED WITH THE GRADUATE CENTRE FOR STUDY OF DRAMA at the University of Toronto I was struck by the very considerable number of students who saw themselves as budding theatre directors. They were typically full of theories, full of confidence, and full of themselves. Most of them had little or no experience of acting, had seen few productions either amateur or professional, and had little sense of spoken language. Usually they did possess intelligence, a knowledge of the writings of Brecht, Artaud, Peter Brook, Grotowski, and Eric Bentley, and often a highly developed visual sense in addition to their boundless enthusiasm for their own ideas. The Centre had selected them not for any theatrical aptitude but purely on the basis of their academic credentials. In fairness it must be said that it is difficult to know who has the makings of a theatre director, indeed almost impossible.

I made it my business to give these students opportunities to work on productions with me and with visiting directors and to encourage their academic masters to allow them to direct their own productions in both our theatres. I warned them that directing is complex, that it involves a great deal of hard work for a very meagre financial reward, that in Canada at that time it was not a viable way of making a living. They did not choose to listen to this, and maybe they were right. Out of dozens of these young enthusiasts perhaps five went on to have, if not brilliant, at least interesting careers as directors. Another handful became drama professors and have had a satisfying experience directing student productions at a dozen universities across the land.

What goes into the making of a director? As the young playwright says in *Shakespeare in Love*, "It's a mystery." It requires a certain sensibility involving a strong visual sense that is not merely pictorial but architectural; a feeling for the musicality of spoken language, its rhythms, tempi, and structure; a knowledge of the history and tradition not just of the theatre but of art, culture, society, and civilization. It necessitates the ability to tell a story clearly, economically, and effectively. It also calls for a sensitivity to actors, their individual character and potential to embody certain qualities, physical, intellectual, emotional, and spiritual. It demands an ability to command respect and exercise authority, to organize a complex group of artists working to produce a result that the director must envision before he begins but that changes and grows during the process, to understand when to demand a certain effect and when to stand back and let some aspect of the work find its own shape. Finally, it requires the manipulative skill to accomplish all this within a finite timeframe so that the show is ready for an audience on a predetermined opening night.

It is a tall order; many of the necessary qualities are innate, but even so, the requisite skills cannot be acquired in short order. A great director may have a stunning success in his early twenties, like Peter Brook and Elia Kazan; in both cases they were fortunate enough to ride on the reputation of established stars: for Brook, Alfred Lunt and Lynn Fontanne, while for Kazan, Florence Eldridge, Frederic March, and Tallulah Bankhead, all of whom, by this stage in their careers, were virtually undirectable. But the process of becoming a fully mature and confident director takes time and a considerable capacity for perseverance. It also requires courage.

There is a popular theory, especially in academic circles, that actors do not make the best directors, but there is much evidence to the contrary. Of the major directors who have worked at Stratford many have been fine actors: Brian Bedford, Douglas Campbell, Jean Gascon, William Hutt, Richard Monette, and John Neville could all act rings around most of the performers they were directing. Brian Macdonald was a dancer before he moved on to choreography and staging. David William also had a career as an actor though not at Stratford. Of the others, John Hirsch, Michael Langham and Richard Rose were not actors; Tyrone Guthrie and Robin Phillips began as actors before deciding their major talent lay elsewhere. While it is possible to be a fine director without having first trodden the boards, it puts a director at a disadvantage if he does not have first-hand experience of the actor's process. How can he ask actors to do things he has never tried to do himself? It is also true that many actors beginning to direct do not get much beyond coaching. At some point there must be a leap back to see the bigger picture.

One of the misconceptions of many beginning directors is that they command and the actors do their bidding. There are some directors who do work this way: the

152

Romancing the Bard

celebrated American Robert Wilson is a case in point. Wilson is essentially a painter-puppeteer. He creates extraordinary visual experiences for the viewer using human figures as one of a number of resources. As his actors do not get to express emotions or ideas, he does not usually attract performers of the very highest order. But the job of the director in a theatre dedicated to the fullest exploration of the human condition is not to force his interpretation on the actor but to bring out the actor's own finest performance. If the director is intent on realizing his own conception of a particular role, he should get up on the stage and give his own performance.

In his book on acting, Tyrone Guthrie puts it this way: "Absolutely I do *not* want [the actor] to concede that, by virtue of my office, I am always right. That would be absurd. But I do hope that he will concede me the right sometimes to be wrong; that if my point of view of the play or even of the actor's own part differs from his, then, if after a reasonable argument we can reach no agreement, he must either play the part as directed, or play it in his way in another production." This is reason grounded in authority.

A director may help an actor to give a performance that he didn't realize he could do. This requires trust and close collaboration and usually a lot of manipulative skill on the part of the director. Manipulation has become a dirty word, but what else is one to call the process by which a director achieves a unified and cohesive interpretation of a play? Such an interpretation may exist in the director's imagination from the outset, but the individual actors, concerned as they must be with their own roles, cannot be expected to grasp it in its entirety. Many directors are said to be Machiavellian, and many are. The important thing is that the director should exercise his manipulative skills in the service of the play and not for his own personal gratification, be it sexual, political or intellectual.

It is in the nature of things for actors to resist directors, unless, let us say, the actor is the director's wife, with whom he is besotted. The exercise of directorial authority is complex and frequently problematic. In the early days of Stratford, Tyrone Guthrie encountered little resistance. Canadian actors felt privileged to be working with one of the acknowledged master directors of the English-speaking theatre and eagerly accepted his suggestions.

But Fred Euringer, in his vivid chronicle of Canadian theatre in the 1950s, *A Fly on the Curtain*, suggests that Guthrie, Langham, and Campbell were all bullies:

153

Inspired Interpreter or Tyrannosaurus Rex?

Guthrie in the style of a regimental sergeant-major, Campbell more like the coach of a rugby team, Langham the headmaster of a boys' school. This was of course the style of an era when authority was much more readily accepted than it is today— and not just in the theatre. Teachers threw chalk brushes at their students or smacked them about the ears with rulers, shouting "Dumbo" or "Blockhead." Parents wouldn't have dreamed of complaining of child abuse. Office boys might be required to drive the boss to Muskoka for the weekend as part of their job. Nurses worked twelve-hour shifts, six days a week.

Actors then accepted that they would be told what to do by a director and told off if they didn't satisfy him. Directors customarily gave actors bits of business and line readings; they expected it and learned from it. But even in the early days some actors were more independent than others. Eric House and Douglas Rain worked out their characterizations on their own and arrived at rehearsal knowing what they wanted to do. The story goes that Rain would eventually ask that it be written into his contract that he didn't have to take direction but finally agreed to accept six specific commands: upstage, downstage, stage right, stage left, louder, softer.

Different directors communicate in different ways. Some love to expound and theorize, while others merely suggest. David Gardner recalls that when he was playing a poet in the 1955 production of *Julius Caesar*, he asked Michael Langham how he saw the character. "I want him to be the epitome of decadence," came the reply. Puzzled, Gardner went offstage and waited for his entrance. Tyrone Guthrie was standing in the wings and whispered, "A scarecrow, dear boy." Guthrie's image instantly sparked Gardner's imagination, but another actor might have found Langham's intellectual concept more helpful.

A canny director will often realize that a certain actor is in tune with what he is doing and leave her alone to get on with it. But he may suggest "shadings." He may say, "That was marvelous, darling, but you know, I preferred what you did Monday," suggesting something completely different than anything she has yet tried. He may tell her she really looks best in profile in an attempt to get her to look at the actor with whom she is playing her big love scene. He may tell her that if she does that again, she needn't come back after lunch. Or he may say all of the above in rapid succession. One way a director can exercise control is by keeping his actors guessing. Robin Phillips was a great master of this technique.

Phillips had many ways of breaking down his actors' reliance on tricks and gimmicks. In rehearsal he would have Bert Carrière improvise on the piano underneath their lines, signalling by a series of pre-arranged gestures. Once, while Maggie Smith was rehearsing as Queen Elizabeth in *Richard III*, Phillips signalled for ragtime. Smith turned to Phillips with an outraged expression but he commanded, "Keep going." Her mounting irritation undercut her grief, adding a whole new dimension to the scene. The underlying trust that existed between Phillips and Smith made such tactics possible. It is unlikely she would have accepted them from another director.

Where Phillips was often outrageous, John Hirsch was confrontational. He challenged his actors at the first sign of laziness, conventionality or phoniness. Seana McKenna recalls him shouting, "Seana, why are you giving me this leading lady acting? If I want a leading lady, I hire somebody else. I want YOU." McKenna observed that Hirsch's brutal, sometimes bludgeoning tactics are more typical of eastern European than Canadian directors, and because of her Polish background she responded more easily to it than some others. Richard Monette had more difficulty acceding to Hirsch's imagistic demands:

"Richard, what are you doing?"

"You asked me to be natural."

"In this scene you are a microphone."

Monette tried the speech again.

"No, no, Richard. You must be a *naturalistic* microphone."

Guthrie, Langham, Phillips, Hirsch, William, and Monette all had the gift of eloquence. They could expound on the theme of the play, the historical context, the social background, the relevance to world issues, the psychological intricacies with wit and ingenuity, eloquence and fervour. Indeed, one stage manager said that the Festival should sell tickets to David William's rehearsals, so insightful and allusive were his comments. His published notes for his 1967 production of *The Merry Wives of Windsor* give a taste of this quality.

William was perhaps the last of the primarily intellectual directors at Stratford. In the present era his erudition has gone largely unappreciated by young actors and his insistence on laying down rigid blocking and specific line readings was thought to be constricting. Monette's techniques are much more immediate, relying on salty comment and outrageous humour. In 1999, when directing *A Midsummer Night's Dream* he demanded a quicker pace in the first fairy scene. The actors ran the scene again and took even longer. During the next run of the scene Monette stood up and started to undress. The actors stopped in their tracks. Monette explained, "You're so boring, I've decided to take off my clothes and amuse *myself*."

Styles change from one decade to another and also from one individual director to another. Ultimately, what matters is what's up there on the stage. How it gets there is the result of daring, imagination, tact, planning, management, and luck. Casting is a vital element: if a director gets the right actors in the major roles, half his work is done before the first rehearsal; if he makes too many mistakes in assigning roles, sometimes nothing can save the production. Some roles are certainly more difficult to cast than others. It has been said that anyone can give some account of Hamlet; it must also be said that almost no one manages to give a totally satisfying portrayal of Macbeth or Othello. Over the years this seems to have been true at Stratford.

It is also more difficult to give fresh life to a play that the audience may have seen half a dozen, or in the case of the critical fraternity, several dozen times. In the 1950s and 1960s, plays like *All's Well That Ends Well*, *Love's Labour's Lost*, *Pericles*, *Cymbeline*, *Timon of Athens*, and *Troilus and Cressida* were a revelation. Many of them had never been done before, at least professionally, in North America. Now the audience looks for a fresh interpretation. This is even more true of plays like *Twelfth Night*, *The Merchant of Venice* or *King Lear*. A more or less conventional staging of these plays satisfies the hordes of students who descend on Stratford in May and September and constitute a significant sector of the Stratford audience, but the mature audience wants something more. Part of the problem of Stratford's success is that it now tries to be all things to all people. Inevitably it disappoints some of them.

One criticism one hears is that Stratford no longer excels at interpreting Shakespeare. A production like Joe Dowling's *A Midsummer Night's Dream* in 1993 shines out like a daring deed in a dingy world. Punchy, raunchy, and fast-paced, it experimented with contemporary music, trendy gear, and highly colloquial speech patterns that delighted not only the young but supposedly stuffy bankers and dowagers. Dowling is one of the few visiting directors who have lit up the Festival stage in recent years. Why did he not return the next year? Why are there not more visitors like him?

156

Romancing the Bard

The answers are complicated and throw into relief one of the Festival's most per-plexing problems. In the early years when there was only one theatre and three pro-ductions, scheduling was fairly simple. Guthrie or Langham directed, or sometimes Douglas Campbell. Their styles differed somewhat but they were known quantities to both actors and production staff. They knew the plays and they knew the system. A number of young English directors came in to do single shows. They often felt that the Canadian actors "didn't know how to act," and their efforts met considerable resistance. The exception was David William, whose *Twelfth Night* and *The Merry Wives of Windsor* were bright and lively and cleverly exploited the talents of the best actors in the company. William also showed shrewdness in spending time to get to know the production people, thus gaining their cooperation.

Meanwhile, other directors came up more or less through the ranks: Tom Brown, George McCowan, Jean Gascon, and John Hirsch. They brought welcome variety: different colours, different accents. Langham was wary about giving untried Canadians major shows. Fred Euringer tells the story of how he went to Langham shortly before rehearsals were to begin for *Timon of Athens* in 1963. At the last minute, English director Peter Coe wired saying he would not be coming and Euringer, who had been working on the text for months, wanted to be given a chance to stage it. Langham decided he would do it himself with Euringer as his assistant but at the last moment switched horses to Michael Bawtree, a young Englishman he knew well. Euringer left the professional theatre.

Jean Gascon was more disposed to develop local directing talent. He gave major productions to William Hutt, and to David William and Michael Bawtree, both of whom had settled in Canada, André Brassard, Albert Millaire, Stephen Porter, Kurt Reis, Keith Turnbull and John Wood and provided workshop opportunities to some twenty aspiring directors including Timothy Bond, Martin Kinch, Clarke Rogers and Paul Thompson. Robin Phillips continued this tradition, assigning shows to Brian Bedford, Pam Brighton, Zoe Caldwell, Marigold Charlesworth, Bill Glassco, Arif Hasnain, Pamela Hawthorne, John Hirsch, William Hutt, David Jones, Peter Moss, John Palmer, and John Wood with varying degrees of success. He also worked with a variety of people as co-directors, among them Keith Batten, Urjo Kareda, Peter Moss, Gregory Peterson, Steven Schipper, Eric Steiner, and David Toguri. There is no

157

Inspired Interpreter or Tyrannosaurus Rex?

doubt he was serious about training. Many of the people he worked with, like many of the people Gascon encouraged, would go on to make vital contributions to the Canadian theatre.

One of the problems in Phillips' regime was that everyone wanted to be directed by The Master. This undoubtedly flattered his ego and he probably directed more shows than he should have. His co-directors were given rehearsals to supervise, but often the actors refused to take them seriously. Phillips' belief that any problem could be solved if the will were strong enough, together with his individual charisma, allowed him to make incredible demands on his actors and technicians; sometimes actors would play one role at the Festival Theatre, then cycle to the Avon to appear there in the last act. But in the end his insistence on absolute control worked against the development of strong young directors. As Gina Mallet put it, "Robin had to be the only cat in the alley."

Hirsch, Neville and William continued to try out Canadian directors: Jeannette Lambermont, Des McAnuff, Richard Ouzounian, Brian Rintoul, Richard Rose, Guy Sprung and Richard Monette. Some did only one show, others several. Most proved themselves competent, but few did work of commanding brilliance. The exception was Brian Macdonald, whose inventive staging of musicals, particularly the major works of the Gilbert and Sullivan canon, became the highlight of Festival seasons in the 1980s.

Monette has taken a different approach. Perhaps influenced by the glory days of the Royal Shakespeare Company in Britain when the directorate was shared by a brilliant clutch of directors that included John Barton, Peter Brook, Terry Hands, and Trevor Nunn, Monette established a stable of directors to whom he made a commitment. They have been given several shows to do, modern and classical, in the three different theatres. This has provided them a chance to experiment, to grow, even to fail, if necessary. Antoni Cimolino, Martha Henry, Jeannette Lambermont, Diana Leblanc, Marti Maraden (until she left to take over the artistic direction of the National Arts Centre in Ottawa), and Richard Rose—these directors form an in-house contingent: they know the company, the system, and each other. They do not necessarily meet at regular intervals but are in touch with each other and with Monette.

Monette discusses casting and concept with these directors, but once they are in rehearsal he leaves them alone with the actors, rarely visiting before the show is in previews unless invited by the director. For this he has been criticized by Board members, especially in the case of the 1999 *Macbeth*, directed by Diana Leblanc and featuring Rod Beattie as a kind of modern-day entrepreneur who seems more at home carrying a briefcase than a broadsword and actually appears before the banquet scene in a barbecue apron. He is besotted with his Lady, an ambitious social-climber as portrayed by Martha Henry. They even burst into a Gershwin love song at one point. The production was lambasted by critics and traditionalists (but popular with younger audiences and, by the end of the run, sold out). Board members told Monette he should have stepped in to modify the show, but he insisted, "This was an experiment. We need to experiment. And to realize that not all experiments are successful."

The company also needs the stimulus of working with exciting outsiders. Monette has pursued big-name directors at home and abroad from Terry Hands to Robert Lepage, Mike Nichols to Atom Egoyan. They usually express interest and discuss projects, but so far none of them has bitten the bullet. The reasons are complex. Many of them don't want to work as part of the current Stratford repertory system. Although Monette tries to give directors the actors they want, at least in the principal roles, they must accommodate their minor casting to the actors in the existing company. Almost all the actors are triple-cast; this means the director only has his full cast to work with one day in three. He may be able to work individual scenes in a play like *Long Day's Journey Into Night* or *Who's Afraid of Virginia Woolf,* but in the big Shakespearean plays it is impossible to try to stage scenes when half the cast is missing.

The system militates against the momentum that builds up when rehearsing a single show. Rehearsals are spread out over three months, which sounds luxurious, but in fact there may only be six or eight rehearsals with a full cast before the show goes into "tech," when the lighting, costume, and prop people grab the director's attention so that he can no longer give full concentration to the needs of the actors. The old hands in the company accept this, but it is a shock to visiting actors, and many established directors consider the system intolerable and simply will not accommodate themselves to it. Peter Brook rehearses a new show over a period of eighteen months to two years and forbids his actors to be involved with other projects in any way.

159

Inspired Interpreter or Tyrannosaurus Rex?

Robert Lepage develops a production over a similar stretch of time, changing it from day to day in rehearsals that continue throughout the run, so that no one performance is like another. The design is flexible and changes as the director and actors explore the text. At Stratford the design decisions are made long in advance, often before the show is cast.

Then there are purely personal considerations. Directors at Stratford must be in residence for four months. If they rehearse one day in three this means a lot of sitting around, perhaps discussing roles with actors over coffee, perhaps working on the next project. If the director has a spouse and family elsewhere, he is out of touch for quite a long time. If he wants to go home, it means a two-hour drive to Toronto and a flight to wherever he lives, returning within forty-eight hours, all at the director's own expense. And the fees are not terrific: Stratford's actors are well paid, but this is less true of directors. Twenty-five or thirty thousand Canadian dollars is not a tantalizing reward for spending two months of preparation and four months in rehearsal in the bleak mid-winter of southwestern Ontario.

It has been said that Stratford's most significant failure has been in training imaginative, capable Canadian directors of Shakespeare and other classical texts. The problems are clear, the solutions less so. Monette is embarking on a new program to train directors, fully cognizant of the difficulties of identifying suitable candidates, especially in a country where young directors may do shows in St. John's, Ottawa, Saskatoon, and Victoria, so that the only person in the country who is liable to be able to see a reasonable sample of their work is the theatre officer of the Canada Council. Once they are chosen, there is a the problem of challenging aspiring directors while maintaining their interest and holding onto them for long enough to get a reasonable return on the investment of training them. If it took Michael Langham the better part of five years to fully master the use of the Stratford stage and earn the committed loyalty and respect of the company, how is a young director going to master his craft in one year or even two?

Nevertheless, Jeannette Lambermont has been charged with drawing up plans for a training program involving a system of mentoring for perhaps three or four apprentice directors a year, in which ideally they would work on shows with two different directors and then do a show of their own, perhaps with the Conservatory, but involving at least some seasoned actors. For it is a very different game working with keen young hopefuls and tougher, less flexible old pros. Key to the success of the plan is the use of the projected Fourth Space.

Monette's determination to come to terms with the problem of training is consistent with his concern to move ahead and improve the quality of work. But the system is resistant to change. Production people are used to doing things in a certain way. The audience expects a certain type of product delivered in a certain style. Will they support truly experimental work? It's one thing to pay ten dollars to see an offbeat take on, let us say, *Don Juan* or a new script on the problems of Inuit lesbian mothers on a rainy Sunday afternoon at Toronto's Tarragon or Passe-Muraille; it's quite another to drive two hours to Stratford and shell out thirty or forty dollars or more.

Herbert Whittaker has for some years advocated that Stratford should do a kind of high season for the cognoscenti, modelled on the early years of the Festival: two superbly cast and brilliantly directed classics running for perhaps four weeks, to be supported by the more populist work of the rest of the season. It would be bravely, uncompromisingly elitist. That would be the beauty of it, but in today's politically correct world it could also be the death of it. Yet it seems clear that some kind of break-through in programming is required if the very best artists, actors, and directors are to be attracted to work at Stratford. The system has become unwieldy, inflexible, almost out of control. And yet, if you are running an organization with a $30-million budget, selling nearly three-quarters of a million seats, employing 800 people and making a profit of nearly $5 million a year, are you going to break the mould and start all over again? I don't think so.

Inspired Interpreter or Tyrannosaurus Rex?

Lucy Peacock as Titania, Ted Dykstra as
Nick Bottom, Yanna McIntosh as First Fairy

162

Lucy Peacock as Titania

S hakespeare's most magical play has been performed almost continually since it was written, often in altered and almost unrecognizable forms. Composers from Henry Purcell to Benjamin Britten have used it as the basis for an opera, though the most celebrated score remains Mendelssohn's. There have been famous productions in this century by Max Reinhardt, Peter Brook, and Robert Lepage, among others. There have been film versions featuring stars from Mickey Rooney to Calista Flockhart. Stratford has produced this play no less than eight times in fifty years and it never fails to delight with its brilliant juxtaposition of comedy and fantasy.

Director: *Joe Dowling*

Sheila McCarthy as Helena,
Stephanie Morgenstern as Hermia

It is the favourite play of visiting Irish director Joe Dowling, who determined in 1993 to make it totally contemporary, painting in broad strokes for the benefit of an audience whose average age he calculated would be under twenty-five. His principal consultant was his own fifteen-year-old daughter. His production evoked an enormously positive response from the teenagers who crowded the theatre for school matinees, and it excited older audiences as well with its hip clothes, pulsing rock music, and unabashed sexiness.

The relationship between the brash, cocky Theseus of Wayne Best and his sultry, sullen conquered bride Hippolyta as portrayed by Alison Sealy-Smith set the tone as they squared off in the initial scene at court. These were no lovebirds but a pair of seasoned scrappers, ready to carry their battle into the bedroom.

Once in the woods, the air was heavy with erotic vibrations as a huge phallic growth appeared that would be climbed upon and slid down by mortals and fairies alike in their capricious games of lust and power. The Oberon of Colm Feore was no effete poseur but vigorous and quick-tempered in his dealings with Lucy Peacock's haughty, sensual Titania. For all the pettiness of their quarrel, these fairy monarchs possessed a stature and nobility the humans lacked.

Into their realm came the four young lovers, who would spend most of the night in their underwear, pawing and groping, scrabbling and skirmishing. Their words were Shakespeare's but their attitudes owed something to the style of sitcoms. The comedy was broad but real, rooted in the hearts or perhaps the solar plexuses of the young actors: Sheila McCarthy, Stephanie Morgenstern, Sean Powers, and Mark Ruel. Emotionally the women were ahead of the men, quicker to discover their feelings, sharper in expressing them. This became very much a play of women's battle for self-fulfillment and advantage.

In its driving search for a free expression of the female impulse the production willingly sacrificed ethereal delicacy for earthy immediacy. Keith Thomas' music may have lacked mystery but it provided a persistent hypnotic beat that moved the story forward. The dances were straight from a disco, and the Puck of Frank Zotter spoke his lines in the rhythms of a rapper.

The mechanicals were not silly old codgers but young and fresh-faced, led by Ted Dykstra's callow, optimistic Nick Bottom. Even in his ass's head he was an attractive young egotist and Titania's infatuation with him was made the more believable. Among his cohorts, Brian Tree's Peter Quince and Barbara Bryne's Starveling stood out, and the enactment of the playlet of Pyramus and Thisbe *had the naive charm of willing amateurs, desperate to please and blissfully unaware of their inadequacies.*

And at the end when the fun subsided and the young lovers sorted out their tangled claims, there came a happy moment when Hippolyta thawed and favoured Theseus with a smile that warmed the whole company.

This was Shakespeare neither vulgarized nor compromised but pushed into new shapes and at the same time thoroughly enjoyed. Dowling's sharp intelligence made Shakespeare's brightly imagined world immediate, real and totally of the moment.

AFTER HOURS

TYRONE GUTHRIE BELIEVED THAT A THEATRE COMPANY SHOULD BE LIKE A GREAT BIG FAMILY NURSERY in an English country house, complete with games, treats, scoldings, spoonsful of medicine, and no doubt an occasional spanking. He, of course, was Nanny: a six-foot-four nanny with a moustache and a powerful bark of command. Like all good nannies, he looked out for his charges twenty-four hours a day, supervising their activities while the big people were engaged with more serious "adult" matters. The image was apt: there is a sense in which all actors are children surrounded by outsize toys; their love of play is what impels them to become the characters they enact. The catch is—these children have discovered sex.

The tradition of actors as a company of mountebanks, a strolling cry of players, goes back a long way, at least to the early Renaissance, when troupes of *commedia dell'arte* performers toured the cities of Europe, their costumes and properties piled on a cart, their stages rickety structures that could be quickly set up in town squares and just as hastily dismantled if they had to move on in a hurry when their broad comedy offended local dignitaries or one of their members got into a scrape in a tavern or seduced somebody's daughter. In the sixteenth and seventeenth centuries, actors still toured as a matter of necessity; cities were not large enough to provide a year-round audience. Shakespeare's company went on the road in times of plague; Molière's company toured provincial France before he won the favour of Louis XIV and was invited to play at court.

Until well into the second half of the twentieth century actors continued to tour in North America as well as England and Europe. They patronized favourite pubs, theatrical boarding houses, and hotels that catered to "the profession." Actors have always thrived on gossip and swapped tall tales of their exploits, just like lawyers, sportsmen, and even clergymen, but the significant difference was that the theatre community included women. Because these women drank, smoked, and were emotionally involved with the men they worked with, they rarely attained the highest levels of social acceptance. Because they were attractive and vivacious they attracted

Romancing the Bard

many admirers and probably didn't regret for a moment their lack of respectability.

The coming of a company of actors in 1953 set the small, conservative city of Stratford on its ear. The clean-living, church-going natives of the town had their own ways of entertaining themselves but these did not include fancy restaurants, let alone bars. They played baseball and attended church socials. They sang in choirs and met to discuss worthy books. They visited each other's homes and served tea and homemade biscuits.

In the beginning they willingly opened up these activities to the newcomers. Both actors and audience-members were boarded in private homes' though on the condition that they didn't smoke, drink or have visitors of any sex. The late Alf and Dama Bell began to give garden parties that continue to this day. The ladies of Knox Presbyterian fed the actors and laid on home-cooked suppers in the church basement that became one of the most refreshing aspects of the Festival for out-of-town visitors. The chief organizer was a certain Mrs. Elgiva Adamson, who also arranged study groups to familiarize people with Shakespeare's plays. She attracted an enthusiastic audience of local women and wrote her own booklets about the plays, in which she expurgated all references to physical cruelty or passion. Guthrie heard about her activities and was furious, but when told Mrs. Adamson was a very unhappy woman who had suddenly blossomed in her new role as Shakespearean expert, he bit his lip and, in Tom Patterson's words, "refrained from comment, which was never easy for him."

The good citizens of the town were delighted to see Alec Guinness riding his bicycle, or Tony and Judy Guthrie having a picnic in the park (though Guthrie was once fined for drinking whiskey in his own back garden), but they were less amused by the shenanigans of some of the lesser actors who had nowhere to go after the show. In the first year, Irene Worth hosted parties; she would get home, open the first four cans on her pantry shelf, throw the contents into a pot on the stove and produce ample if unpredictable casseroles that staved off starvation for some of the more poorly paid members of the company. Guthrie was also a frequent host and while he was in residence he was able to keep the lid on things, but his successors did not have the same authority. There was gossip about late night carousing and suspected bed hopping. Boys will be boys, and actors will be actors. William Needles recalls, "There was an underlying distrust between us and the local people from the beginning. I won't say they hated us, but they could certainly be hostile. Some actors were roughed up by local youths. You didn't want to go out alone at night."

A major change came with the arrival of the actors from Quebec. They were horrified to discover they could not get what they considered edible food and drink at the hotels and restaurants of Stratford. On the second day of rehearsal Gabriel Gascon was missing; it seemed that he was so disgusted at the prospect of adjusting to these gastronomic conditions that he had taken off back to Montreal. His brother Jean went after him and brought him back in a car laden with bottles, and the two brothers rented a large farmhouse outside the town where they entertained throughout the season. Louis Negin recalls being invited to a party: "Gabriel was cooking a wonderful ragout and I stood beside him at the stove, fascinated. I remember saying, 'I think you're wonderful.' Gaby, who didn't have much English, turned and gave me a great big kiss. I fainted."

Eventually it became very chic to live in the country. Pat Galloway's farm was later to be the setting for many festivities. "We partied a bit too much, but we were a big, happy family who thoroughly enjoyed each other's joys and sorrows," she recalls. She still entertains a sizeable clutch of Stratford's longtime regulars for Christmas dinner. Other actors acquired country properties which gave them a private space for play but also retreat and recuperation: Berthold Carrière, Lewis Gordon, Seana McKenna and Miles Potter, Stephen Ouimette, Nicholas Pennell. In Stratford itself the situation moderated as married actors set up housekeeping, made possible by longer seasons and larger salaries: Douglas Campbell and Ann Casson, Michael Langham and Helen Burns, Bruce and Mary Swerdfager, Joseph Shaw and Mary Savidge. And there were romances within the company, some fleeting, others more durable.

Actors come together to work in very intimate conditions. They must open themselves emotionally to each other and often they are in close physical contact. Backstage they share dressing rooms and see each other in confined quarters and various states of undress. It is rather like a cross between a Caribbean cruise and a military barracks. Liaisons are almost inevitable. Stratford was no exception: Frances Hyland and George McCowan, Max Helpmann and Barbara Chilcott, Christopher Plummer and Tammy Grimes, somewhat later Martha Henry and Douglas Rain, Seana McKenna and Miles Potter, Peter Donaldson and Sheila McCarthy, Martha

Romancing the Bard

Henry and Rod Beattie. Not all these matches began at Stratford but they became part of the social fabric.

These partnerships are often professional as well as personal. The actors hear each other's lines at home, discuss and work their scenes together or offer suggestions for scenes with other actors. They look out for each other's careers, pool their resources, their connections, their finances. It is part of a great tradition: Alfred Lunt and Lynn Fontanne, Douglas Fairbanks and Mary Pickford, Laurence Olivier and Vivien Leigh, Jessica Tandy and Hume Cronyn. The theatre is often likened to a family. Where better to learn about the craft of acting than at the family dinner table? Genes and skills are passed on from one generation to the next. The Barrymores and the Redgraves are famous examples. In Canada we have the Campbells, the Davises, the Needles, the Neville-Dinicols, the Wright sisters.

At Stratford, as elsewhere, not all the partnerships have been heterosexual. A whiff of homosexuality has pervaded the theatre from the earliest days. There has been much speculation about the Greeks, whose male actors received lavish gifts and other attentions from wealthy patrons, and the Elizabethans when young gallants flirted with the boy actors. There is certainly evidence in Shakespeare's work that he was alive to the erotic possibilities of male relationships. In the English-language theatre of the twentieth century, homosexual playwrights have been major figures: Wilde, Coward, Williams, Albee. At Stratford over half the artistic directors have been homosexual. It is not surprising that this has had a continuing influence on the work.

"Back then we didn't know what homosexuality was, darling. Nobody mentioned it," recalls Mary Jolliffe. But Guthrie's sexuality must have influenced him, at least unconsciously, in his choice of actors. The 1953 company contained half a dozen homosexuals. They may not have proclaimed their preferences at the time, but they would come out of the closet eventually. As with the heterosexuals, gay actors influence each other. They look out for each other and provide a network, a "grapevine" that passes on gossip, contacts, opportunities. Their liaisons, though sometimes brief, are often very instructive; professional skills are passed on. The model here is Platonic: the older man providing a model and encouragement for his young lover to emulate.

Over the years there has been an attempt to accommodate the partners (of whatever sex) of the major actors in the company. This policy has sometimes had an impact on morale; it's not how talented you are but whom you sleep with. It's no different in other artistic venues—Broadway, the West End, Hollywood, Toronto—and there is evidence that there are real benefits to the company. A happily mated actor is more apt to settle down and stay with the company and to be more cooperative in rehearsal. Meanwhile the partner receives opportunities to improve in his or her craft. Actors grow by acting and sometimes those chosen for their connections rather than their obvious talents become useful and accomplished company members. Not every good actor shows great potential in the beginning. And not every actor in the company can be a star. They also serve who only stand and listen.

By the mid-1960s the centre of social life for the actors was the Chalmers Lounge at the Avon. Here actors gathered to unwind after performances. It could be rowdy. Diane D'Aquila recalls, "The Chalmers was not patronised by the townies. Some members of the company were there every night. Jack Creley and Roly Hewgill would have these tremendous arguments. 'Hold that thought,' one of them would say, go and have a pee in a potted plant, pick up a refill at the bar and go back at it. Sometimes they came to blows. Nobody ever left till the bar closed. Then they'd stagger home together, just in case they attracted the wrong kind of attention from the town toughs."

The British model was evident in the pub atmosphere of The Jester's Arms on Ontario Street (now Bentley's) which offered Guinness and other British brews on tap and darts in the backroom. Many of the actors played cricket; the annual match against the team fielded by the Shaw Festival continues to be a major event to this day, consolidating the not unfriendly rivalry between the two festivals. A good number of actors have worked for both companies, and Shaw's artistic director Christopher Newton received much of his early acting experience at Stratford when Monette was also trying his wings. The two maintain an ongoing communication. There is an unwritten understanding that neither will raid the other's company, though occasionally they have met to do a little horse-trading.

Robin Phillips inaugurated a more sophisticated social era. The swinging sixties did not arrive in Canada until the beginning of the 1970s and Phillips set about to make the infrastructure of Stratford more welcoming to an upscale public. He believed this would encourage people to visit the Festival for longer periods and ultimately to pay higher ticket prices. Everyone in Stratford would benefit. The quality of life would be improved and the cash registers would jingle. There would be more money for the merchants as well as the theatre box-office. The model and the hub for this new social order would be The Church, a first-rate restaurant developed and managed by Phillips' partner Joe Mandel in an abandoned ecclesiastical building a block from the Avon Theatre. It was modelled on the trendier eateries of London and offered chic California-influenced *nouvelle cuisine* imaginatively presented by handsome young waiters to the strains of Mozart and Vivaldi.

Here Phillips held court. His new regime, seemingly democratic but actually rather hierarchical, took as its paradigm an eighteenth-century royal household, that of Louis XIV perhaps, or Frederick the Great. During working hours there were rituals to be observed: warm-ups and voice classes, dance and fight rehearsals, Alexander sessions and massages, fittings for costumes and wigs and of course acting rehearsals, which often continued until late in the evening. But on the weekends some of the more affluent actors dined at *The Church* and the more impoverished were seen there sometimes as Phillips' guests. The Court was, in effect, on view to the public. William Needles recalls with a touch of asperity, "We were assigned tables according to our positions in the company. Those in favour got to sit with Robin or close to his table. I usually found myself just outside the ladies' washroom."

The success of The Church motivated other restaurants, notably Rundles and The Old Prune, whose proprietors set up a school for chefs. Many of its graduates have gone out into the world beyond but others have stayed in Stratford and the result is a proliferation of eateries and stores selling gourmet provisions: Balzac's, Bistro au Jardin, Keystone Alley Cafe, Pazzo, Ragueneau, Trattoria Fabrizio, Vidalia and the York Street Kitchen offer a variety of gastronomic experience far surpassing any other Ontario city of comparable size. Robin Phillips' vision has indeed been realized and it strengthens the interaction between Festival performers and audiences. One day my wife and I were having lunch with Joseph Shaw and Ann Stuart. Inevitably our conversation centred on theatre gossip and because Joseph is a bit deaf we were shouting at the tops of our lungs. We lingered over coffee till mid-afternoon and when we got up to go, the people at the next table cried out, "Don't leave. Your conversation was so fascinating we've missed our matinée."

John Hirsch also ruled Stratford like a king, a despot in fact. The image of the Sun King gave way to that of a Borgia Pope or a Byzantine Empress. He did not

171

make public appearances in the manner of Phillips but spent his leisure time plotting and scheming with a coterie of favourite gossips, caustic queens in their parlours masticating malicious tidbits. He could not of course visit The Church, because this was the hangout of Phillips and his closest cronies. It came to be spoken of as the Court-in-Exile. Such was Hirsch's green-eyed rancour that it was said he arranged to have a carton of cockroaches let loose in The Church's kitchen, then called the health inspectors.

Neither John Neville nor David William had Robin Phillips' capacity for socializing; William in particular was withdrawn and reclusive, but the social patterns of Phillips' era persisted, becoming ever more popular in character. Actors increasingly organized parties of varying size in their houses. By the 1980s a good many of the established actors owned their own homes. Today they spend eight to ten months of the year in Stratford, and even those who no longer work for the Festival on a regular basis maintain residences. Colm Feore works mainly in Hollywood, yet lives a stone's throw from the Festival Theatre. It provides a welcome haven away from the madness of Tinseltown and a safe environment with good schools for his children.

The rise of the bodybuilding craze in the 1980s began to be reflected in Stratford. Actors have always been concerned about their appearance and now a well-developed body has become *de rigueur* for young performers, although a good voice is still a better entrée to the company than impressive pecs and abs. Gyms sprang up in Stratford, backed up by a clutch of masseurs and chiropractors, to service the demand of younger members of the company. They still spent leisure hours swimming at the quarry in St. Mary's, a favourite sunning spot since the early days of the Festival, but nowadays it has become a place to display the effects of all those hours spent doing press-ups and crunches.

The other principal playground today is a bar called Down the Street, established by two members of the technical staff in the early 1990s. Here members of the company gather nightly after the show to drink and gossip, see and be seen. Many nights Monette is on deck, Scotch and cigarette in hand, surrounded by a clutch of the regulars, Bert Carrière, Roy Brown from props and, until his untimely death in October 2000, Michael Mawson, director of the Conservatory. Monette will converse with his actors: one night Brent Carver, another Michelle Giroux. Eyes are batted, tall tales are traded.

Romancing the Bard

More mogul than monarch, father than Fuehrer, Monette is unquestionably the most approachable artistic director the Festival has ever had. Some critics say he runs the Festival from this bar, and certainly in the small hours connections are made and ideas floated. But for all his accessibility Monette is a cat who ultimately walks alone. No one accompanies him back to his house on Douglas Street (though they may drop him at the door after a half-hour conversation in the car) and even his oldest friends need not expect rewards or favours unless they can deliver the dramatic goods. Today, as in the days of Guthrie, Stratford is still a family. The ultimate decisions are made by Big Daddy Monette, but his final choices are defined not by the interests of any individual member but by the good of the enterprise as a whole. He is infinitely open to suggestion, a long-suffering listener and a veritable magpie when it comes to picking up bright ideas embedded in the mounds of verbal debris that pile up around him.

John Colicos as Timon of Athens

TIMON OF ATHENS · 1963/1964

This, the darkest of all Shakespeare's plays, has been hailed by some critics as the most contemporary in its sensibility. The story of a generous host and free-spirited patron of the arts who feasts and subsidizes a whole society, only to find himself scorned and abandoned once his wealth is spent, is a parable about greed, ambition and the nature of friendship.

Director: **Michael Langham**

Designer: **Brian Jackson**

Martha Henry as Phrynia, William Hutt as Alcibiades, Rita Howell as Timandra

*M*ichael Langham boldly set the play in the present day and with the help of designer Brian Jackson evoked the high- and lowlife haunts of a great and corrupt city: Havana before the revolution, hangout of mafioso bosses, international sophisticates, and Ernest Hemingway, with perhaps a hint of London, which in 1963 was just starting to swing. Here were grand banquets where the wine flowed like blood, gaming tables where fortunes changed hands in an hour, and steamy bathhouses where unconventional couplings occurred in shadowy corners. The production juxtaposes air-raid sirens, barbed wire, and ticker-tape machines with sumptuous candlelit feasts and

175

Timon's banquet

haute couture gowns, evoking opulence, decadence, violence and, ultimately, sterility.

The proceedings were greatly enhanced by an original jazz score composed by the mighty Duke Ellington, whose syncopated rhythms, dissonant chords, and elusive melodies dissolved into each other providing a sonic surround that swirled and swept and seemed to hang in the air. It inspired choreographer Alan Lund to invent an original dance step, somewhere between the mambo and the twist, that Ellington christened "the skillipoop," a word that in black argot signifies something like "messin' around."

But the glory and challenge of Timon is its language, ornate, convoluted, studded with bizarre images and corrosive epithets. John Colicos possessed the vocal skills to deliver it, his rich baritone vibrating as he moved from the grandiloquent extravagances of the profligate philanthropist in the first part of the play to the searing rage and scatological excesses of the misanthropist he becomes in the second half. The unsparing honesty of Colicos' portrayal somehow made the two halves of this dual personality cohere as we followed his brutal journey through the dark forests of contempt and loathing down into the depths of ultimate self-knowledge.

William Hutt's Alcibiades, physically modelled on Fidel Castro, matched the scale and grandeur of Colicos' Timon, and his power to suggest this vainglorious and self-inflated military posturer strongly motivated Timon's explosive tirades. Douglas Rain provided the blunt candour and tough-minded provocation that made the philosopher Apemantus his perfect foil. Martha Henry as Phrynia and Rita Howell as Timandra were lissome, slippery whores cynically clutching at any advantage that presented itself.

We saw a world of wealth no longer morally grounded, power at the beck of a momentary whim, beauty chasing its own reflection and lust rampant: not a pretty picture but a potent one. When the company took this production to Chichester it astonished the British critics, as yet unaccustomed to such radical interpretations of Shakespeare. Some praised, some condemned, but none was indifferent. This was as close to the avant-garde as Stratford would come in the next decade.

A WORLD TOO WIDE:
STRATFORD REACHES OUT

NO SOONER WAS THE STRATFORD FESTIVAL PERCEIVED TO BE A SUCCESS than there was an engulfing desire to have this success extended to and acknowledged by the world at large. This hunger for a wider audience was motivated both by generosity, a wish to share this rewarding experience with others, and by insecurity, the need to receive confirmation that the work was indeed as good as it was said to be by the people who had attended the performances of the first season.

The first manifestation of this desire was the formation in 1953 of the Canadian Players, a touring company set up by Douglas Campbell and Tom Patterson using a nucleus of players from the Stratford company to tour with a repertoire of classical plays that favoured Shakespeare and Shaw. They unabashedly took on the big works – *Macbeth*, *King Lear*, *Saint Joan*, *Man and Superman* – and travelled not only to major cities but to smaller towns and villages and to remote outposts in both Canada and the United States. In organizing the tours, Campbell was inspired by the stories of the early explorers and pioneer settlers of his adopted country of Canada, and he believed deeply that art was the backbone of civilization and should be available to everybody.

The conditions of these tours, which continued throughout the first ten years of Stratford's existence, have been vividly described in Fred Euringer's *A Fly on the Curtain*: the fleabag hotels, the ten- and twelve-hour bus-drives in the dead of winter, with the actors singing to keep their spirits up and then setting up for performances in school gymnasiums, church basements or dilapidated hotel ballrooms. The pay was low, the food lousy, and the hours intolerable, but there were moments of magic. Campbell's huge Falstaffian face lights up as he recalls a performance almost fifty years ago in Pembroke, Ontario, when two older women in the front row started to laugh in the first five minutes of a comedy at exactly the right places, leading the entire audience so that for the whole evening the hall rocked with merriment and at the end rang with applause. The actors knew they had done something memorable that neither they nor the audience would ever forget.

As a touring version of the Stratford company, the Canadian Players were rough and ready, and proud of it, but Guthrie himself came up with a much more grandiose scheme in 1956: a production of Christopher Marlowe's *Tamburlaine the Great* to open in Toronto and then travel to New York City. The cast, members of the Stratford company supporting the British stars Anthony Quayle and Coral Browne, included Barbara Chilcott, a young Colleen Dewhurst, William Hutt, and William Shatner. *Tamburlaine* opened at the Royal Alexandra in Toronto to an audience somewhat discombobulated by the ferocious lashing of slaves, the pulling out of tongues, the deflowering of virgins, and Douglas Rain bashing out his brains against the bars of his cage. The vast spectacle was barbaric, brilliant with brandished banners and whizzing arrows and, in Guthrie's words, "quite wonderfully horrid." It went on to the Winter Garden in New York with the aid of producer Robert Whitehead, where, in spite of a first-night audience that included Greta Garbo, Alec Guinness, Marlene Dietrich, and Tyrone Power, it failed to do good business and was withdrawn after only twenty performances. This outing cost Stratford $51,000, and although the play was roundly condemned by the critics, the production and performances were lavishly praised and the publicity it gained the Festival was invaluable.

The next such venture was a visit to the Edinburgh Festival in the same year with *Henry V* and *Oedipus Rex*. The critics used phrases like "alarmingly robust" and "invigorating freshness of attack" but criticized the speaking of the verse as crude and unintelligible and particularly disliked the Québécois accents. Michael Langham believed that the British critics were determined to patronize the colonials. But his production of *Henry* was more favourably received than Guthrie's *Oedipus*, whose masks were described by Kenneth Tynan as "Toby-juggish" and by *Punch* as suggesting "a school of very old, Asiatic baboons." The tour did little to bolster the Canadian company's reputation in England, and nothing of similar scope was attempted for nearly a decade.

Instead, Langham inaugurated a small touring company that took *Two Gentlemen of Verona* and Donald Harron's Canadianized adaptation of von Kleist's *The Broken Jug* to London, Toronto, Montreal, and New York. But the plays were obscure and the productions uninspired; the venture played to small houses and lost money. In these early years Stratford's attempts to reach out to wider audiences was neither strengthening the company nor enhancing its reputation. Then came Guthrie's rollicking version of *H.M.S. Pinafore* in 1960, which played to sold-out houses at the Avon and with its proscenium staging and single set proved admirably suited to touring. Guthrie arranged for it to visit Montreal, Panama City, and England, and later New York. Guthrie's equally fresh and inventive *Pirates of Penzance* also toured to London and New York. The Festival did not benefit financially from these productions; the fact that they were managed by experienced commercial producers no doubt contributed to their success.

In 1964, the four-hundredth anniversary of Shakespeare's birth, Stratford again invaded the hallowed precincts of the English stage, responding to an invitation not from the Royal Shakespeare Company but from the Chichester Festival. The Chichester theatre, which had opened in 1962 and was largely inspired by Stratford, possessed a somewhat differently configured thrust stage. The plays chosen were revivals of Langham's *Love's Labour's Lost* and *Timon of Athens*, and Gascon's newly staged *Le Bourgeois gentilhomme*. The actors attacked the plays with gusto and the critics warmed to them. Hutt was praised for his silvery Don Armado, Rain for his Holofernes (a "perpetually ruffled owl of pedantry"), and Colicos for his "handsome, sonorous, utterly sincere" Timon. But it was as a company that the Stratford actors were most highly regarded: for the constant fluidity of movement on the open stage, for their sense of ensemble, for their articulate speech and physical grace. Ronald Bryden wrote, "They've worked together until their integration is flawless and they play their instrument like a Stradivarius." The haughty English were, if not utterly conquered, at least somewhat seduced by the charms of the Canadian company.

In 1967 the nation was gripped by Centennial fever and the government was prepared to pay handsomely for the birthday party. The Canada Council coughed up a substantial subsidy and a winter tour took *The Government Inspector* and *Twelfth Night* across the country from Victoria to St. John's. In October, *The Government Inspector* starring William Hutt and *Antony and Cleopatra* with Zoe Caldwell and Christopher Plummer played at Expo. These ambitious outings spawned the notion that the Stratford company should take its rightful place as Canada's national theatre.

In Ottawa the monumentally oppressive bulk of the National Arts Centre was already taking shape under the guidance of Hamilton Southam. Following the image-enhancing Expo appearance, it was announced that what was now to be called the Stratford National Theatre of Canada would provide a winter season of English-language plays and spend half the year in Ottawa. The evanescent dreams of cultural nationalists from Herbert Whittaker to John Hirsch seemed about to become solid reality. But it was not to be, at least not for long.

Stratford did send a number of its productions to Ottawa, *A Midsummer Night's Dream* in 1968, *Hamlet* and *The Alchemist* in 1969, *The Merchant of Venice*, *The School for Scandal*, *Cymbeline* and *Tartuffe* in 1970, *Much Ado About Nothing* and *The Duchess of Malfi* in 1971, *As You Like It* and *Lorenzacchio* in 1972. They also mounted original productions in the small N.A.C. studio and in 1970 two modern plays, Brendan Behan's *The Hostage* and Boris Vian's *The Empire Builders* as well as John Hirsch's children's show *Sauerkringle*. But the strain of running two large theatres was to be too much even for the freewheeling exuberance of Jean Gascon. By 1972, Stratford was mounting nine fully staged productions in three theatres. The offices, rehearsal rooms, production workshops, and, most importantly, the trained staff were all in Stratford. Productions could not be built in two places at once without enormous extra cost and an atmosphere of ongoing chaos. So it was necessary to treat the N.A.C. as essentially a touring house (as the British Royal Shakespeare Company based in Stratford-upon-Avon has treated the Barbican theatre in London). Inevitably, members of the Ottawa-based production staff of the N.A.C. began to resent this arrangement, especially as they began to develop confidence in their own abilities.

During the Gascon years the Stratford shows that went to Ottawa also visited other venues. Between 1968 and 1972 these Festival productions went to the Maisonneuve Theatre in Montreal, the Mendelssohn Theatre in Ann Arbor, Michigan, the Studebaker Theatre in Chicago, the Krannert Theatre at the University of Illinois, and the Guthrie Theatre in Minneapolis. In 1969, Jean Gascon's production of *Hadrian VII* starring Hume Cronyn went on a forty-six week tour of major American cities. In 1973, Stratford made a major European tour sending *King Lear* with William Hutt and *The Taming of the Shrew* with Pat Galloway and Alan Scarfe to Copenhagen, Utrecht, The Hague, Warsaw, Krakow, Moscow, and Leningrad, subsidized by the Department of External Affairs. They played before royalty in Copenhagen and received a nine-minute standing ovation in Leningrad, enjoyed packed houses, and returned with a strong sense of well-being and exhilaration.

The next year they took Molière's *The Imaginary Invalid* to Australia, touring to four cities. The European tour had been prestigious, but this tour was fun. Australian hospitality was spontaneous and extravagant and the Canadian actors' love affair with their fellow Dominion was, according to William Hutt, "flagrant." It was a happy finale to Gascon's expansionist policies for the Festival, but the concept of Stratford as a touring company was doomed. The cultural euphoria that developed in 1967 was fading. Arts and academic budgets were beginning to be trimmed, nationalism and separatism were on the rise, and this would affect the way Stratford's subsidies were perceived on Parliament Hill and at Queen's Park. Robin Phillips kicked off his first season with a tour of *The Comedy of Errors* and *Two Gentlemen of Verona* that went to the West as well as Montreal, two areas of greatest discontent with Ontarian cultural domination; the next year, *Hamlet* and *The Tempest* travelled Ontario. But they would be the last tours of Shakespeare for a decade.

After 1976, Phillips concentrated on developing small productions that could be sent off to larger centres, following the model of *Hadrian VII*. An early run at this was Robin Phillips' production of *The Guardsman* with Maggie Smith and Brian Bedford that played Los Angeles before coming to the Festival. Phillips left after opening night, and the two stars, playing in an enormous auditorium, broadened their performances until the show became a parody of Phillips' original intention. When they returned to Stratford he reasserted his authority, and *The Guardsman* became a light-textured but ruefully truthful comedy and one of the hits of the season. The experience was not lost on Phillips, who thereafter honed and polished small shows until the actors had confidence in his vision before they were sent out to triumph abroad. Highly successful were *Foxfire* in New York and *Virginia* at the Haymarket in London in 1981. But Phillips' plan to take *King Lear* with Peter Ustinov to the same venue collapsed when some of the cast refused to go. Ustinov sued the Festival, a suit finally settled out of court.

After Phillips left, the vision of Stratford as a touring company persisted and a major tour of *King Lear* and *Twelfth Night* was organized in 1985 with visits to Los Angeles, Seattle, Chicago, Palm Beach, Fort Lauderdale, and Washington, D.C. The company was composed of Festival stalwarts led by Douglas Campbell and including

Mervyn Blake, James Blendick, Patricia Collins, Colm Feore, Max Helpmann, Seana McKenna, Richard McMillan, and Nicholas Pennell. It was conceived as an important marketing tool to woo American audiences to come to Stratford, but it met with a rather tepid response and racked up a substantial loss, variously interpreted by different administrators but amounting to at least $100,000. Although the tour had been strongly supported by the ambitious Board Chairman Peter Herrndorf, the realization was driven home that large-scale touring was a thing of the past.

For the next fifteen years Stratford would confine itself to occasional transfers. In 1982, Noel Coward's *Blithe Spirit* with Brian Bedford, Tammy Grimes, and Carole Shelley, and in 1984 Terence Rattigan's *Separate Tables* with Domini Blythe and John Neville went to Toronto's Royal Alexandra for successful runs as part of that theatre's subscription season. In 1996, plans to transfer *Alice Through the Looking Glass* to Toronto's Winter Garden fell through when Sarah Polley was unavailable to play Alice. Discussions are underway for a remount of *Elizabeth Rex*, to play in both Stratford and Toronto. There has also been a plan to remount *Fiddler on the Roof* in Toronto, but both schemes depend on the availability of Brent Carver, who is much in demand and consequently unwilling to commit himself very far in advance.

Other productions have visited the academic communities of Ann Arbor and Dartmouth and been well received. Monette's production of Feydeau's *A Fitting Confusion* went to Edmonton in 1996 and Marti Maraden's staging of *A Man for All Seasons* featuring Douglas Rain played the National Arts Centre in 1998. The 1996 production of *Barrymore*, co-produced with Garth Drabinsky and starring Christopher Plummer, had a highly successful run in New York but the transfer of *The Miser* and *Much Ado About Nothing* to Manhattan's City Center in the autumn of 1998 was less successful. New York critics were condescending and audiences thin. The 2001 transfer of *The School for Scandal* to Chicago was a happier experience, in part because it appeared as part of an established subscription season.

Rising salaries and more stringent union regulations have contributed to the rapidly escalating costs of touring, as have the increase in fares, hotel rates, and restaurant prices. But another factor slowly seeped into the collective consciousness of Stratford's administrative and artistic leaders. It was first clearly articulated by Hope Abelson, a Board member from Chicago, who came to the Festival every year and who characterized a visit to Stratford as a vivid and unique experience. If she wanted to see stars, she explained, she could travel to London or New York; if she wanted contemporary experimental work it was available at home. But her annual visit to the Festival was an important cultural ritual in her life. She did not want it to come to her, she wanted to go to it, somewhat as one makes a pilgrimage to a shrine, be it Lourdes or the Parthenon.

A Festival offers a particular experience to those who participate. Usually accompanied by friends or family, they set off a block of time and see several shows. They discuss their perceptions and ideas about it over lunch or dinner, meet old friends they saw at the same time last year or new friends they will hope to see again in future years. It is a holiday, but something more because the participants are artistically nourished and stimulated. They are surrounded by other people undergoing the same sensations and emotions. They become part of an ever-changing community that has come together and received a gift.

In our fast-paced world, the Festival experience has potent appeal: for a brief time cell-phones are shut off, e-mails go unread, TV serials are unwatched; there is a concentration of attention on a particular kind of aesthetic experience. Most people come to Stratford only once a year for a few days, but if the shows are really good, the afterglow lingers and they will return to recapture a magical moment lovingly remembered.

Stratford was not the first arts festival. It was preceded by Bayreuth, Salzburg, Glyndebourne, Edinburgh, and Avignon, to name a few. But it was one of the first established in North America. Festivals have since proliferated across the continent, and Stratford itself has spawned more than one. The autumn Film Festival began at Stratford in 1956 and flourished under the guidance of Tom Patterson, Louis Applebaum, John Hayes, and Gerald Pratley during the next decade, before it moved to Toronto. The short-lived but brilliant summer festival of opera at the National Arts Centre under Mario Bernardi was a direct extension of the work he did with Gascon at Stratford from 1965 to 1967.

The Shaw Festival at Niagara-on-the Lake also took heart from the success of Stratford, and its development has owed more to a combination of imitation and reaction to its elder sister than to the inspiration of the earlier Shaw-dominated Malvern Festival in England. Even the semi-annual International Theatre Festival at Harbourfront in Toronto owes much of its inspiration to Stratford's success; its current director is Stratford alumnus Don Shipley, who played one of Martha Henry's children in her Stratford debut performance as Lady Macduff.

Stratford still offers a unique experience to those who come to it, and it might do well to realize it is better served by letting its public make the pilgrimage to its shrine than by pursuing them far and wide. But the urge to reach out, to spread the Gospel, is strong and hard to counter, especially in today's media-dominated world.

Indeed, it was inevitable given the interplay between stage and film in Britain, where actors parlayed their theatrical prestige into film careers, that Stratford actors would want to follow the same starry route. Lorne Greene, William Shatner, Christopher Plummer, and John Colicos took off and disappeared into celluloid heaven. In 1956, Guthrie directed a film based on his staging of *Oedipus Rex*, which was shown at the Edinburgh Festival alongside it and is generally recognized to be the first dramatic feature film shot in Canada by Canadians. Back home the CBC turned to Stratford to collaborate on a TV feature in 1957: *Peer Gynt*, starring an energetic Bruno Gerussi in a badly mangled script that failed to please anybody.

In 1960, the CBC televised Tyrone Guthrie's production of *H.M.S. Pinafore* in its Toronto studios under the skilled direction of Norman Campbell. It proved so popular that other tapings of G&S productions rapidly followed: *The Pirates of Penzance*, *The Gondoliers*, *The Mikado*. Norman Campbell became the guru of the TV transfer with his recreation of Stratford productions on tape (although CTV produced the first televised Shakespeare production in 1967 with Michael Langham's neo-Brechtian anti-war *Henry V*). CBC televised John Hirsch's swashbuckling *Three Musketeers* in 1969 and two productions in 1981 of *H.M.S. Pinafore* and *The Taming of the Shrew*.

Hirsch had been head of TV drama at CBC and had the connections to make a deal between the Festival and the national broadcaster, but the reaction to *Shrew* was mixed. The decision was made to shoot a live performance, and although Norman Campbell exercised ingenuity in cutting to close-ups, there were built-in problems. It was impossible to shoot the large-scale scenes without the audience being seen across the stage behind the actors. In addition, the vocal projection necessary to be heard in a 2000-seat house made the actors seem forced and stagy on the small screen.

The Festival's 1994 production of Eugene O'Neill's *Long Day's Journey into Night* was selected by Rhombus Films for a sensitive recreation of the play in cinematic terms. The young film director David Wellington restaged the piece on a set built to replicate the essential qualities of the stage design and redirected the actors to produce effective film performances. The deal between Rhombus and Stratford was brokered by the energetic and aggressive publicist Janice Price, who helped put the financing in place. But the producers failed to acquire full American rights and the film, though it won many awards in Canada, will never have full international distribution. Rhombus is currently developing a production of Timothy Findley's *Elizabeth Rex*, a much more complex and costly proposition because of its large cast, period clothes, and more ostentatiously theatrical flavour.

Another media connection has been an annual collaboration between Stratford and CBC radio, with live performances by Stratford actors in the Toronto Glenn Gould Studio being taped for broadcast for radio. The plays have ranged from original scripts about Blake, Yeats, and Chekhov to recreations of stage productions of *The Tempest* and *Twelfth Night*, modern classics like *Waiting for Godot* and *Under Milk Wood*, adaptations of works by Mark Twain and Gogol, and compilations of poetry and memoirs. It provides a valuable outreach for the Festival, bringing its work to inaccessible corners of the nation. But the theatricality of the stage militates against the intimacy of the best work on radio; often the result is a hybrid not completely satisfying to anyone.

The desire to harness Stratford's theatrical creativity to the media began early and will no doubt continue. Guthrie, Phillips, and Hirsch in particular all had large ambitions in this area and the experience to back it up. Tom Patterson spent considerable time and effort working on a scheme for a film production studio in Stratford. Many producing organizations have approached the Festival and there have been discussions with such major players as Atom Egoyan, Norman Jewison, and Robert Lepage. But film and stage are very different animals with vastly different organizational requirements, financial structures, and audience expectations. Gifted directors and actors can move from one medium to another, but the existing Stratford plant cannot cope with the complications of film production in addition to its existing duties. Nor is there anyone on staff with the knowledge and aggressive outlook to drive a film production program.

In the last year the Royal Shakespeare Company has put together an impressive group of American contacts with the avowed aim of marketing Shakespeare worldwide, producing films, television, and DVDs. Can the Stratford Festival be a player in this burgeoning international market? What is needed is a dynamic young producer, a Garth Drabinsky or James Campbell in the making, who will wheel and deal in Los Angeles, Toronto, New York, Vancouver, Rome or wherever, and then roll his Winnebagos up to the back door of the theatre and carry off the actors for six weeks shooting in Saskatoon, Prague or Manila. Is this a real possibility? Hard to say. But the dream of Canadian movie-making seems almost as indestructible as the Festival itself. To paraphrase Celine Dion as her plangent soprano becomes the iconic voice of Canada throbbing around the globe, "The dream will go on."

Peter Donaldson as Jamie Tyrone

Eugene O'Neill continues to be revered as America's first great playwright, and his late masterpiece provides as definitive a challenge for a mature actor as *King Lear* and for an actress as *Hedda Gabler*. It is an ordeal for both actors and audience, as it is meant to be. But there is dark humour and tongue-tied poetry as well as melodrama. The play is a challenge, like Everest, like Mars.

The four disillusioned people in this disjointed family play out their desperate struggle to reconnect without giving up their cherished illusions and psychological defences. The play demands intense concentration and unwavering emotional truth, and Stratford's 1994 production under the sensitive direction of Diana Leblanc delivered this, giving us an utterly engrossing realization of the tortured individuals tethered to each other by buried emotional needs and an unwavering determination to follow dreams that only fitfully touch the rough surfaces of reality.

The family feeling in this production was intense, so much so that when it was suggested that one cast member, Martha Burns, who played the maid, might have to be replaced in the second season, the company declared they could not possibly do the show

Director: **Diana Leblanc**

Designer: **Astrid Janson**

Martha Henry as Mary, Tom
McCamus as Edmund, Willia
Hutt as James Tyrone, Peter
Donaldson as Jamie

with another actor. This bonding of actors provided an emotional centre from which radiated every move, every grimace, every inflection.

Not that we were aware of moves, grimaces or inflections. What we tuned into was the psychic force of a world peopled by characters whose grip on reality was tenuous, shifting, out of control. All of them knew the others to their very core, yet none of them really knew themselves.

William Hutt had the stature, the vanity, the impulsive changeability of the successful nineteenth-century actor James Tyrone. He also had a great warmth of feeling under his assumption of crusty irascibility and the underlying humour of a man who has known many shifts of fortune, many successes, many disappointments.

Martha Henry brought a similar knowledge of life's vicissitudes to Mary Tyrone: we saw the ghost of the innocently passionate romantic she must have been, turned into a desperately lonely woman who retreats into a drug-dependant haze and yet battles on, a cunning, charming, manipulative, caring, determined survivor.

It is usual in this play for one of these characters to dominate and yet in this production the balance was maintained, a balance constantly shifting, a marriage imperfect, painful, jagged as in life.

Peter Donaldson embodied the self-despising, cynical, hard-drinking Jamie, whose protective shell is cracked momentarily by Tom McCamus' vulnerable but unyielding Edmund, still hopeful and resolutely tough-minded as the two brothers drink their way through the night in the haunted house by the impervious, unknowable sea that is O'Neill's great metaphor for the universe in which man struggles to maintain and realize himself.

And yes, Martha Burns had just the right air of slovenly cheerfulness as the maid Cathleen. A perfect cast, perfectly attuned to each other and the rhythms of this towering, punishing, exhilarating play.

Diana Leblanc seems to have known instinctively how to shape and orchestrate, what to highlight, what to demand, when to let the actors find their own way. Astrid Janson's set met the players' needs and reinforced the author's intentions. Shutting off the back end of the overlong Patterson stage evoked the dark labyrinth of the family's past, out of which they struggle fitfully toward the light.

In the second year of the production there was some over-elaborate ornamentation, particularly from Martha Henry, that detracted from the delicate balance of the first season, but the film returns to the purity of the original performance. David Wellington's production perfectly realizes the stage version in another medium, proving as with Kazan's film of A Streetcar Named Desire *or Mike Nichols'* Who's Afraid of Virginia Woolf? *that a great stage play need not be rewritten for the screen.*

The film brings one of the glories of Stratford to a wider audience than any tour could hope to achieve. Will this prove to be a portent of the future or a one-time phenomenon?

Martha Henry, William Hutt

KEEP YOUR COUNCIL:
CULTURAL POLITICS AND ECONOMIC REALITIES

VINCENT MASSEY MUST BE ACKNOWLEDGED AS THE CULTURAL FATHER OF HIS COUNTRY. This shrewd, austere, discriminating patrician was a committed Anglocentric, whose suave demeanour even British peers admitted "made one feel a bit of a savage," but underneath the hauteur was more than a trace of the pioneering evangelistic Yankee farmers from whom he was descended. His contributions to the arts in Canada were many, including a timely donation of $10,000 to the Stratford Festival in its first year when the committee members were on the verge of throwing in the sponge.

But his most influential cultural achievement was the production of the Massey Report. Profoundly influenced by the British model of state cultural support for the arts which he had observed while serving as Canadian High Commissioner in London during the Second World War, Massey's report recommended the establishment of what was to become the Canada Council, a government agency charged with the task of promoting and funding Canadian scholarly and artistic endeavours.

The Canada Council was hailed by art-lovers and of course by artists. The idea that they might actually be paid something substantial for their labours was heady, intoxicating. In the early 1960s the sum of $1000 (the amount I received in my one and only grant), while not enough to send me to Europe for a year of basking in old-world artistic ambiance, was still an impressive sum — enough to buy a new typewriter and six months' supply of whiskey.

Soon after the Canada Council was put in place, most of the provinces, not to be outdone, set up their own councils, and many major cities followed suit. All governments thought they wanted a stake in culture. The heyday of arts subsidy coincided with the country's centennial celebrations in 1967. Expo '67 featured a large arts component, showcasing new film technology, importing performing companies from around the globe, displaying the latest and most extravagant architectural designs.

Romancing the Bard

At the same time, theatres and galleries were built across the land, rivalling Ottawa's new National Arts Centre, which was expected to become Stratford's winter home. Smaller theatres, dance companies, publishing houses, music groups, and art galleries proliferated. And they all had their hands out. Artists were quickly learning a new artform: how to concoct applications that appealed to arts council juries.

From the beginning, arts-council grants were supposed to be "arm's-length." Governments did not want to be seen to be telling artists what they should create. The agencies were not looking to beget propaganda but rather Art. This was not the Soviet Union, where artists had to dance to the tune of a philistine dictator. In order to safeguard the ideal of governmental non-interference, juries were set up composed entirely of artists. The applicants would be judged not by bureaucrats but by their peers: musicians evaluating musicians, painters evaluating painters, and so on.

Juries were put together by arts-council officers who tried to get a representative cross-section while they themselves maintained an impartial stance. But it was not possible for jurors to ignore completely the personalities of the applying artists, and in the relatively small artistic communities of Canada someone on any jury usually knew at least some of the candidates. It was also inevitable that jurors would have their own prejudices and preferences. My experience is that jurors bend over backwards to be fair. Indeed, George F. Walker once stated that Canadian juries are "boringly fair." Is this preferable to being outrageously unpredictable?

Fair or not, one result of the growing influence of arts councils has been to politicize the arts. It was inevitable that juries dealing with public money would take into account the prevailing orthodoxy and strive to be politically correct. It is in some ways easier to evaluate a submission in terms of its compliance to understood criteria that give preference to the work of racial minorities or representatives of geographically remote or disadvantaged areas than to judge the artistic quality of the work. This is even more true in the case of institutions than it is with individual artists.

Therefore the requests for funds from a high-profile institution like the Stratford Festival are approached by jurors with definite preconceptions. Some consider Stratford elitist; others think of it as primarily a tourist attraction. Because it gets larger grants than most other arts organizations, it is envied. Because even these large grants represent only a small part of the overall budget, it is argued that the grant is

Keep Your Council: Cultural Politics and Economic Realities

not important to the organization. Why not do away with it altogether and give the money to people who need it more? And who might be more appreciative?

One former arts-council officer makes the argument that Stratford is less deserving than, for example, the Thunder Bay Symphony, which brings culture to an otherwise under-serviced and comparatively isolated area. Its members are not only artists but also involved in the community. They teach music to students, work in the high schools or are church organists. Their integration into the community gives them a special importance in fostering culture where it is most needed. The concern here is not with artistic excellence so much as social relevance.

Faced with this kind of argument, governments gradually came to see arts funding as increasingly controversial and a potential source of political embarrassment. They realized that, although the arts community is highly vocal and has ready access to the media, it is comparatively small. There is a large section of the populace who don't care whether the arts are supported or not.

Meanwhile, government subsidy had become a fact of life in the arts, especially after the councils picked up the tab in 1970 and paid down the deficits of several major performing arts organizations. The understanding was that there would be no more deficit budgeting. In fact, performing arts companies like Stratford began to practice what came to be called "zero budgeting." To be eligible for government grants they had to be seen to be "not-for-profit." Thus they had to walk a tightrope between profit and loss; they had to budget so that their revenues would cover their expenses but not show an inordinate gain at the end of the year. The impossibility of this situation led to a good deal of fancy footwork in the accounting department and took up time and energy that might have been better employed in artistic rather than actuarial creativity.

The king of zero budgeting at Stratford was Gary Thomas. A Stratford accountant who was brought on board in the Phillips years, he was not promoted to general manager (as he had hoped) and was therefore denied access to the Board. When Peter Stevens arrived, he immediately realized that he needed Thomas as an ally and granted his wish. As general manager after Stevens decamped, Thomas was in a strong position. He knew the workings of the Festival and got on well with the staff. The Board welcomed the stability and air of competence that

Thomas supplied. It did not bother them that he preferred baseball to drama; rather it was seen as evidence of his down-to-earth common sense.

The Board at this time consisted of Stratford businessmen and rather more high-powered entrepreneurs from outside: Toronto, London, Ontario, Montreal, Chicago, Detroit, New York. Occasionally artists were asked to sit on the Board: Nicholas Monsarrat, Hume Cronyn, Nicholas Pennell, Norman Jewison, but most of the members were inexperienced in the intricacies or even the rudiments of theatrical production. John Uren, a publicist trained by Mary Jolliffe, who stayed on through most of the 1980s, recalls that many of these magnates said very little at meetings. When Uren questioned Board members Peter Widdrington and Robert Gordon about this, they replied, "Hell, most of us don't know anything about running a theatre. We don't want to look stupid." They were there to facilitate the making of art, not to criticize. But as the number of women on the Board grew, this changed. The women might have been no more knowledgeable but they were not afraid to ask questions. Feminism began with women asking questions men didn't want to answer.

At the same time the running of the theatre became increasingly complex. There was much more paper work: grant applications, union negotiations that led to more restrictive work hours, and a proliferation of elaborate contracts. Both IATSE, the stagehands' union, and the musicians' union were quick to make demands once Stratford had established itself as a going concern. For a while some stage-hands were making two or three times as much as the average actor. In time the seamstresses and dressers, prop-makers, and wig-dressers would all be unionized. Today a costume-fitting can only take place in the presence of a dresser and the head of wardrobe. These people must also attend all photo-calls. There is now one stage manager for every five performers. Rehearsals must stop at an exact time or the company goes into overtime and everyone must be paid time-and-a half. All shows must be under three hours to avoid crippling overtime charges.

Actors' Equity has had a good relationship with Stratford, at least partly because it was a clutch of Stratford actors who fought for and participated in the birth of the Canadian union. Prominent Stratford actors continue to take an active part in negotiations. In recent years Actors' Equity has fought for and gained higher salaries for performers as well as the right for actors to be paid if they spend time on publicity

195

activities, such as being photographed or interviewed. The artistic management and the Board are sympathetic to the actors' demands, but it all contributes to a greater commercialization of Stratford, not just in the administrative departments but also in the attitudes of the actors themselves.

Another development that Gary Thomas had to deal with was the introduction of the GST, which required more frequent and complicated reporting to governments. Administration became more complex: there were meetings to plan, project, prioritize, schedule, revise, and re-schedule, progress reports to make, post-mortems to conduct. Thomas presided over all this. He saw that the slots for publicity, marketing, casting, production management, educational activities, and finance were covered and gave people a fairly free hand. His efficient administration satisfied the Board. But not John Hirsch.

Hirsch was by nature demonstrative, combative, declamatory, and suspicious to the point of paranoia. When the 1981 season posted a record loss he insisted on more high-priced help. When he learned that John Hayes had been brought out of retirement because no one else could draw up a rehearsal schedule, he insisted on a producer with artistic background, so the Board agreed to hire Gerald Eldred. The next year he brought back Mary Jolliffe, who by this time had been chief publicist at the Guthrie in Minneapolis, the Metropolitan Opera, and Expo '67. She was not about to take a lot of guff from Hirsch and left within a year, but before she went she rehabilitated Tom Patterson, who was recognized as Founder of the Festival. The re-naming of the Third Stage and an island in the middle of the Avon in his honour would follow in due course during the tenure of David William. Jolliffe's protégé John Uren succeeded her and ran lively sales campaigns that outraged the Old Guard, who considered his tactics inappropriate and sometimes downright vulgar, as when he invoked the image of the McKenzie brothers (Canadian, eh?) in an ad in the *New York Times*. Douglas Campbell fumed, "I will not be marketed like a pork chop," to which Uren cheekily retorted, "Hey, Dougie, you're the biggest chop in the window." But Uren's sales stratagems worked. And vulgarity didn't bother Hirsch, who was not hung up on Anglo notions of "good taste."

Hirsch believed that his job was to create art and that it was up to the government to pay for it. In fiercely passionate speeches he denounced philistines and bureaucrats. These tirades were as dramatic as anything heard on the Festival stage:

196

What the place needs is the support, the love, the care, the concern of every single person who cares about theatre in this country. Institutions are incredibly precious…. They can get weak, die, disappear. We must stop in this country rejoicing in troubles and difficulties…. We can't afford it, because we ain't got that many good things around. So what the hell is going on?

The essential thing is to ensure that good things go on. All things are in trouble all the time. *I* am in trouble all the time. It takes me two hours in the morning to pull myself together because of what happened the night before. I have to tell myself, "Come on, Hirsch, get up, shave, make a speech, get something going." Not to sit and moan and nitpick and analyze and put everything down, *which is so much fun*, because then you don't have to be good, you can just say, "This is shit, it's terrible."

The place was in trouble, it collapsed. A was guilty, B fucked up. But all that is gone. What can *we* do about what happened? What can we do now and who is going to come and help? That is why I told you the story of my life. If anybody has a reason to sit and moan, it's me—a Jewish orphan left alone to starve at thirteen, wandering around… what more terrible thing can happen to anybody?

The appeal to the personal was very much part of Hirsch's style, and few of his hearers could resist it. Guilt! Passion! Revenge! It was a potent combination and justified some very high-handed dealing. As Uren has said, "Hirsch did some terrible things, but in the belief that what he was creating at Stratford mattered so much it justified anything he might do." Meanwhile Thomas kept the ship afloat, his phlegmatic practicality providing a balance to Hirsch's erratic emotional outbursts and temperamental turbulence. The Board tried to recover its poise and credibility; they sat back and weathered the storm. They did not, however, solve the problem of habitual deficits. And they could not control Hirsch's extravagance, which far exceeded that of any of his predecessors.

John Neville displayed a very different style. He was a committed socialist who wanted to place Brecht alongside Shakespeare, but he was also an autocrat. When Julian Porter commented that his first season built around the three late romances (*Pericles*, *Cymbeline*, and *The Winter's Tale*), an idea borrowed from Stratford-on-

197

Avon, might not prove easy to sell, Neville responded, "Mr. Porter, I do not advise you on how to run a political campaign. Please do not presume to advise me on how to run a theatre."

But when his first season ended in the red, Neville was quick to try to remedy the situation. He began to do big, popular musicals on the main stage: *Cabaret*, *My Fair Lady*, and *Kiss Me, Kate*, initiating what would become the cornerstone of future Festival financial planning. He saw to it that the major crowd-pleasing comedies were programmed in each season (what critic Urjo Kareda defined as the Stratford "rinse-cycle" of programming). He invited Robin Phillips back to run the young company at the Third Stage and to direct an annual production in the big house, ensuring a high standard of work and the publicity that Phillips unfailingly attracted. And he recalled John Uren to mastermind marketing these ventures. Most important, John Neville used his innate charm and tact to improve the relationship between the Festival and the town, which had deteriorated during the Phillips and Hirsch years.

Professor Ross Stuart of York University has a theory that since Robin Phillips, Stratford has usually appointed its artistic directors ten years too late in their careers (at least until the advent of Monette). This was certainly true in the case of David William. In spite of his familiarity with the Festival (he first directed there in 1966 a stylish production of *Twelfth Night*), when he was finally in command of the Stratford company William took the position that this company should be above financial considerations. It should, in effect give the public what was good for it: Middleton's *The Changeling*, Euripides' *The Bacchae*, Beaumont's *Knight of the Burning Pestle*, Eliot's *Murder in the Cathedral*. His programming also included some crowd-pleasers: *Gypsy*, *Treasure Island*, *Shirley Valentine*, *Letter from Wingfield Farm*. But they failed to balance the budget.

From the mid-1980s, the Board began to tackle the Festival's escalating financial problems. Peter Herrndorf, who saw himself as a working president rather than a fig-urehead, established the principle that the artistic and financial leaders should make separate reports to the Board. But it became apparent that there was no one figure who could say no to the artistic director. Gerry Eldred tended to be a liaison between the moneymen and the artists. This responsibility then devolved upon Colleen Blake. Both Eldred and Blake worked sympathetically and sensitively with the artists but a pattern had been set: the artistic director chose the season; Blake and Thomas costed it. Then they projected box-office revenue based on the previous season and set the ticket prices so that they could balance the budget. Between 1975 and 1990 ticket prices tripled. But still there was a shortfall, aggravated in part by a sharp escalation in union demands. This began after the 1980 crisis when management acceded to excessive demands just to get the season on. But Gary Thomas was finding it more and more difficult to stand up to the artistic director and the unions. Relationships remained cordial, but at a price.

Board presidents William Somerville, Murray Frum, and Tom O'Neill realized that something had to be done. When William's final season lost nearly $2 million, the Festival's reserves and bank credit were exhausted. Colleen Blake realized that she could not carry on as before and went to work for the Shaw Festival in Niagara-on-the-Lake. At about the same time, production manager Paul Shaw left and went to Garth Drabinsky's production company LiveEnt. It was made clear to incoming artistic director Richard Monette that a new system of budgeting would have to be instituted. The writing was on the bathroom wall.

To deal with the financial problems a triumvirate was formed consisting of general manager Gary Thomas, financial officer Ev Mueler, and the new production manager Vito Zingarelli. They worked together on Monette's first season and showed a small profit, but their attempt to be tougher met with resistance. After two seasons Zingarelli left, saying the situation was impossible. Thomas and Mueler carried on, but things came to a head when Julia Foster, the first woman president of the Board, received forty faxes from members of the company and staff complaining about the system's unworkability. Foster approached Thomas, who was less than two years from retirement, and they agreed that he should concentrate on planning for the renovation of the Festival Theatre. Foster and the Board set out to find a new general manager.

Two new figures within the organization emerged as possible candidates. Publicist Janice Price's drive and imagination had established her as the most effective marketer since Mary Jolliffe. She instigated a demographic analysis of the audience in terms of age, income, geographic origin, and educational background. It was not the first such study but it was certainly the most detailed. The Festival discovered that forty per

199

cent of its audience came from below the border, that the older audience members strongly favoured comedy, and that most of the people who saw the musical did not want to see Shakespeare. Price presided over the revamping of the Festival's image and an aggressive new marketing strategy.

Monette's personal assistant Antoni Cimolino started as an actor with the company and played Romeo in Monette's 1992 production. He worked as Monette's assistant on several shows and mastered the intricacies of casting, scheduling, and costing productions. When Monette moved out of the "broom-closet" he occupied during William's tenure and into the executive office, Cimolino went with him. The two worked closely together planning the seasons. When Monette returned to the stage in Eduardo de Filippo's *Filumena*, Cimolino directed him. He followed this up with a sensitive and finely calibrated *Night of the Iguana* featuring Seana McKenna as a quintessential Tennessee Williams heroine.

Julia Foster interviewed both Price and Cimolino for the job of general manager. She was particularly impressed by Cimolino's grasp of financial matters: "He'd certainly done his homework and learned an incredible amount in a short time," she recalls. "Price was very quick too. But they didn't have sufficient in-depth experience." Neither got the nod. Price left and soon became director of public relations for New York's Lincoln Centre. Meanwhile, Cimolino stayed on to work with Monette. The job went to Mary Hoffsteder, an experienced administrator in the field of education. She would stay for three years.

There was no longer an aura of frosty silence in the executive offices. Monette might sound off in private but his public style was persuasive, humorous, and easygoing. He liked people to enjoy their work as much as he enjoyed his. He would go anywhere to meet anyone who could be useful to the Festival. Already an accomplished raconteur and a brilliant mimic, he became a highly entertaining speaker. He relied increasingly on Cimolino to provide him with facts and figures and on literary manager David Prosser to polish his public utterances.

The system began to work more smoothly. And every year the Festival made more money. Times were good, audiences grew, budgets increased but so did profits. In 1999 the Festival showed an unprecedented surplus of over $4 million. The budget was now in the range of $30 million, the greatest part of which (approximately

200

$18 million) went to production (sets, costumes, and effects), more than triple the budget for actors even though they were better paid than those on any other stage in the country. Top performers commanded salaries in the range of $2000 to $3000 a week; even apprentices earned $800 a week. This was a far cry from the Festival's first year, when the most highly paid Canadian performer Amelia Hall received $1000 for the whole season and apprentices were paid $40 a week.

In the 1990s, all levels of government continued to cut back on grants. The high-powered businessmen who sit on arts-council boards have started to apply their growing conviction in the supremacy of a market economy to artistic institutions. The establishment of the Ontario Lieutenant-Governor's Awards by the Hon. Henry Jackman put an official stamp on this viewpoint. The awards are given not for artistic excellence but for fund-raising performance. (Stratford has won the top award several times.) Jackman's point is that if the leaders of the community want the arts to flourish they must dig into their pockets. His dictum has had its effect. In 2001 Murray Frum, Isidore and Rosalie Sharp, Joey and Toby Tannenbaum, and Ken Thomson all made extraordinarily large bequests to arts organizations in Toronto. And Michael and Kelly Meighen donated an unprecedented $5 million to Stratford to be added to its growing endowment, which has accumulated $12 million toward a target of $50 million. In the same season Raphael and Jane Bernstein and Sandra and James Pitblado each contributed $1 million towards the renovation of the Avon Theatre. Notwithstanding her generosity, Board president Sandra Pitblado emphasizes that the Festival must continue to pursue "financial comfort" while practising fiscal prudence.

Today the total contribution of the arts councils to the Festival's budget is just over three per cent. It has begun to be said that the Festival could manage without government support but Monette remains tenacious in his belief that all levels of government have an obligation to support the arts. And he points out that the Festival now brings into the town of Stratford revenues in excess of $350 million a year. But the Festival itself is now a profit-making concern, and in spite of its ever greater complexity, every year it manages to get the season on without cancellations or delayed openings or highly publicized squabbles.

One reason that the system functions as well as it does (and no one pretends it is perfect or that there aren't still sizeable pockets of discontent) is that Monette and

Cimolino have developed a very close working relationship. They see eye to eye on many issues. They frequently spend one or two hours a day planning, projecting, refining, and doing damage control. Cimolino is both sharp and tough, but his knowledge and decisiveness are respected. He came up through the ranks. He's a born manager, a hard worker. He's also an artist and totally loyal to Monette, whom he respects as "an inspired programmer." Monette cheerfully accepts the compliment and retorts, "I make the money that Antoni spends."

Romancing the Bard

Three Comic Masterpieces

The earliest of Shakespeare's aristocratic comedies contains his most densely intricate word play and his most elaborately courtly manners and language. These qualities attracted the subtle, incisive intelligence of Michael Langham to the text. As Jean Gascon said of this production, "Michael has taken the text like a lemon and squeezed it dry."

Murray Scott as Moth, Paul Scofield as Don Armado

Director: *Michael Langham*

Designer: *Tanya Moiseiwitsch*

*F*ive actresses con-
tributed individual
notes, a fact echoed
by Tanya Moiseiwitsch's
stylish Carolingian dresses
in richly contrasting shades
of white. Joy Parker was a
proud, elegant Princess of
France, Mia Anderson a
pertly petulant Maria,
Michael Learned a graceful
Katherine, Zoe Caldwell an
audacious, fun-loving
Rosaline, and Kate Reid a
saucy Jaquenetta. Their

Jack Creley as Holofernes,
William Needles as Nathaniel

suitors paled slightly in comparison although John Colicos was a bold thrusting Berowne whose high spirits challenged and matched the zest of Zoe Caldwell. These two working together or separately would dominate the next few years at Stratford.

Backing them was an ensemble of Stratford's strongest players: Mervyn Blake as the exuberantly foolish constable Dull, Jack Creley the pedantic Holofernes, William Needles a slyly cautious Nathaniel, Douglas Rain a courtly Boyet, and Murray Scott the winningly precocious page Moth. But it was Paul Scofield as the fragile, feathery Don Armado who breathed most purely the rarefied air of antique romance. Ensnared in his own fantasies, he

Douglas Rain as Boyet with Mia Anderson as Maria, Zoe Caldwell as Rosaline, Michael Learned as Katherine, Joy Parker as the Princess of France

floated through the production, tentative, tremulous, delicate as gossamer, until he found the object of his quest and did final battle with Eric Christmas as the clown Costard.

The whole production had the quality of a minuet, with John Cook's music underlining and supporting the formality of Langham's blocking and Alan and Blanche Lund's evocative choreography, until the arrival of Garrick Hagon as Marcade brought news of the King's death and the play modulated into a sombre key. The lovers exchanged vows in a dying light under falling leaves : a last touch of nostalgic magic that still lingers in the minds of Stratford play-goers even now after forty years.

The lovers bid farewell: Mia Anderson and Peter Donat; Leo Ciceri and Joy Parker; John Colicos and Zoe Caldwell; Gary Krawford and Michael Learned; Douglas Rain as Boyet, Garrick Hagon as Marcade

206

The magic moment when love bursts into bloom is at the heart of this most lighthearted, lyrical and love-shot of Shakespeare's comedies. Rosalind, the smart but deeply smitten heroine is, of all Shakespeare's women, the most self-aware, the boldest and yet the most vulnerable. "O coz, coz, coz, my pretty little coz," she cries, "that thou didst know how many fathom deep I am in love: but it cannot be sounded: my affection hath an unknown bottom, like the Bay of Portugal."

Director: **Robin Phillips**

Designer: **Robin Fraser Paye**

Maggie Smith as Rosalind

Brian Bedford as Jacques with Richard Partington, Gerald Isaac, Leslie Yeo

*M*aggie Smith brought all her wit to bear on this role, fluttering her fingers, knocking her knees, wringing her wrists, even though under Robin Phillips' stern commandment she dutifully abandoned the quest for laughs, emerging funnier than ever, self-mocking, rueful, rampant in her pursuit of the object of her irrepressible heart's desire, touchingly smitten and smarting at her own fragility.

In this production Phillips' identification with his heroine was complete. United in the audacious pursuit of unexpected love, Phillips and Smith rode the roller coaster of emotion and submitted unflinchingly to the experience of a wild tumultuous fancy that led they knew not where.

Domini Blythe as Celia,
Bernard Hopkins as Touchstone,
Bob Baker as Le Beau, Maggie
Smith as Rosalind

*Robin Fraser Paye's physical setting was lush and pastoral: a huge broken
tree, toppled by unexpected storms, his costumes wildly romantic and fanciful.
We were reminded of Gainsborough figures lolling on the new-mown grass,
Marie Antoinette happily astray in her dairy. Through the branches of the tree
wafted the notes of the suggestive score composed by Berthold Carrière,*

*The flight of untethered invention was anchored by the astringent cynicism
of Brian Bedford's Jacques, the earthbound pragmatism of Bernard Hopkins'
Touchstone. But soaring fancy triumphed, carrying us into a world of lovers'
rapture, transient, but for the play's all too brief duration, utterly irresistible.*

Goldie Semple as
Katherine, Colm
Feore as Petruchio

210

Lightly mocking nostalgia coloured Richard Monette's take on this tale of bourgeois manners thinly veiling a sharp-edged skirmish of the sexes. The delicious shock of recognition at the appearance of a life-size Alfa Romeo, the sudden childish scrap between sisters over an outsize Teddy bear or the sound of a familiar pop tune owed much to the inspiration of early Fellini but also to sight gags lifted from *I Love Lucy*.

Director: **Richard Monette**

Designer: **Debora Hanson**

Scott Wentworth as Tranio,
William Needles as the Pedant,
Eric Coates as Biondello

211

Kate's homecoming: Scott A. Hurst, Geraint Wyn Davies, Colm Feore, Goldie Semple, Keith Dinicol

*M*onette picked up on the Guthrie tradition of richly bizarre background detail and also paid homage to Jean Gascon's antic and uproarious commedia dell'arte version of The Comedy of Errors in 1963. The grotesque retainers in Petruchio's house, led by Keith Dinicol, Scott A. Hurst and John Wodja, provided a hilarious counterpoint to the conflict of the newlyweds.

Set against this horseplay, the central characters became vividly three-dimensional. Goldie Semple was a haughty Katharina, unappreciated by her philistine family and the bevy of insensitive suitors who courted Kim Horsman's mildly retarded Bianca. Brian Tree, Scott Wentworth, and Geraint Wyn Davies were street-smart but heart-foolish in their grab for a golden-haired heiress, passing over Semple's Kate who was, in the expressive phrase of the period, "a piece of work."

Colm Feore downplayed the provocative and flamboyant antics usually associated with her tamer and gave us a commonsensical, straightforward Petruchio. His winning of Katherine came across as a triumph of reason in a mad world. His genuine affection was sufficiently evident for Kate's ironically inflected speech of submission in the final act to be interpreted as a recognition of his fundamental good will.

With this production Monette established his characteristic mix of high jinks and human warmth and set the tone for the comedies that would prove to be major crowd-pleasers in the years to come. The ultimate accolade came from Tanya Moiseiwitsch: "Tony Guthrie would have loved it."

THE CHEESE STANDS ALONE

MONETTE APPROACHED HIS FIRST YEAR AS ARTISTIC DIRECTOR full of innovative ideas and projects, among them a production of *A Midsummer Night's Dream* on Patterson Island in the Avon River aimed at young audiences and using a cast of native Canadians to play the fairies. Another idea was the erection of a small tent theatre where new work could be showcased. It was this sort of imaginative vision that won him the job, but when he tried to carry out some of these projects he was told firmly by general manager Gary Thomas, backed by the Board, that this was impossible. His job was to put bums in seats in the existing theatres.

Nothing in Monette's background prepared him to be the financial saviour the Board was seeking. He was born and grew up in the east end of Montreal, the son of a smalltime French-Canadian promoter and his volatile, unstable Italian wife. All four of his grandparents were illiterate. "Until I was fourteen I spoke a mixture of *joual,* Abruzzi dialect and English street slang," he says. "I decided to learn how to speak one language properly." He chose to master English. He went to study with the Jesuits at St. Ignatius Loyola. They gave him rigorous training, instilling in him a concept of excellence, but also bent the rules so that he could take time off to perform and write special exams later. He felt no qualms at turning his back on the French language: "I had to make a choice. My father wasn't a patriot. He was a little guy who worked for the English. He wanted me to be on the winning side."

At sixteen he arrived on the doorstep of Eleanor Stuart, the voice teacher of Christopher Plummer, John Colicos, and Leo Ciceri and a leading actress at Stratford in the first decade. She asked briskly, "What can I do for you?"

"I want to be an actor like John Gielgud and Laurence Olivier."

She took in the cherubic face, the green pussycat eyes, the nasal tones, the mangled vowels, the urgency underlying the singsong cadences that would later prove so compelling in his portrayal of Hosanna.

"Well then, Mr. Monette, we have a great deal of work to do."

This was in 1960. By 1967 Monette was a member of the Stratford company, playing Eros alongside Christopher Plummer in Michael Langham's production of *Antony and Cleopatra*. In the meantime he had played a variety of other roles, including Hamlet at the age of 19 at Toronto's Crest Theatre. "I worked hard to master English, all the nuances, all the colours. It's a life study. I'm still working on it." This wholehearted commitment is typical of Monette, who has always plunged headlong into whatever he is working on at the moment. He has played major roles in Toronto, London, and the United States, but most notably at Stratford when he returned in the Phillips' regime to star as Hamlet, Romeo, Caliban, Parolles, Prince Hal, and Benedick, as well as character roles in *The Importance of Being Earnest*, *Hay Fever*, *The Devils*, *Foxfire*, and the one-man tour de force *Judgement*.

Although he made reasonably good money, he kept little or no track of it. He lived from hand to mouth, partying hard, putting nothing away for the future, although he did acquire a house, heavily mortgaged, in joint ownership with his then partner Domini Blythe. His affairs were in the hands of a manager whose accounting was infrequent and often incomprehensible. Then calamity struck in the form of stage fright. In the middle of a performance he was convinced he was experiencing a heart attack. When the curtain came down he was rushed to a hospital but the doctors could find nothing physically wrong. He decided to take a break from stage acting and turned to voice work and directing. The chance to direct at Stratford came in the Neville era, when he was offered *The Taming of the Shrew*, starring Colm Feore and Goldie Semple. He set the production in the 1950s, the era of Gidget and Lucy, exploiting the clothes, the pop songs, the repressed but smouldering manners of that time. It was nostalgic, funny, and humane. Not since Guthrie's cowboy version or the pairing of John Colicos and Kate Reid in 1962 had the audience taken such delight in this comedy. At the same time it went straight to their hearts.

In the next season Monette was asked to take on Vanbrugh's *The Relapse*, with Brian Bedford as Lord Foppington. He commented that Bedford was undirectable; the next day the actor challenged him in the green room. Monette's retort was, "Brian, I know you're undirectable, but don't worry. I'll put you downstage centre and just move everybody else around you." The two formed a bond that would benefit them both in the years ahead. This production again demonstrated Monette's sense of style, command of staging, and ability to handle actors with wit and grace.

There was some thought that Monette might be a suitable successor to John Neville, but the Board opted instead for David William as more experienced and stable. William, a highly articulate man with lofty ideals and a clear vision of what he believed the Festival should be, was also aloof and acerbic. His witty and evocative orations to his cast did not always translate into vital and imaginative productions. William made brave choices, but broke no new ground. And he had to contend with the worst economic recession since the Dirty Thirties, as well as the introduction of the GST.

Monette was fortunate that William had to steer the ship through these troubled waters while he was able to gain experience of production and the backstage workings of the Festival. He was aware of being a possible heir apparent and privately agonized over whether he wanted the job. At one point he and Martha Henry discussed the possibility of joint rule, but Monette was convinced that the job must be done with a single strong captain at the helm. The unsuccessful partnership of Gascon and Hirsch and the fate of the Gang of Four no doubt reinforced this conviction. He bided his time and the call came.

Monette's 1993 appointment was widely hailed. He was accessible, younger than his three predecessors, a Canadian, popular with the theatre community, an actor's actor. "King Richard succeeds to the Throne" ran one Toronto headline. Characteristically, he preferred to be known as *"Le Grand Fromage."* He soon set about strengthening the company by brokering the return of Martha Henry, who had quit the scene when the Gang of Four was abruptly dismissed, and wooing major actors such as Tom McCamus, Stephen Ouimette, and Seana McKenna. In his first season he gave two women, Diana Leblanc and Marti Maraden, shows to direct. He wanted to involve as many former artistic directors as possible and offered shows to Robin Phillips and Michael Langham as well as retaining the services of Brian Macdonald and casting David William as Malvolio in his own production of *Twelfth Night*.

These gestures of good will did not have completely felicitous consequences. David William behaved in a high-handed, disruptive manner and has not been seen at the Festival since. Robin Phillips negotiated to direct *Othello* and *Cyrano*, then pulled out mere months before rehearsals began, leaving Monette scrambling to find alternative directors for shows that were already largely cast and planned as co-productions with Edmonton's Citadel Theatre. Phillips' contention was that they could not find a suitable actor to play Othello, but his decision destroyed the rapport he had enjoyed with Monette in the past.

Michael Langham did not accept a show until the following year, when he directed *Measure for Measure*. He proved caustic with actors and demanding with production people. Some felt that Langham should be given special licence in view of his eminence and past service to the Festival, but many of the younger actors were not of this mind. Brian Macdonald delivered sparkling and popular musical shows but schemed to build his own musical theatre empire and eventually stormed off in high dudgeon, giving acrimonious interviews to the press. Monette came to realize that he could not treat his predecessors as part of a large convivial family. He was in fact very much on his own.

Monette's first season boasted some stunning successes. Diana Leblanc's *Long Day's Journey into Night* provided a magnificent vehicle for Martha Henry and William Hutt, receiving rave reviews and selling out. James Reaney's inventive fantasy based on *Alice Through the Looking Glass* delighted children and adults alike and contained wonderfully detailed comic turns by Douglas Rain and Tom Wood, as well as an intelligent and charming Alice from Sarah Polley. Colm Feore achieved matinee idol status as the Pirate King and Cyrano. Stephen Ouimette offered a sensitive, intimate performance as Hamlet, fifteen years after he had been promised the role by the Gang of Four and deprived of it by John Hirsch. And for the first time in several years the season ended up in the black. The profit was not large, but financially the Festival was moving in the right direction.

In the next four years there were more outstanding shows: the giddy and spirited musical spoof *The Boyfriend*; a bitter-sweet, meticulously detailed *Waiting for Godot* featuring the finely matched comic talents of Tom McCamus and Stephen Ouimette; a mature, humane *King Lear* from William Hutt; a gorgeously nostalgic *Camelot* starring Cynthia Dale; the delectable Italian puff pastry *Filumena*, featuring Monette himself opposite Lally Cadeau; the "geriatric" version of *Much Ado About Nothing* showcasing the mature wit and wisdom of Brian Bedford and Martha Henry; *The*

Night of the Iguana, exploiting the sensitive intelligence of Seana McKenna and the rascally charm of Geordie Johnson; an impeccable performance from Douglas Rain as Sir Thomas More in *A Man for All Seasons*.

Monette explored and extended his talent for his specialty: comedy with heart. The Festival began to be permeated with his personal touch, a combination of warmth, humour, and a certain florid opulence, just as Michael Langham's years had been characterized by intelligence, stringent wit, and textual lucidity, and Robin Phillips' regime embodied restrained elegance counterpointed by emotional daring and sexual energy. Monette would be criticized for vulgarity, for being a popularizer, for "dumbing down" the Festival. Once it was clear the Festival was back on the road to fiscal health, even members of the Board began asking, "Richard, what about *art*?"

Monette was concerned with pleasing his audience but he was also giving expression to his own sensibility, which owed less to an English concept of good taste as understood by a 1950s society that valued polished manners, gamesmanship, and an innate knowledge of what was "U" or "non-U," than to his youthful experience in Montreal: the outrageous chicanery of Duplessis and Camilien Houde, the bawdy, brash wit that pervades Michel Tremblay's plays, and the songs of La Bolduc. Monette responds emotionally to Shakespeare, Oscar Wilde, and Puccini, but also to Lerner and Loewe and Walt Disney. These influences are strong in his work. They have also shaped the sensibility of his audiences. The theatre-going public at the beginning of the twenty-first century may still hanker for the dying splendours of post-Imperial Britain but it is moving on. It has embraced *Star Wars*, Andrew Lloyd Webber, and Seinfeld. "Good taste is still good taste," maintains one eyebrow-raising senior actor, but the concept his statement implies probably wouldn't have meant much to Sophocles, Shakespeare or Molière and has been knocked on the noggin by Brecht and Mamet.

By his third season Monette began to be attacked by the press. First in the ring was Kate Taylor, who published a recipe in the *Globe and Mail* for "saving Stratford." Her suggestions included a shorter season, dropping the musical and popular productions, and getting rid of Monette. He contemplated a riposte in which he would advocate that the editors "save" the *Globe and Mail* by getting rid of advertising, the Sports and Business sections, and Kate Taylor. Taylor, however, was expressing an opinion that began to be heard frequently in Toronto. Critic emeritus Herbert

Whittaker advocated a special short season aimed at those who truly loved and understood great theatre, and several cultural caryatids could be heard to say, "We don't go to Stratford anymore. It isn't what it was."

Then came Urjo Kareda's portrait of Monette in *Toronto Life* under the headline "Sold Out", the implied ambiguity of which was undermined by Kareda's cleverly constructed but ultimately disparaging portrait. (One shrewd reader observed that underlying this piece was an inescapable sense that Kareda wished he *were* Richard Monette.) Kareda recalled Monette's passionate partisanship in early days, the audacity of his portrayals of Hosanna and Hamlet, the "kamikaze" quality that he seemed to have abandoned in pursuit of the comfort and assurance of safe choices guaranteeing him the support and love of his actors and his increasingly middlebrow audience.

There is some truth in this. Monette does want to attract and please larger audiences. He does want the Festival to be a popular success. His whole life has an aura of "rags to riches," echoing *Cinderella*, Charles Dickens, and the misfit heroes of Robertson Davies' novels. He also does see his company of actors as a family, the family he never had. He designs his seasons around them, counsels them ("Take the fuckin' movie, kid. I'll hire you back next year") and sometimes spats with them. His relations with William Hutt and Joseph Shaw, Martha Henry and Rod Beattie, Brian Bedford and Tim MacDonald, Lucy Peacock, Lally Cadeau, Domini Blythe, Antoni and Brigid Cimilino, his former assistants Jason Miller and Paul Leishman, his new development director Andrey Tarasiuk and planning manager Ivan Habel, younger actors Graham Abbey, Donald Carrier, Michelle Giroux, Claire Julien, Michael Therriault, and Nicolas Van Burek, as well as many others, are close and continuing. He entertains them to dinner, drinks with them after shows at the bar, gives them expensive presents. Some think he is too accessible, and too easily influenced by what his actors want. "A soft touch."

First and foremost an actor, Monette has approached his job at the Festival as a role to be played: *Le Grand Fromage*. He sees himself less as a monarch divinely ordained to rule than as a chosen leader, a sort of Trudeau of the Theatre. He has absorbed certain things from all the predecessors under whom he has worked: from Langham technical mastery of the stage and a strong sense of the importance of rhythm and meaning; from Gascon a sense of fun that pervades his rehearsals as he employs a ready wit and a deadly skill in mimicry to keep his actors amused and alert

219

to the sting of his mockery; from Phillips a realization of the deep underlying emotions that drive both tragedy and comedy.

As he has immersed himself in his chosen role and perfected it, his confidence has grown: his assurance as a speaker, his audacity in sounding off or blowing up when it is least expected, his persuasiveness in pursuit of his goals. He can totally convulse his entire cast with a sudden quip. He can charm a TV audience with his easygoing banter. He can present a lucid explanation to a Board and defend it with passionate commitment. He can also be a totally silent observer when he finds himself among strangers or unleash a histrionic tirade, one part vitriol to two parts hilarity. In public he almost always comes across as larger than life: Falstaff meets Don Corleone. Anyone who tries to take a bite out of le Grand Fromage stands in danger of a slight taste of rat poison.

With the Festival's substantial profits in 1999 ($4.2 million) and in 2000 ($5.1 million) Monette is in a strong position to realize some of the dreams he cherished when he began his tenure. He may not get his Natives on Patterson Island, but he is getting a Fourth Space in which he will be able to exercise his Conservatory trainees and showcase new work. The real challenge will be to find dynamic teachers, recruit skilled dramaturgical staff, and above all to identify young and imaginative directors. Although he has a splendid lieutenant in Antoni Cimilino, too many of his advisors are fallen into the sere, the yellow leaf, and are also self-seeking. Monette's record in giving opportunities to Canadian directors is impressive, but only Martha Henry and Antoni Cimilino have delivered a fully satisfying Shakespearean production and all but two are over forty. Where are the Wunderkinder?

Yes, the Festival has become commercialized. With declining government subsidies and the insistent emphasis on a market economy, this was inescapable. There is a very real danger of pandering too much to the lowest common denominator, but the Festival is no more mercenary than the University of Toronto or the Royal Ontario Museum in battling to attract big-time donors, increase attendance, and gain higher public profile. Monette's programming may not be everybody's idea of what a classical theatre should be doing, but a season that includes *Hamlet*, *Medea*, *Tartuffe*, *As You Like It*, and *Titus Andronicus* can hardly be accused of being nothing but trash. Monette may be populist, but he is in touch with the times. As William Hutt has put it, "Richard has brought the theatre to the people and the people to the theatre."

The "lusty month of May": Cynthia Dale as Guinevere

CAMELOT · 1997

One of the most enduring legends in the English-speaking world, the story of Arthur and his Knights of the Round Table is as magical today as it was in the time of Mallory or Spenser. It calls up an age of innocence, a dream-scape of a better, simpler, nobler past.

The untried youth who claims his birthright when he pulls the sword from the stone, the mysterious wizard Merlin who guards his secret, the wicked enchantress Morgan-le-Fey and her bastard son Mordred, Arthur's bride, the beautiful Guinevere who falls under the spell of the perfect knight Sir Launcelot and brings the whole golden world tumbling

Director: **Richard Monette**

Designer: **Desmond Heeley**

221

down are mythic figures who are fated to be invoked over and over. The Kennedy era was compared to Camelot, and so was the reign of Robin Phillips at Stratford.

The marriage of the mystical and the earthy in these stories has attracted storytellers from Walt Disney to Robertson Davies, and if anyone imagines this potent mix no longer lays hold on youthful imaginations they have only to reflect on the Harry Potter phenomenon.

It was T.H. White's brilliant idea to retell in The Once and Future King *this tale in colloquial terms easily accessible to today's young people without trivializing it. And it was Lerner and Loewe's inspiration to adapt it to a musical that glows and shimmers in song and marries wit, nostalgia, and unabashed sentiment in their inimitable manner.*

In Camelot Monette found all the elements of his ideal family show: humour, spectacle, adventure, heart. It is an unapologetic dream of childhood played out in adult terms. It harks back to one of Jean Gascon's most memorable shows, Pericles, in which Monette appeared in his first season back in Canada after a five-year sojourn in England.

The chemistry of the Camelot actors took instant hold. From his first moments on stage Tom McCamus was a brave, vulnerable, forthright Arthur whose bright articulation of songs like "I wonder what the king is doing tonight?" and "How to handle a woman" had the sincerity of youth and the warmth of an incorruptibly honest man.

Cynthia Dale's bright beauty and simple freshness made Guinevere irresistible in her flighty, frivolous girlishness and gave danger to her developing passion as she found herself following the unpredictable dictates of her heart.

Dan Chameroy was a splendidly handsome and vocally ringing Launcelot. Michael Therriault, making his Stratford debut as Mordred, was insidiously snide and deliciously nasty.

The action accelerated in a swirl of rich colour and pageantry as the parade of Desmond Heeley's gorgeous costumes swept on and off the stage. Here was opulence, elegance, grandeur. Heeley's final Festival show revealed him at the peak of his powers and rivalled anything he had produced in his forty years at the Festival.

At the end of the show, when the little boy closes his book as the fallen Arthur sings the title song about the vanished dream that once was Camelot, we feel we have indeed been taken on an enchanted journey into a bright world that we would like to believe existed -somehow, somewhere, long ago, and far away.

Cynthia Dale as Guinevere, Tom McCamus as King Arthur

PERICLES · 1973/74

Director: *Jean Gascon*

Designer: *Leslie Hurry*

Nicholas Pennell as Pericles

T his fairy tale is more like a composite of the dark twisted underworld of the Brothers Grimm and the extravagant eroticism of *The Arabian Nights* than the graceful courtliness of Charles Perrault or the stylized posturings of Jean Cocteau. Jean Gascon brought to his production of *Pericles*, the first professional production in North America, a decidedly Gallic sensibility derived from the Parisian theatre he had experienced in the 1940s, imagistic productions like the André Obey *Nöé* of Michel Saint-Denis or the *Christophe Colombe* of Claudel mounted by Jean-Louis Barrault.

*A*nd yet this free-flowing production was remarkably true to the printed text of Pericles, corrupt and incomplete as the scholars generally assert it to be. A key element was the retention of Gower, the medieval poet who tells us the tale. In this role, the eccentric actor Edward Atienza was granted licence to assume total responsibility for the production, peering owlishly at the audience, fussily admonishing and instructing them in his own interpretation of events, wandering through the scenes and freezing the actors while he adjusted some detail of their performances. He led us through the action, justifying its theatricality while establishing an intimate rapport with the audience.

We moved from tournament to shipwreck, from court to rocky seashore to tawdry brothel. Leslie Hurry's fine painted costumes and evocative props suggested the exotic east in an enchanted time out of time. Gil Wechsler's

Pamela Brook as Marina, Amelia Hall as the Bawd

225

lighting gave richness and depth to the stage pictures, painting actors, defining space with changing colour and shadow. Gabriel Charpentier's music glimmered and shivered like moonlight on water, sunlight on polished silver.

In the title role of Pericles, Nicholas Pennell was noble, resonant, sweet-spoken, emotionally open. He embarked upon an adventure of the heart and, though betrayed along the way, was rewarded by the love and generosity of Martha Henry's brave Thaissa and the filial devotion of Pamela Brook's delicate Marina. The reunion of father and daughter at the end of the play was simple and moving, a rich fulfillment of the questing spirit and undefeated trust of this heroic prince.

Around him pranced and postured an array of semi-mythic characters: Tony van Bridge as the jocular, deceitful Simonides; Richard Curnock as a repulsive Pandar; Amelia Hall as a raucous, garish, flat-footed madam, presiding over her stable of hideously decayed whores; Powys Thomas as the faithful lord Cerimon; Angela Wood as the stylish, perfidious Dionyza. They were attended by fishermen, lords, pirates, and questing knights, played by an agile company of young actors, some of whom would make major contributions in the years ahead: Patricia Collins, Lewis Gordon, Barry MacGregor, Marti Maraden, Richard Monette, and Jack Wetherall.

This production was much admired by critics and scholars for its beauty, its imaginative and fluid staging, its emotional depth, its simplicity and fidelity to the playwright's text and intention. Robertson Davies considered it among the half dozen finest achievements in the Festival's first twenty years: "What emerged was a splendid mythical tale of Fortune's favour, Fortune's desertion, of danger, love and desolating loss, which at the end were healed by agencies which were magical, spiritual, and in the true sense of the word, natural. I have seen the play several times before, but never as it was done here, and I thought, Canada has something to teach the world about Shakespeare, just as Shakespeare has much to teach Canada about itself."

AFTER THEY'VE SEEN L.A.

FIFTY YEARS AGO, CANADA HAD THREE CULTURAL CAPITALS: London, Paris, and New York. Now we have moved on: today this position is occupied by Los Angeles, the town that generates the sitcoms and teen-flicks in which young Canadians find their role models, that sets the beat they groove to, that promotes the lifestyle that defines the emerging generation. It is in L.A. that our aspiring artists, or at least entertainers, find stardom, and with it wealth and worldwide recognition. They may hang their hats in rural Quebec or even Stratford, Ontario, but the road to celebrity lies through Hollywood. So it is inevitable that actors leave theatres like Stratford and head south, as they have done for generations.

Canada's continuing cultural colonialism is partly inevitable, partly choice. The question of what sort of country we are and want to be is complex and constantly evolving. Our country being vast and our population concentrated in a few relatively small areas, most of which lie on or close to the American border, the United States has easy electronic and physical access to the bulk of our population. The Americans see Canada primarily as a natural extension of their home market. They are further aided in their cultural imperialism by the fact we do not have a large enough population to run the kind of country we are trying to run. If we were 100 million instead of 30 it would be feasible to be more culturally competitive with our neighbour to the south.

As Canada continues to fill up with a significant number of immigrants from many parts of the world, most obviously at the moment from Asia, Africa, eastern Europe, and the Middle East, we are faced with the challenge of absorbing new cultural influences and adapting to different traditions. The newcomers adopt our language but affect the way it is spoken and understood. They have different attitudes toward music, dance, poetry, and drama and the place they play in social life.

This provides a changing context in which Stratford fashions its art and finds itself examined. This institution, which has from its inception been seen by some as a kind of cultural flagship, is not always judged simply by the excellence of its work but

227

also for its ability to give shape to the values and identity of a nation, a nation which is still seeking its identity, a nation in the making. This patriotic image of Stratford exerts a continuing pressure that finds expression in a variety of ways. The Stratford company remains primarily Caucasian, but a real attempt is made to recruit visible minorities. Actors from different ethnic backgrounds are auditioned but they are still being judged to a large extent by standards established by the British founders of the company: above all the ability to speak verse clearly, intelligently, and musically. Stratford does employ actors from different racial backgrounds, though in fact relatively few "ethnic" actors choose to audition.

Eventually a more highly integrated company may evolve as actors from different races and cultural backgrounds acquire the experience and skills and find ways to interpret classical texts in a manner that convinces directors and excites audiences. Political correctness may be an admirable concept but in the short run it may have an inhibiting, even stultifying effect on artistic expression. Is it a necessary stage in the evolution of a truly integrated company that will reflect the cultural reality of Canada as it evolves in the twentieth-first century? Other theatres besides Stratford are struggling with that question.

In response to this trend, at Stratford a greater emphasis is being placed on training. Richard Monette understands that if talented actors are going to come and go just when they become most useful, there must be fresh faces to take their place. The pristine charms of the young and eager must be backed by vocal technique and physical agility. Shakespeare's young lovers cannot be played by callow youths who cannot parry a thrust, whether verbal or martial; his heroines cannot be played by tongue-tied ingénues, no matter how beautiful, who cannot turn a phrase or handle a train.

The Stratford Conservatory, established by Monette in 1999, is only the tip of the educational iceberg. The second directive of the Festival's Charter is "to provide facilities for education and instruction in the arts of the theatre." Tom Patterson recalls that the first grant from the Ontario Arts Council was conditional on demonstrating "that this Stratford Festival is educational," reflecting the governmental priorities of that era. In a broad sense everything the Festival does could be said to be educational. Audiences as well as actors are educated by the very experience of theatre. Special student performances began as early as 1959, when the

Canada Council Train was initiated to bring students from across the country to see performances.

The train lasted only four years, but now each season there are over 50 student performances with kids bussed into town from American and Canadian schools and colleges. They see the show and meet some of the actors afterwards for question-and-answer sessions. These student performances build the audiences of the future, but they also hook some young people permanently. A dozen or more theatre professionals, from stage manager Ann Stuart to actor R.H. Thomson, have told me they remember going to Stratford as children and deciding, "That's what I want to do with my life." For kids like this who are already snagged, the Festival offers one and two-week practical summer sessions for ages 13-18 as well as study courses at the university level, some of them for academic credit. Stratford maintains a formidable educational infrastructure under the direction of Pat Quigley. There are lectures, seminars, and study groups available to the public involving visiting scholars, critics, and writers.

At the apex of this structure is the Conservatory, which trains a dozen carefully selected (and paid) young performers over a two-month period in the autumn, some of whom are then brought into the company. The selection of these happy few is crucial, and Monette usually involves himself in the auditioning process. He relies on his gut feeling about them as much or more than the information offered by their résumés, but is only too aware of the difficulty of assessing young talent. As he puts it, "You hire a singer, she can sing. You hire a dancer, he can dance. You hire an actor—pot luck."

The Conservatory is grounded in an ideal of training that has been firmly espoused by every artistic director in the Festival's history, though none of them was able to realize it fully. The principal reason for Monette's success lies in his early realization of the need to present his vision to the Board with a financial plan firmly in place. Now that confidence in him is backed by his solid success at the box office, he is determined to push forward and consolidate his gains by the addition of the Fourth Space, which will, among other things, provide a forum for young actors to tackle roles they are not yet ready to undertake in the bigger houses.

Michael Langham's demand for more adequate actor training was not considered a priority by the Board in the 1950s when its members were preoccupied with getting a theatre built and running a season, but it did play a role in supporting the formation of the National Theatre School in Montreal in 1960. Initially inspired by the guidance of internationally acclaimed director Michel Saint-Denis, its realization relied to a great extent on the hands-on involvement of Jean Gascon. Diana Leblanc remembers auditioning for Gascon when she was 17. She had chosen a speech from Racine's *Bérénice*, and before she could finish Gascon leaped up on the stage and played out the scene with her.

Gascon's aim was nothing less than the creation of a unique Canadian style of acting that would embrace the best of both French and English traditions. It was expected that French- and English-speaking actors would take classes together and initially this was done, especially for work involving mime and masks, two techniques on which Saint-Denis placed considerable emphasis. But there were few actors (Diana Leblanc being a rare exception) who could work credibly in both languages. It is hard enough to master the vocal requirements of a classical actor in one language. And the rise of separatism politicized the school, driving a wedge between the Québécois and the Anglos.

In 1987, not long before his death, I interviewed Gascon and he recalled, "In the early sixties we had this vision of a transcendent Canadian style that would combine the vivacity of the French with the more cerebral control of the English." It proved a bit like yoking carriage-horses with Clydesdales, and it soon became apparent that even if the students were prepared to co-operate, the teachers were not. After the Quiet Revolution came the PQ, and a majority of Quebec's leading theatre artists lined up with the separatists. Gascon sighed, "I see now we were deluded but it was a noble concept. In the end nationalism destroyed it all."

In spite of Gascon's disillusion, the students of the National Theatre School continued to be closely connected with Stratford. Many of its artists have taught there, most notably the bardic Welsh actor Powys Thomas, who inspired a whole generation of young actors. NTS students have been frequent visitors at Stratford, participating in workshops and discussion groups. The school has carried on running parallel French and English programs, although currently it is undergoing an extensive overhaul and many English-speaking instructors have left. There will apparently be greater emphasis in the future on the physical and imagistic, less on text. Peter Wylde,

230

a longtime teacher, opines that this will lead to the decline and probably the demise of the English section. But for the past 40 years the NTS has been the foremost training institution for theatre practitioners in the country. It has provided Stratford with some of its finest actors, from its first graduate Martha Henry through Colm Feore, Seana McKenna, and Lucy Peacock to Michelle Giroux and Paul Dunn.

Having undertaken a study of various theatre-training institutions in Canada and the United States several years ago, I am convinced that the best schools are the ones that make the greatest demands. Students who are lax or uncooperative are booted out; there are always others at the door waiting to come in and fill their places. Any school can teach students only if they are ready and willing to learn. But given keen appetite on the part of the individuals in it, a class in any given year is dependant on chemistry in much the same way as the cast of a particular production. A group of students who have a strong rapport learn from each other. The instructor is merely a guide, opening windows, pointing out possible paths to be taken. And a real artist, even a young one, knows intuitively when he needs help and seeks out the mentor who can provide it. He also senses when it is time to move on.

Today there are many schools across the country which purport to offer professional theatre training: ten in Ontario alone. If each turns out twenty graduates a year, it is obvious that they will not all find work as professional stage actors. For this reason most of these schools do not spend much time on preparation for classical work; they are more concerned with how to audition for television commercials. They are perceived and funded by the provinces as vocational training schools and television is where most of the job opportunities lie. These schools do graduate people who end up working for Stratford: Wayne Best, Juan Chioran, Claire Julien, Geordie Johnson, Stephen Ouimette, Michael Therriault. As actors come to terms with their own talent, they seek and find the environment in which they can best express themselves.

Monette's Conservatory is intended to fight the decline in the teaching of the interpretation of classical texts, and build on and further refine the basic training offered by theatre schools. There is a strong emphasis on vocal work. The voice is still the classical actor's primary asset. Looks will fade or at least change, physical agility will decrease, though that process can be mitigated by exercise, but the

231

After They've Seen L.A.

individual voice is a unique gift. Monette's own magnificent instrument was already there in embryo when he first went to Eleanor Stuart for years of intensive training; he claims that cigarettes and whiskey have done the rest.

So it is not surprising that Monette looks for vocal quality above everything else in an actor or that he counsels his young actors to increase their range and expressivity. After Michael Therriault played Mordred in *Camelot*, Monette took him aside. "You're very talented, Michael, but you sound like Mickey Mouse. If you're going to have a shot at the big roles in the years ahead, you've got to work on your voice." Therriault went to the voice coach, who believed his lower range could be developed, but he would have to work several hours every day and give up singing for at least a year. Therriault loves singing, but he agreed to the coach's terms, and indeed his voice is stronger and his range extended. When Monette gave similar advice to a young actress, she decided against committing herself to a similar program. Monette shrugs, "She's very sweet and attractive in ingénue roles but she'll never play Cleopatra."

The Festival spends a million dollars a year on company training, a sum roughly equivalent to its Canada Council grant. There are daily warm-ups, regular vocal sessions for all company members, ongoing work in Alexander technique and Laban, classes in movement and intensive scene study. Some of the leading coaches in the world come to the Festival to teach: from England, vocal instructor Patsy Rotenberg; from the United States, Uta Hagen, who in 2000 lit into the young Stratford actors denouncing their laziness and lack of physical stamina. There are a number of actors who do not attend classes or even warm-ups on a regular basis. Sometimes they're too hung-over, sometimes they just can't be bothered. One young actor observed, "Bill Hutt doesn't do warm-ups," to which Rod Beattie drily retorted, "Bill's whole life is a warm-up."

Beattie's comment masks an almost Puritanical belief in the actor's duty. He deplores the decline in the idealism and commitment he experienced under Robin Phillips' regimen: "Working with Robin was like riding a racing bicycle. There wasn't any freewheel. If you didn't pedal it, it would pedal you. You might have thought the work would get easier, but it didn't because more and more was demanded of you." Beattie is only one of many actors who still think of Robin as the ultimate guru; even Monette has acknowledged that Phillips taught him more about acting than anyone else he has ever worked with. William Hutt and Martha Henry are only two of the senior actors who still speak of their years with Phillips as a turning point in their professional development.

Phillips took particular delight in directing young actors. He invited the third-year students from the NTS. to spend a month with him at Stratford. One student recalled, "It was without question the single most valuable learning experience of our training.... [He] managed to draw more out of us than we realized we had to offer. While this left us drained at the end of every day it somehow also had an invigorating effect—making us eager to give that much more." This sentiment has been echoed and re-echoed by actors as varied in style as Sheila McCarthy and Albert Schultz.

When Phillips returned in 1987 and 1988 to direct a young company at the Third Stage, he did what was arguably his finest work in Canada. Without the necessity of keeping major stars happy or attending to all the complications and machinations of master-minding the Festival, he concentrated on his actors and produced at least two magical productions, *Romeo and Juliet* and *As You Like It*. Some of the young actors he worked with would go on to create the Soulpepper Company. While it has not knocked the spots off Stratford in quite the way some Toronto critics have suggested, it has given us some fine productions, including *Don Carlos*, *Our Town*, *Endgame*, *Platonov* and *Uncle Vanya* and it provides an alternate opportunity for actors to do serious classical work without tying themselves up for as long a period as Stratford demands.

Rod Beattie is not alone in his belief in the actor's need to commit himself whole-heartedly and unsparingly to his exacting craft and art. It is shared by other performers as well as designers and technicians. Their idealism is challenged by the demands of union officials and administrators who must look out for interests that have little to do with art and everything to do with the management of money, resources, and, above all, time. The struggle between the artist and the administrators that existed from the beginning will go on. At Stratford, Guthrie won the first round for the Muses, but there is no guarantee of their ultimate victory.

Stratford, like every other arts institution, has had to come to terms with changing technical conditions and human attitudes. Colm Feore is every bit as dedicated as Beattie, but in recent years he has more or less abandoned the stage for the lure of the silver screen: "Richard offered me a short season, but there's no such thing. You have to rehearse at least three months and perform for at least three months.

233

After They've Seen L.A.

During this period you start at ten in the morning and often finish at eleven at night, six days a week. It's exhilarating but it eats up everything you've got. If it doesn't, you're not doing the job. It's not just that at this stage in my career I can't afford to be unavailable for that long. It's also that being here for half the season is like being half pregnant. If you can't be totally involved, it's better to make way for someone who is. Anyway Richard has learned no one is indispensable. People will come here to see good shows no matter who's in them. It's given him freedom and it's given him power."

This sounds reassuring, but Stratford still needs actors of maturity and stature to play the big classical roles. Will Feore come back? He believes he will, eventually. Christopher Plummer has made a commitment to appear in the 2002 anniversary season. For other leading actors from past years such as Robin Gammell, Kenneth Welsh, and Geraint Wyn Davies the likelihood is not great. They have been away too long and developed other responsibilities—to their families, to their associates in the world of film and television, to other interests. "For a while I used to get that seven-thirty feeling," confides Robin Gammell. "Shouldn't I be somewhere else—at a theatre making up? But it goes in time. Like the craving for cigarettes or whiskey, you get over it." Yes, the show must and will go on, but not necessarily with the same actors. Training at Stratford intensifies but the drain continues as the parade passes by. Plummer, Colicos, Monette, Carver, Feore, Abbey: who's next? What rough talent, its hour come round at last, slouches toward Stratford to be born?

Romancing the Bard

ROMEO AND JULIET · 1960

Director: *Michael Langham*

Designer: *Tanya Moiseiwitsch*

ROMEO AND JULIET · 1987

Director: *Robin Phillips*

Designer: *Patrick Clark*

ROMEO & JULIETTE · 1990

Directors: *Robert Lepage, Gordon McCall*

Designers: *Don Griffiths, Del Surjik,*
Irene Coupland

1960: Julie Harris as Juliet,
Bruno Gerussi as Romeo

ROMEO AND JULIET

S hakespeare's most popular play contains his
most immediate and compelling love poetry and
some of his bawdiest humour. It is no accident
that it formed the framework for the immensely
popular film *Shakespeare in Love*, or that it has been

*S*tratford has mounted Romeo and Juliet *seven times in its fifty-year history and consistently attracted an enthusiastic audience. The play seemingly cannot fail and yet its essence is not easy to capture. Much depends on spontaneous emotion and individual chemistry.*

The first production in 1960 remains a landmark. The great American actress Julie Harris was an incandescent Juliet: simple, intelligent, fragile and emotionally open, igniting and then ignited by the recklessly capricious passion of the youthful Bruno Gerussi's Romeo. Both actors had something of the outsider, creating for themselves a private world of emotional immediacy that could not last.

236

1960: William Needles as Benvolio, Bruno Gerussi as Romeo, Christopher Plummer as Mercutio

Kate Reid's garrulous, gritty, salty-tongued Nurse underscored Juliet's early innocence; Douglas Rain's icy Tybalt was a perfect foil for Gerussi's fiery Romeo. Christopher Plummer's flamboyantly extravagant Mercutio was flip, hip, and caustic; his death, a sudden cry of rage tinged with bitter mockery, sounded a note that echoed and re-echoed in the second half of the play.

The production captured the public's imagination. Performances were sold out. People lined up the night before to buy the rush seats that went on sale every morning. Michael Langham's ascendancy was established. The striking tableaux that opened and closed the show and highlighted the meeting of the lovers, the vigour of the fight scenes, the sense of control undercut by the sudden eruption of passion — all of these displayed technical mastery allied to psychological and emotional depth. Langham emerged as rightful master of the Stratford stage.

1960: Julie Harris, Bruno Gerussi, with Kate Reid as the Nurse

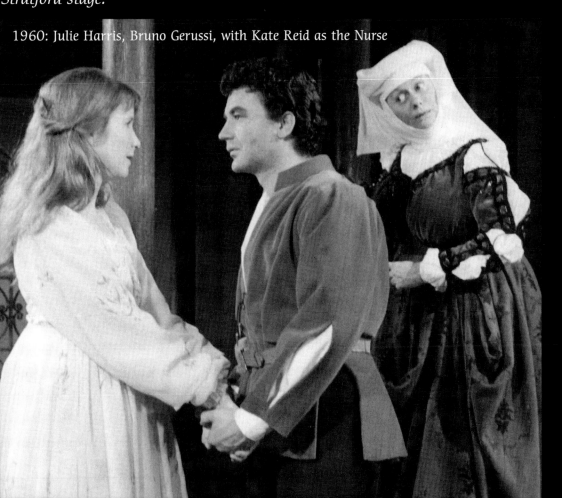

Robin Phillips' production of *Romeo and Juliet* at the Patterson Theatre in 1987 also featured unconventional casting. Susan Coyne and Albert Schultz's young aristocrats were emotional outsiders within a privileged world, drawn together by irresistible attraction and intellectual affinity. The innocent arrogance of these young lovers, in over their heads, daring everything on a sudden throw of the emotional dice, was compelling.

1990: Céline Bonnier as Juliette

1987: Susan Coyne as Juliet, Albert Schultz as Romeo

238

1990: Randy Hughson
as Benvolio

The dramatic stakes were high but the staging was simple, suggesting the cool elegance of an Antonioni film, light and shadow, hot afternoons under spreading white awnings, steamy nights when the sirocco stirs the netting above the bridal bed. Sudden gusts of wind, sudden twists of fate. The lovers' lives held in the inept hands of their well-meaning, inadequate mentors: Nancy Palk's sardonically fatalistic nurse, William Webster's bumbling Friar Lawrence. The production hailed the second coming of Robin Phillips to Stratford, a brief resurgence fated not to last, which would nevertheless crystallize the ambition of a new generation of young actors whose influence would continue at Stratford and beyond.

A third production of the play, entitled Romeo & Juliette, *visited Stratford in 1990. Co-directed by Quebec's Robert Lepage and Saskatchewan's Gordon McCall, it played in a tent and featured Quebec actors as the Capulets, speaking a text translated by Jean-Marc Dalpé, opposite Anglophone kids as the unruly Montagues who made their first entrance in a beat-up jalopy tossing beer-cans out the window. The balcony scene was played on the back of a pick-up truck.*

The electricity generated by the willful, headstrong Juliette of Céline Bonnier gave urgency to the brief love-affair and motivated the extraordinary scene of the discovery of her death played with full-out intensity by Anne-Marie Cadieux and Patric' Saucier as her parents. Here, for a fleeting moment, Jean Gascon's vision of a theatre uniting the passionate vivacity of the Québécois and the raw energy of English-Canadian actors was realized.

BRAVE NEW WORDS

THE STRATFORD FESTIVAL WAS SET UP TO INTERPRET THE CLASSICS: its early leaders, Tyrone Guthrie, Tom Patterson, and Michael Langham, were very clear that this was its mandate. But almost immediately the Canadian nationalists wanted to clamber aboard the bandwagon. Nobody claimed there was a trove of Canadian masterpieces out there waiting to be performed, but if the major theatre in the land would not consider performing native works, so the argument ran, there would never be any.

Herbert Whittaker led the nationalist parade and cracked the Festival's seemingly impenetrable classical facade by setting up a playwriting contest jointly sponsored by Stratford and the *Globe and Mail*, whose winner would receive not only a cash prize but also a performance of his work on the Festival stage. The winner, Donald Lamont Jack's *The Canvas Barricade*, was duly presented in 1961 with a cast that included Zoe Caldwell, Douglas Chamberlain, Jack Creley, Peter Donat, Amelia Hall, Douglas Rain, Kate Reid, Eleanor Stuart, and John Vernon: the cream of the company.

The play was bright and irreverent, colourfully costumed by Mark Negin and tightly directed by George McCowan. Harry Freedman provided a lively score that included a variety of songs and dances for which Alan and Blanche Lund provided sprightly choreography. The actors gave it their best shot and the critics praised their vivacity and charm. But the public stayed away; all six performances were poorly attended. The brave experiment of producing an original Canadian work on the Festival stage has never been repeated.

However, at about this time Stratford did begin to concern itself with Canadian plays, both previous successes that it either imported or remounted and also workshops of untried plays. There is a long history of revivals, from Gratien Gelinas' *Tit-Coq* in 1956 to Timothy Findley's *The Trials of Ezra Pound* in 2001. There have also been workshops of new scripts such as John Herbert's *Fortune and Men's Eyes* in 1965 (the Board refused permission for a Stratford production because of its graphic depiction of sex between male prisoners) and Lee MacDougall's *High Life* in 1997 (also considered "unsuitable" because of its farcical treatment of criminal elements). Both plays went on to have critical and commercial success in Toronto and beyond.

In between there were a formidable number of productions of new works staged in the smaller theatres: operas, children's plays, and adaptations of novels or classic plays written in other languages. In 2001 the total number of full-scale productions involving the work of Canadian writers stood at 66. Well-known artists involved included Roch Carrier, Gabriel Charpentier, Hume Cronyn, Timothy Findley, Elliott Hayes, John Murrell, Michael Ondaatje, Dan Needles, Sharon Pollock, James Reaney, R. Murray Schafer, Harry Somers, and Michel Tremblay. The number of workshops runs into the hundreds and involves many more well-known names.

The list is impressive, but new work does not have the same position at Stratford as it does at the Royal National Theatre of Great Britain, which has commissioned and performed work by such playwrights as Alan Bennett, David Hare, Harold Pinter and Tom Stoppard, or The Public Theatre in New York, which has produced work by Michael Bennett, John Guare, and David Rabe. Both these theatres produce classical texts but develop original work that they frequently show in their smaller theatres and then transfer to commercial houses in the West End or on Broadway. Often a close relationship grows up between a writer and the theatre on a basis not of exclusivity, but of mutual support: a sort of open marriage.

The Festival has never sustained this kind of relationship with any of its writers, though there are four playwrights who have each had more than one play performed at Stratford. The first in time was James Reaney, a poet who is a Stratford native son. He was commissioned by John Hirsch (then associate artistic director working with Jean Gascon) to write *Colours in the Dark* for the centennial year 1967. and the entertainment they devised together turned out to be one of the most delightful and imaginative productions in the Festival's history. Although its twelve performances were not sold out it, it went on to be performed across Canada in the next decade and established Reaney as a major Canadian playwright. Sadly this relationship between writer and director was disrupted by Hirsch's acrimonious departure from Stratford after the debacle of his other new work *The Satyricon*, a camp romp that sold well enough but outraged the Board and the critics and overran its budget by nearly eighty per cent.

Twenty-five years later, David William wooed Reaney once again and the result was the magical *Alice Through the Looking Glass*, first presented in 1994 and revived in 1996. Again it delighted audiences and plans were made for it to be transferred to the Winter Garden in Toronto, but they fell through because of casting difficulties. In my estimation Reaney is one of the most imaginative and original voices in the Canadian theatre, and the failure of Stratford to provide a platform for his work is sad, verging on tragic. There has been talk of reviving *The Donnelly Trilogy*, which Reaney wrote in the 1970s and which toured the country in a lively and imaginative production directed by Keith Turnbull. We can only hope this becomes a reality.

Sharon Pollock's play *Walsh*, presented at the Third Stage in 1974, is concerned with the dilemma of an officer in the North West Mounted Police who greatly admires Sitting Bull, the victor of the battle with Custer of the American cavalry at Little Big Horn; Walsh has been ordered to return Sitting Bull to the United States and is reluctant to do so. The play deftly deals with the attitudes of both Americans and Canadians toward natives and underlines the tensions between the two countries. This play, based on actual events, is typical of most of Pollock's work and of a whole school of Canadian playwriting in the 1970s and 1980s, a school in which Pollock was probably the biggest fish. Her later Stratford plays, *One Tiger to a Hill* in 1990 and *Fair Liberty's Call* in 1993, draw on similar actual political situations. Pollock is a forceful personality, outspoken and deeply committed to libertarian and humanist concerns; the productions of her plays at Stratford have been directed by John Wood with care, understanding, and fidelity to her intentions, but they have not succeeded in grabbing the attention of a substantial audience. This suggests that the Stratford audience is not looking for moral conviction or intelligent debate of political issues.

Sharon Pollock was a favourite writer of David William, who had a greater interest in producing Canadian work than most of his predecessors. William was responsible for scheduling productions of Michel Tremblay's *Les Belles Soeurs* and *Bonjour, là, Bonjour* and for commissioning an adaptation of Robertson Davies' novel *World of Wonders*, finally fulfilling that writer's dream of having an original work produced at the Festival he had done so much to promote and foster.

William appointed as his literary manager Elliott Hayes, son of former general manager John Hayes. Elliott Hayes began his literary work at Stratford as early as 1981 when he devised a script of Shakespearean excerpts to be performed by Nicholas Pennell. It played at the Third Stage the next year under the title *A Variable*

Passion. Hayes followed this with *Blake,* a selection from the English visionary poet's work. It was directed by Richard Monette with music composed by Loreena McKennitt. Blake was impersonated by Douglas Campbell. The show was performed at the Third Stage in 1983, toured to Ottawa, and was part of the first CBC Stratford broadcast series in 1994.

Hayes proved to be the most committed and imaginative literary manager at the Festival since Urjo Kareda. He was himself a writer and he championed other young writers, sometimes directing workshops of their scripts. He adapted Robert Louis Stevenson's *Treasure Island,* which David William staged at the Festival Theatre in 1991, and Davies' *World of Wonders,* which was performed at the Avon in 1992. This production was a wonderful spectacle, if somewhat confusing in its storyline, and it introduced Richard Rose's work as a director to the Festival. Rose would become an important contributor to the Stratford scene. His strongly imagistic style has usually worked better with new scripts than with classical texts. His production of *Glenn,* the intricately structured analytical take on the life and work of pianist Glenn Gould, is one of the most original works the Festival has yet produced and was highly successful at the box office. Rose's adaptation of Robertson Davies' early novel *Tempest-Tost,* about amateur theatricals in a town modeled on Kingston, Ontario in the 1950s, also proved extremely popular in the 2001 season.

Hayes also wrote several original plays. His *Homeward Bound,* produced at the Patterson Theatre, was a somewhat Albee-esque bittersweet comedy. It was a critical and box-office success and has been performed by a number of regional theatres in Canada and the United States. An earlier play, *Hard Hearts,* was workshopped at the Festival and later performed in Toronto. Hayes was working on a screenplay based on Robertson Davies novel, *A Mixture of Frailties,* when he was killed in a car crash in 1995. His loss was a blow to Monette, with whom he had formed a close working relationship when they collaborated on *Blake.* Up until 2001 there has been no one working on play development for the Festival who possesses a similar degree of savvy or insight into the dramaturgical process.

Timothy Findley was an actor in the Festival company in the first season and, along with Richard Easton, he was spirited off to London by Alec Guinness to try his fortunes there. Easton stayed for several decades working with major actors including John Gielgud and Ralph Richardson and eventually returning to play the

243

lead in Tom Stoppard's *The Invention of Love* on Broadway, winning a Tony award. Findley came back across the pond much sooner and before long abandoned acting to concentrate on a career as a writer. Like Robertson Davies he has had greater success as a novelist than as a playwright, though he penned several screenplays for CBC television, and his early plays *Can You See Me Yet?* and *John A. Himself*, a vehicle for William Hutt, were professionally staged. He then wrote a play for Hutt and Martha Henry, *The Stillborn Lover*, which premiered at the Grand Theatre in London when Henry was artistic director.

This play centres on a diplomat whose career has been compromised by a liaison with a young Russian spy and conflates the real life stories of two Canadian foreign service officers, Herbert Norman and John Watkins. The loyal but disturbed wife who is battling the early stages of Alzheimer's disease provided Henry with a splendid acting opportunity that she exploited to the hilt. The play proved popular with audiences and was revived as part of Stratford's 1995 season, before being made into a television movie. Findley then began work on a new play, *Elizabeth Rex*, for Martha Henry and Brent Carver involving a confrontation between Queen Elizabeth and a young actor in Shakespeare's company.

Henry elected to direct this piece rather than starring in it and she supervised workshops and revisions over a four-year period. The role of Elizabeth I was taken by Diane D'Aquila. The play was skillfully staged as part of the 2000 season and the two leading performers gave outstanding performances. The reviews were "over the moon" and the play sold out. Plans have been made to revive it, possibly in collaboration with the Mirvishes, and also to film it. The success of this play prompted the Festival to stage another Findley work, *The Trials of Ezra Pound*, based on a radio script Findley had written for the CBC and expanded into a stage play. Again it provides a splendid acting role, which David Fox seized upon with alacrity.

Findley's success is gratifying and is certainly no flash in the pan. He served a long apprenticeship as both actor and screenwriter and is therefore accustomed to listening to directors, but he has the stature to stand up to them, if need be. He has settled in Stratford, where he spends about half the year and is thus available for ongoing dramaturgical work. He has also been shrewd in his choice of subject matter. A play which has both the Bard and Good Queen Bess as characters and a gender-bending theme has more obvious audience appeal than, say, a play about the quiet desperation of frustrated housewives in rural Ontario. (Of course, Alice Munro handles this material brilliantly, and with her name attached to it, it might also sell very well.) An interesting test at the box office in the 2001 season is *Good Mother*, a new play by the award-winning young actor and playwright Damien Atkins about a family dominated by a forceful woman who suffers a stroke, with the highly talented Seana McKenna in the central role.

The other major success story of Canadian writing at the Festival is the Wingfield phenomenon. The partnership of Rod Beattie, his brother Douglas Beattie as director, and writer Dan Needles goes back to their boyhood forty years ago when they played ball-hockey together in North Toronto. I first encountered them as a team when they were all in a production of *Hamlet* that I directed at Hart House Theatre in 1972. Though not exactly passion's slave, Rod Beattie was a highly articulate and corrosively edgy Hamlet, the qualities that he would use to such good effect in the Wingfield plays.

Although they may seem episodic and full of random comment, the five plays are in fact tightly structured, the result of many months of collaboration between the three. The wit and observation express Needles' own unique vision, but hours are devoted to building a storyline in which the stakes escalate in the second act and a payoff is contrived to provide an effective climax. These plays owe much to the fact that in Canada many people are not very far removed from the rural experience. When I first saw the show in Orangeville, Ontario, the audience was made up of local people, delighted by this accurate reflection of themselves and their friends, but skeptical of its wider appeal: "You couldn't do this in the city. They wouldn't get it." A month later the show opened for a brief run at the Arts and Letters Club in Toronto, whose members opined, "You couldn't do this in the country. People would be insulted." The shrewd mix of the two milieux is a key element in the shows' appeal, even though the town-and-country opposition has been used by playwrights for centuries, notably by one William Shakespeare.

Now that Monette has secured his new Fourth Space he is determined to place greater emphasis on new work and to develop an audience for it. The lessons to be learned from recent successes seem twofold. Audiences will come to see new work if it has a sufficiently intriguing subject and is performed by well-known players. (In other words, the rules are roughly the same at Stratford as on Broadway or in

245

Hollywood.) Writers must work hard to develop the special skills required by the demanding medium of theatre and need skillful guidance. The number of people who can provide such guidance is small indeed, perhaps because in this country there isn't much of a pay-off, either financially or in terms of professional kudos or advancement. Both Canadian Stage and the Tarragon Theatre in Toronto have done intensive work on play development. Tarragon has been more obviously successful, partly because it operates a small house of less than 200 seats, which is easier to fill than the 875-seat Bluma Appel Theatre, although Canadian Stage does do new work at its smaller Berkeley Street Theatre).

Tarragon has also been more successful in attracting writers of genuine ability. Bill Glassco and Urjo Kareda have been very shrewd over a thirty-year period about uncovering and cultivating new talent, and this has paid off. Good writers and directors attract each other as inevitably as mating animals, and there is an inner circle. Years ago I remember Robert Gill, Hart House Theatre's director in the 1940s and 1950s, being accused of running an elite club, to which he replied, "It's true and the entrée is talent." Like actors and directors, writers build a career by networking, finding people with whom they can work, getting their work seen, picking up awards. The work has to be sold and commissions go to those who can grab attention for themselves, who are thought to be "hot." But in the end, they have to deliver. The work has to be good. As Tom Stoppard puts it, "The play has to *work*. It has to be truthful. The audience must *believe*."

Andrey Tarasiuk is Stratford's newly appointed Director of New Play Development. He is serious and extremely hard-working and has had more than twenty years' experience in Toronto at the Tarragon and Toronto Free theatres and then at Theatre Direct, developing such plays as Colin Thomas' *Flesh and Blood*, Fabrizio Filippo's *Waiting for Lewis*, and Thomson Highway's *A Trickster Tale*. He inherits a small stable of mature writers led by Findley and Needles and a gaggle of playwrights who have been commissioned by the Festival for new plays that have not yet seen the light of day: Robert Cushman, Jason Sherman, David Young.

Tarasiuk and Monette have devised an ingenious scheme to showcase the work of very young playwrights at the new Fourth Space in the anniversary season. Four playwrights have been commissioned to write one-act plays, each of which will be paired with a short piece by a well-known author: Jean Cocteau's *La Voix Humaine*,

Jean-Paul Sartre's *No Exit*, a hitherto unproduced script by Federico Fellini, and a new play by Timothy Findley based on his characters Minna and Brag. The young authors chosen are Stratford actor Paul Dunn, recent NTS graduate and Montreal writer Celia McBride, rabbinical student turned Dora-winning playwright Anton Piatigorsky, and aboriginal Winnipeg writer Ian Ross. There will also be a production of *The Death of Cupid*, the first part of an original verse trilogy *The Swanne*, written and directed by the gifted and controversial Peter Hinton.

However, the new Fourth Space will not just be dedicated to new work. It will be both a laboratory and a playground. It will replicate in miniature the thrust stage of the Festival Theatre to give aspiring directors experience in working in this kind of space. It will allow for the production of plays unlikely to fill a larger theatre: Aristophanes' *The Clouds*, Marlowe's *The Jew of Malta*, Ghelderode's *Chronicles of Hell*, for example. Monette himself will lead off with a production of Niccolo Machiavelli's *Mandragola (The Mandrake)*.

There will be opportunities for unconventional casting: Michelle Giroux as Hamlet, Stephen Ouimette as Cleopatra, Peter Donaldson as Don Juan, Seana McKenna as Richard III. (These examples are purely my fantasy, but I would happily go to see any of them.) And there will be readings and small-scale productions of original scripts, adaptations, and translations of work that may or may not go on to be done in one of the larger theatres. Production values will be minimal, with costumes and props pulled from stock. Emphasis will be on acting and directing, not design or technical experiment. Runs will mostly be short and ticket prices will be kept low.

Tarasiuk is only one of the people who will be closely involved in this work but he is a key figure. He firmly believes Stratford now has the opportunity and the responsibility of creating new work to complement its classical repertoire as a major part of its mandate. He is determined to set up the infrastructure to commission, develop, and program new plays from a variety of playwrights, not necessarily all Canadian. In this he has the strong support of Monette, who lobbied vigorously for both the small space and the approval of the Board to expand the mandate at the strategic moment of euphoria over the reception of *Elizabeth Rex*, a play whose ultimate literary worth remains to be proven in the larger arena but whose importance to the Festival has been crucial. Monette is as unashamedly opportunistic in his bid to expand the Festival's programming as he has been in expanding its audience, budget, and artistic stable. Like all successful conquerors he is supremely confident of the value of his vision: "We're the biggest theatrical company on the continent and we owe it to ourselves to ensure we are the best. And we will be."

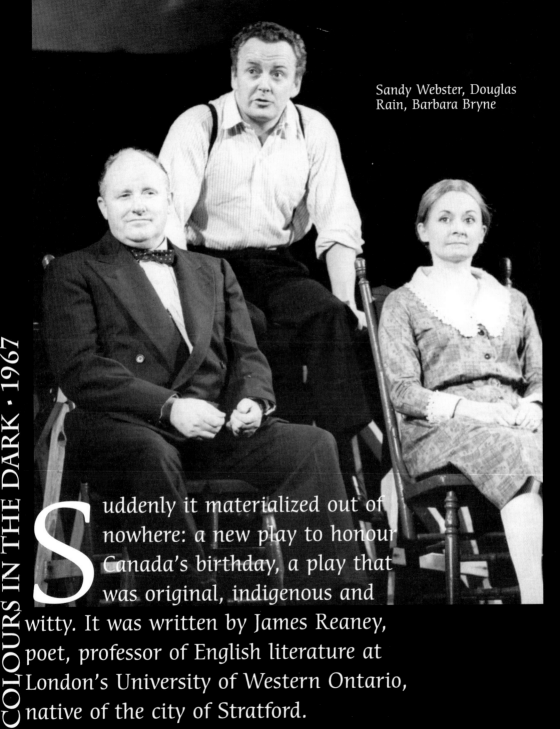

Sandy Webster, Douglas
Rain, Barbara Bryne

*S*uddenly it materialized out of
nowhere: a new play to honour
Canada's birthday, a play that
was original, indigenous and
witty. It was written by James Reaney,
poet, professor of English literature at
London's University of Western Ontario,
native of the city of Stratford.

Director: **John Hirsch**

Designers: **Don Lewis & Eoin Sprott**

Douglas Rain and the children play Blind Man's Bluff

*O*n opening night, the Avon Theatre slowly filled with a disparate
group: Stratfordians who remembered Reaney as a boy, alternate
theatre people from Toronto who were not Stratford habitués,
Reaney's students from London—a far cry from the usual boiled-shirt and
bare-bosomed first-night crowd at Stratford. They were handed black-eyed
susans and assaulted by a soundtrack that was a medley of snatches from
1930s and 1940s radio: Charlie McCarthy, the Happy Gang, Oxydol's
Own Ma Perkins, the Lone Ranger riding to the beat of Rossini's William
Tell overture.

The lights dimmed and the play began to unfold like a Christmas concert in a Stratford classroom, complete with recitations, drills, playlets,
and chorus numbers. The hero was James Reaney as an infant, a boy, an
adolescent, and a mature man. He was also a poet whose journey paralleled the awakening of the Canadian imagination, an awakening soul
who followed the path of Everyman, Bunyan's Pilgrim, Milton's

Hanging out washing

Adam/Christ. In a collage of images, a rapid succession of forty short episodes, a compelling rush of words, the story unfolded.

There were evocative images devised by director John Hirsch and his designers Eoin Sprott and Don Lewis, gleaned from children's art, Eskimo prints, old photographs, Mennonite quilts, Haida masks. And music by Allan Laing that drew on hymns, popular songs, and folk tunes: a xylophone brought to life a set of dishes; a simple march evoked a parade.

A kaleidoscope of colours with symbolic significance brought into focus sharp social commentary: white for birth, red for the anger of an outraged schoolmaster, yellow for energy and the brio of a music lesson, orange for the Orange Day parade, purple for the Dance of Death. And there were magical effects: babies flew through the air, life-size puppets rescued a child swallowed by a bear, one character crawled into a log and emerged as a luna moth, two chairs on the empty stage rocked by themselves.

Douglas Rain with native spirits

The performers included a group of children with whom Reaney had been working for months in an improvisational group. Together they devised several scenes: the berry-picking episode where the child is swallowed, and the scene about the set of dishes owned by a family, where after four generations only one cup is left. The kids were joined by six professional actors from the company, each of whom played many parts, like the protagonist of Shakespeare's Ages of Man.

Memorable were Barbara Bryne as the querulous Granny Crack, Martha Henry as the sympathetic Mother and the mysterious Wind Lady, Mary Hitch as Bible Sal, Heath Lamberts as a cheeky boy, Douglas Rain as an angry schoolmaster, and Sandy Webster as the loquacious Professor Button. These were people drawn from the town of Stratford and the countryside around it, no less fantastic in their eccentricity than Falstaff, Sir Andrew Aguecheek, Juliet's Nurse or Macbeth's witches, but rooted in native soil, unique but utterly recognizable examples of Canadian Gothic.

At the end the of the opening night the audience clapped and, slowly, raggedly, rose to their feet, not in the manner of the obligatory ovation accorded all Stratford premieres but in a genuine tribute to welcome home a native son, who slowly shambled out onto the stage to acknowledge their welcome for the first real Canadian masterpiece to be commissioned and realized at Stratford. Who would have guessed the next one would be such a long time coming?

TEARING IT APART:
THE CRITICS ARE HEARD FROM

TYRONE GUTHRIE ATTRIBUTED THE INITIAL SUCCESS OF THE STRATFORD FESTIVAL in large part to the positive reaction of the American critics, specifically Brooks Atkinson of the *New York Times* and Walter Kerr of the *Tribune*. Atkinson's initial review of *Richard III* expressed marked reservations about Guinness' performance and Guthrie's conception, which he characterized as "loose and superficial." But he responded more favourably to Guthrie's interpretation of *All's Well That Ends Well* in spite of his opinion that it was a "potboiler," and his wrap-up piece on the front page of the *Sunday Times* was a rave that strongly endorsed this bold new theatrical enterprise, declaring that "the Stratford Festival in Ontario is a genuine contribution to Shakespeare in North America." *Time* magazine was even more emphatic: "Shakespeare has a new home this side of the Atlantic.... The result is a minor theatrical miracle. Seldom have so many Shakespeare lovers owed so much to so few." The Churchillian echo inspired a stream of American enthusiasts who flowed north to the Festival in that first year, a stream that has since swelled to a river of Mississippian dimension.

Atkinson and Kerr continued to review Festival productions, and although they did not commend everything they saw, their treatment of the Festival as a major North American theatrical event did much to put it and keep it on the map. Atkinson's final review for the *Times* in 1960 singled out Stratford and stated, "The Ontario company plays with the virtuosity of a symphony orchestra." Kerr continued to review the Festival until 1976, and in his final year he totally fell under the spell of Maggie Smith in Robin Phillips production of *The Way of the World*. "...When Miss Smith comes on as Millamant ... she prattles about the papers she uses as hair-curlers, about suitors, about landscapes and lying and the unreliability of love ... language is her last line of defence. She's secretly more vulnerable than anyone on stage. She is magnificent." This is the kind of review that draws people into the theatre.

Canadian critics were equally enthusiastic about the opening productions. Here is that bombastic curmudgeon Nathan Cohen: "That excitement, that enthusiasm just kept mounting. We were as one with the actors. It was more than involvement. It was a mingling of soul. We felt that something absolutely original and world-important was going on.... That first night at Stratford was the single most memorable experience I ever had in the theatre." This euphoria was echoed by Herbert Whittaker, Morley Safer, and Robertson Davies. Their laudatory prose was given credibility by the endorsement of the American press. This was not just chauvinistic pride; this was undeniably work that measured up to international standards.

Safer would soon go on to fame on the television show *Sixty Minutes*, but Whittaker and Davies would prove in the early years of the Festival to be important boosters. Whittaker wrote positively about the Festival in the *Globe and Mail*. He also cultivated the confidence of Guthrie and various Festival actors, making suggestions about repertory and casting. Indeed, Guthrie proposed that Whittaker might become a director at the Festival if he were willing to go to England and work with established professionals to learn the ropes, an offer Whittaker declined.

Whittaker would continue to bring his waspish insight and paternalistic concern to bear on the Festival during its first five decades, now praising, now scolding, evermore admonishing and advocating a higher standard of theatrical art. His advice has not always been welcome, but it is still listened to. Monette refers to him with mocking affection as "Emeritus" but pays heed to his comments. And his successors at the *Globe*, John Fraser, Ray Conlogue, and Kate Taylor, have all been influenced by his views, no matter whether they accept or reject his dictates.

Robertson Davies had known Guthrie in England when Davies was a junior member of the Old Vic Company, playing Snout in Guthrie's smash hit production of *A Midsummer Night's Dream*, four minor roles including the Widow in *The Taming of the Shrew*, and doing dramaturgical work. Guthrie dubbed him "our resident pedant." Davies was on hand when Guthrie arrived in Canada in 1952, made himself available for consultation, served as a member of the Board for nearly twenty years, wrote three elegantly phrased and beautifully produced books about the first three seasons in collaboration with Guthrie, painter Grant Macdonald, and

254

others, which did much to promote the Festival, and reviewed Festival productions with pungent wit and judicious learning in the upscale periodical *Saturday Night* for more than a decade.

Davies also penned a short "missing scene" for insertion in Tom Brown and Michael Langham's 1956 production of *The Merry Wives of Windsor* and wrote a version of Ben Jonson's *Bartholomew Fair* set in rural Ontario that was, sadly, never performed. In recompense Guthrie directed a stage version of Davies' novel *Leaven of Malice* with a company of Festival actors that played to enthusiastic houses in Toronto and Boston under the title *Love and Libel* before making a less felicitous appearance in New York. Davies remained a staunch supporter of the Festival until his death in 1995. In 2001 the dramatization of Davies' first novel, *Tempest-Tost*, was complemented by a "Robertson Davies Celebration," a series of dramatic readings emphasizing his early work as a playwright and critic. It was a fitting tribute to Davies' commitment to the Festival and to his position as both icon and animateur of Canadian cultural life.

Nathan Cohen's first-night ecstasy was short-lived. He became the Festival's most vituperative detractor. "Hell-bent for sterility," "Slaughter at Stratford," "crass and contemptuous of the play's content," "vocally and technically flabby," "perhaps unconscious but certainly expanding anti-intellectualism," "muddled, willful, scan-dalous, a shambles," "muted and de-natured," "numbellicitous nonsense ... in the extreme of its inadequacy": these typically ornate, pejorative phrases characterize his comment in the eighteen years he wrote about the Festival, although there were things he admired: Langham's *The Taming of the Shrew* with Kate Reid and John Colicos, Tony van Bridge's Falstaff, Gascon's *The Dance of Death* in which he played the captain opposite Denise Pelletier, and William Hutt's *Tartuffe*.

Nathan Cohen was the first Canadian journalist to adopt the role of the critic as scourge, following in the footsteps of Dr. Johnson and George Jean Nathan. He undoubtedly had high standards and expectations but also an almost sadistic delight in roasting his victims. There is no doubt that many of his readers enjoyed this as much as he did. Any working journalist will have encountered members of the public who say, "If I were you, I'd really let those guys have it." There is a considerable audience that delights in vitriol and venom. Cohen played to them with panache and eventually, with the help of television, he became a bigger star than most of the

255

people he was writing about. In the end he was celebrated not only with a seat in the Festival Theatre dedicated to his memory but with a play by Rick Salutin in which he was ably impersonated by Douglas Campbell, who unerringly reproduced Cohen's inflated persona and over-emphatic delivery.

Cohen's stance has been taken up since by several Canadian drama critics, perhaps most notably Gina Mallet and Kate Taylor. They have embarked upon a self-imposed but noble mission; their desire to uphold standards of artistic excellence and integrity can only be seen as admirable. At the same time it should be noted that they are in the employ of commercial interests, a fact that both Mallet and Taylor freely acknowledged. Mallet once told me she was less interested in getting the facts right than in writing provocative copy. At a recent seminar at the Central Library in Toronto, Taylor stated, "I do not have a primary commitment to the theatre. My job is to sell newspapers." Her fellow panelists Robert Cushman and Richard Ouzounian did not contest this imperative.

How important is the critic to the theatre? Certainly critics have been with us for a long time, beginning with Aristotle, whose doctrine concerning unity of time, place, and action is still widely cited. In modern times critics have played a vital role in shaping theatre. George Bernard Shaw championed Ibsen and the play of ideas before he went on to write some of the most intelligent and provocative English drama of the twentieth century. Kenneth Tynan championed Brecht and John Osborne while Ronald Bryden discovered Tom Stoppard. Urjo Kareda was the first Canadian drama critic who wrote about native playwrights without reference to what was going on in Britain or America, who said, in effect, "This play is good, go and see it." He has championed the work of David French, John Murrell, and Judith Thompson, among others, as writers to be evaluated and enjoyed on their own merits.

For the audience, critics have a clear function. They describe the play and delineate their reaction to it. This gives the playgoer an indication of whether the play is something he wants to see or not. Two primary factors influence his evaluation. Is this the sort of play I would enjoy, given my interests and individual taste? Is it well executed? The reader must make allowances for the critic's bias or agenda and also assess the critic's ability to judge. Is he merely saying he's tired of plays about feminism, gay coming of age, racial intolerance, or middle-class angst? Or is he evaluating this particular production against a broad experience of many kinds of theatre?

256

Given the nature of today's fast-changing world, there are "drama critics" working for major newspapers or other media who a year ago were assigned to the sports desk and a year from now will likely be political correspondents in Beijing or Berlin. They may write well, be insightful and amusing, but their theatrical experience is limited and their judgements inevitably rather shallow. Perhaps this is acceptable to the general public and even to the committed theatre-goer, particularly if he has sufficient background to view the reviewer's opinions in context. In the words of Tom Stoppard, "You have to read the critics *critically* and make the necessary adjustment according to what you know about them. When I was a critic ... I was not a good critic, because I never had the moral character to pan a friend. I'll re-phrase that—I had the moral character never to pan a friend."

Stoppard's comments throw into relief one of the tensions that exists between critics and practitioners in the theatre, or for that matter, any art. Many critics were once aspiring artists themselves. Herbert Whittaker and Nathan Cohen both wrote plays that failed to win approval. Cohen licked his wounds and lashed out at others but Whittaker at least went on directing. Ronald Bryden wrote a lively and entertaining college revue. Robert Cushman is working on a stage version of *The Iliad*. Richard Ouzounian wrote the book and lyrics for the musical version of *Dracula*, which was a resounding success in the 1999 season. Even Kate Taylor, I am told, has a script waiting in the wings. But to be an artist, especially as exposed an artist as an actor, requires courage and persistence in the face of discouragement and rejection. In the words of Tennessee Williams, "If you have talent, you must simply go on, *go on*, regardless of frivolous reaction."

The imbalance that exists between the creative and critical faculties in the arts is, I believe, rooted in our education system, particularly in our universities. Students are trained to exercise their intellectual judgement rather than to follow their intuition. They eventually become so critical of their own work that they stop doing it and turn their attention to analyzing and quantifying the work of others. My own experience over ten years of running theatres at the University of Toronto led me to the unhappy conclusion that the University was on the whole hostile to the practice of the arts. I am not talking about administrators but rather the majority of the professors instructing the students.

However, for an artist to blame his failure on his education, or his parents, or his lovers, or the critics, is a cop-out. He may say, "Why should I listen to someone who knows less about the theatre than I do and who only saw one performance and knocked out a few paragraphs in an hour, when I have spent ten years (or a lifetime) acquiring my professional skills and two months working on this performance." He may refuse to read reviews, as many actors do, especially older, established actors. But he cannot therefore ignore the importance of criticism. Every artist must to some extent become a critic of his own work. He must exercise judgement and a sense of proportion. He must accept direction from the people whose opinion he respects, be it a mentor, a director or a fellow actor. He can ignore the professional critics or indeed counter their arguments, but he must learn how to judge his own work

For a producer it is not quite so simple. The opinion of the press affects ticket sales and he must take this into account. Many producers claim that they do not read critics; Monette is one of them. But he learns about the critical response to any given show from his assistants, and his decisions about programming, casting, and direction are inevitably influenced by this. Theatre people continue to cry out against the critics, from Ed Mirvish fuming in the early days of his ownership of the Royal Alexandra, to Donald Sutherland wailing in the pages of the *Times* when his recent London appearance in *The Enigma Variations* was roundly panned. (He bounced back smartly, however, and six months later was earning accolades for his performance in Jon Robin Baitz' *Ten Unknowns* in New York, a striking illustration of the resilience essential for a successful acting career.)

One way for a producer to insulate his theatre against the slings and arrows of the critics is to pre-sell his shows, and of course it is easier to pre-sell a package than an individual production. The risk is spread for both producer and audience-member. Both Mirvish and Monette have aggressively pursued this policy and the results are reflected in the full houses and satisfied customers they enjoy. Of course, nothing rouses the fury of a critic like a show his opinion cannot destroy.

Inevitably, since I am a practising theatre artist my view of critics is somewhat jaundiced, but it is only fair to point out that several critics have had a highly positive influence at Stratford. Following in the footsteps of Davies and Whittaker, a number of academics contributed to Stratford's success. Berners Jackson wrote intelligent analyses of many productions in the 1950s and 1960s in addition to serving on the Board. Peter Raby and Michael Bawtree did dramaturgical work for Michael

Langham, which involved cutting and researching texts and helping to prepare productions. Both men wrote original scripts based on literary or historical material that were successfully produced, and Raby's script for *The Three Musketeers* has seen two full-scale revivals.

Two critics had a strong effect in shaping policies and practices in the Robin Phillips era. Ronald Bryden and Urjo Kareda are both immensely knowledgeable and sharply articulate writers who have devoted their lives to theatre in its many aspects. Both influenced Phillips' programming and casting, and Kareda in particular was concerned with identifying and bringing along promising young actors and writers. Both men can be prickly, devious, and sometimes loftily dismissive but each possesses a sharp nose for talent and a shrewd sense of what will be theatrically effective. Stratford would have been the poorer without their contribution.

In the last twenty-five years various academics have stepped into the shoes left by Kareda: Michael Schonberg working with John Hirsch, Robert Beard with David William, David Prosser and Peter Wylde with Monette, but none of these has had either the authority or the ingenuity of Kareda. Their time has increasingly been taken up with the practical demands of writing advertising copy and speeches, planning seminars, devising curriculum for the Conservatory or threading their way through the intricacies of contract negotiations.

The recent institution of an annual Visiting Scholar has provided an informed outside view. The opinions and suggestions of Gary Taylor, Alexander Leggatt, and Brian Parker have been interesting and useful, but at the moment there is no one on the inside offering the imaginative input that an experienced theatre man can provide. Instead a sort of complementary infrastructure has grown up inside the Festival which offers lectures, discussions, and historical perspective, both visual and literary. This enhances the educational réclame of the Festival but does not necessarily contribute to its aesthetic development. The techniques and means of promotion become ever more sophisticated but the creative process remains personal, intuitive, and ultimately mysterious. The wind bloweth where it listeth, not where the big bucks beckon.

Monette remains an active listener. He spends time with the many distinguished visitors who come to Stratford, from Stephen Sondheim to Tom Stoppard. There are certain critics such as Ronald Bryden and Robert Cushman who have his ear. Advice is offered by writers such as Timothy Findley, now a Stratford resident, and senior theatre artists who weigh in, more perhaps than they realize. Like a downy bird fashioning its nest, Monette weaves bits and pieces he gathers from all these sources, carefully shaping them to protect his festival against the whips and scorns not of wind and weather but of the critical fraternity. For the critics will not disappear, nor will they topple the Festival as long as it continues to produce good work. Inevitably the anxious but potentially fruitful (or, as Nathan Cohen might have said, "fructiferous") tension between artist and critic will persist.

ELIZABETH REX · 2000

Timothy Findley's drama is in a sense the Canadian play that Stratford has been waiting for since its inception. Witty and imaginative, it is bold in its use of historical and literary antecedents to create something contemporary and controversial. The provocative title suggests the theme: an uncompromising examination of the nature of the relationship between the sexes.

Diane D'Aquila as Queen Elizabeth I

F inaley refuses to accept stereotypical formulations about the sexual nature of either men or women. In this, like good King Wenceslas' page, he follows in his master's footsteps. The poet who penned love sonnets to a young man and the greatest lyric drama in the history of the theatre, who created some of the most memorable women in literature (Katharina, Ophelia, Beatrice, Lady Macbeth, Rosalind, to name a few), and who then went on to limn the most complex and eloquent study of the tensions generated by personal ambition in conflict with sexual obsession — he was surely the most adventurous explorer of the nature of sexual identity in his own or any age.

Findley gives us three memorable characters. The aging Queen is shrewd, tough, imperious, but stricken with repressed regrets for what might have been. Shakespeare is both detached and captivated, mesmerized by the behaviour of the royal termagant he will immortalize as Cleopatra. Ned Lowenscroft, the young actor doomed to perish from the ravages of syphilis, is alternately terrified and courageous, obsessed with the limitations of his own mortality but fearless in his attempt to uncover the truth and come to terms with it. As if this were not enough, Findley gives us a magnificent animal, a bear whom Ned cherishes and defends and who ultimately lays his shaggy head on the great Queen's lap. Findley rejects not only conventionality but also the innate superiority of all things human.

The play, set on the eve of the execution of Elizabeth's last great love, the Earl of Essex, accused of treason for leading a march on London that challenged the supremacy of the Queen's

Diane D'Aquila and Brent Carver

authority, is a tangle of conflicting emotion and intellectual argument. Findley's central premise is expressed as a paradox, when the aging Queen challenges Ned, "If you will teach me to grieve like a woman, I will teach you to die like a man." The two central characters circle each other like gladiators; their weapons are clear, uncompromising vision and naked wit.

As Elizabeth, Diane D'Aquila is raucously regal and terrifyingly razor-tongued, changeable as a chameleon but always engaged. Brent Carver perfectly captures the young actor Ned's hysteria, nervous volatility, willingness to dare all and inability to contain his passions. Like shot silk or oil on water, these characters are engaged in an endless dance of changing shapes and colours.

On the edges of the drama the other characters loom now bright, now dimly: Bernard Hopkins as the shrewdly insinuating physical and moral pygmy Robert Cecil; Scott Wentworth as the handsome actor Jack, deftly putting on the personas of the charming, feckless Essex, the nobly declining Antony, and Ned's importunate Captain off to the Irish wars; Joyce Campion as the wry old tiring-woman Tardy; Peter Hutt as the articulate, soft-spoken onlooker Will Shakespeare. The ever-shifting focus as these characters engage and disengage, confront, collide with or sidestep each other is the particular strength of Martha Henry's fluid and sensitive direction.

But it is Findley's unique voice that rings out strong and clear: a voice of power and originality that speaks to critics and audiences alike and touches them with its emotional truth and essential humanity, a voice that sets a standard of high ambition for the other voices that will demand to be heard

PUTTING IT TOGETHER

"LIFE'S A BANQUET, AND MOST POOR SONS OF BITCHES ARE STARVING." Auntie Mame's Epicurean observation is a favourite quotation of Richard Monette, who sees the programming of a season at the Festival as being like planning a banquet: "Shall we have oysters or smoked salmon, pheasant or beef Wellington? We don't want pâté if we're having bouillabaisse. The oven isn't big enough for lobster Newburgh and boeuf en daube. And we must have a choice of desserts: profiteroles and crème brûlée and, of course, a fruit sorbet to cleanse the palate. Perhaps mango, but no, we served that when we entertained this crowd last year." The analogy holds good, but programming a season as large as Stratford's is more like devising the menu for an upscale restaurant. Perhaps Robin Phillips learned a thing or two about putting a season together from his companion Joe Mandel's experience at The Church restaurant. Or vice versa.

When setting out to devise a season, Monette confers closely with executive director Antoni Cimolino but entertains and solicits suggestions from other trusted advisors such as Brian Bedford, Martha Henry, and William Hutt, as well as sometimes consulting outside observers, critics like Ronald Bryden and Robert Cushman. I have sometimes been part of this process. "Everyone thinks he can program. I get suggestions from members of the Board that range from *The Complete Works of William Shakespeare (Abridged)* to *Gammer Gurton's Needle.*" Monette listens to them all. A bright idea may come from anywhere and these people also make good sounding boards. And, after all, he is not obliged to take any of their advice.

Sitting in a waterfront café in Bodrum on the Aegean coast of Turkey in November 2000, Monette is in the midst of a four-month semi-sabbatical. In the background he hears the sweet, clear soprano of Loreena McKennitt, a Stratford native who is a major star in Turkey. Monette sips his wine as he relaxes, but his thoughts are three thousand miles away, back at the Festival. "We start with Shakespeare and the obvious thing for our fiftieth anniversary season is to repeat

264

Romancing the Bard

on the main stage the two shows that inaugurated the Festival. For *Richard III* we really should have a star." Bedford has done it and doesn't want to repeat it. Paul Gross has expressed interest in playing the role and so has Colm Feore (although he too has already given us a Richard III). Probably neither one will agree to a whole season. Maybe one of them could open and the other take over midway, but neither will want the second slot. Monette could do the second slot himself. It's a role he's always wanted to play. But it's huge, and a split run means a lot of extra rehearsal at a significant cost of time and money. And who will direct? Bedford? No, he has already indicated he will not be available for the anniversary season.

All's Well That Ends Well is easier. It is a show Monette would like to direct himself. Martha Henry as the Countess and William Hutt as the King of France would be good casting, and for Helena there is a choice of Lucy Peacock or Michelle Giroux. Graham Abbey for Bertram, and for Parolles perhaps Monette will reprise the role he played in 1977. Monette is still ambivalent about acting. He seems to have conquered the acute stage fright he experienced in the early 1980s. In 1997 he played the male lead in *Filumena* at the Avon and discovered that the collywobbles had disappeared. There are many people, I for one, who feel that Monette is in his acting prime and should get back up on stage. But acting takes time and Monette's directorial and public-relations duties already fill twelve to fourteen hours a day, seven days a week, fifty weeks of the year. And directing a show in which you also play a sizeable role is problematic, especially on the Festival stage, with a large cast, tricky blocking problems, and major technical demands to be accommodated.

The other Shakespeares? Most likely *Henry VI*, with the three parts consolidated into two evenings. These early plays are repetitive and confusing and have traditionally not been big sellers, but Monette is determined to do all the plays in the Shakespearean canon before his contract is up in 2004, and these plays along with *Richard III* would complete the history cycle begun with *Richard II* in 1999. Done at the Patterson, they might sell reasonably well, especially since the Royal Shakespeare Company production that he has just seen in Stratford-on-Avon and that is to play in Ann Arbor, Michigan early in 2001 might build interest in these rarely seen chronicles. And there is a good opportunity for a young actor in the title role. Donald Carrier? Paul Dunn? Michael Therriault? That will depend on how they shape up in the 2001 season and, of course, who is directing.

265

Then there is the possibility that Christopher Plummer might agree to do a late-opener. Plummer would like this, and there are ongoing discussions. He is now a member of the Board and has a feeling of loyalty to Stratford and to Monette himself, who played Eros to his Antony in 1967, Plummer's last appearance at the Festival in a Shakespearean role. He has yet to play Prospero or Lear. He is in good shape, but realizes that he should tackle these large, taxing roles while he still has the stamina to pull them off. If Plummer does not bite the bullet, what about a late opener with Feore? Marlowe's *Doctor Faustus,* for instance, or Molière's *Don Juan,* two titles never seen at the Festival but with a high recognition factor and both offering roles well suited to Feore's gifts. But will Feore come?

The other central component in building the season is the musical. It makes money that subsidizes the rest of the repertoire and attracts not only those theatre-goers who want something a little lighter to balance their Shakespeare but a separate audience of people who don't want to see anything else. It is the big-time "classical" musicals that these people want to see, the ones with well-known tunes and lots of spectacle. Stratford has had formidable successes with *My Fair Lady, Camelot,* and especially *Fiddler on the Roof* in 2000, which sold out in the second half of the season. Why not follow up with another starring role for Brent Carver? But his availability is notoriously problematic. *South Pacific* is a hit-filled musical that Stratford hasn't done, and it is enjoying a revival in London. It offers a terrific role for Cynthia Dale, who will return to star in *The Sound of Music* in 2001. (This saccharine confection with its yodeling moppets and operatic nuns will be roundly panned by the critics but will regularly sell out anyway. There will be no doubt that Dale's sweet clear voice and exuberant personality are what will carry the show.)

But should the musical remain in the big house? The thrust stage presents formidable problems for a choreographer, but Monette observes that because most musicals were written for a proscenium stage they have to be re-invented for the Festival stage, and he believes this is often a good thing. The *Fiddler* staging, which used a newly-constructed double revolve, offered brilliant images: the people of the *shtetl* danced in a circle that conveyed their in-looking togetherness; the easy transitions from kitchen to farmyard to synagogue using simple props also built a sense of a closely connected community; and the nightmare scene with the ghost seemingly flying out over the audience had a startling immediacy. And Carver, a brave, frail, concerned Tevye standing alone in the middle of the stage talking to his God or wrestling with his conscience was close enough that he could play on a human scale.

There are other considerations besides aesthetics. The musicians' union has decreed that the big theatre must have an orchestra of at least ten, the Avon at least five. Thus, a musical with a big orchestra requires extra musicians at the Avon, but they cannot be traded off against the Festival Theatre requirement; the big house must still hire ten musicians. The Avon with its proscenium stage requires more complicated sets than the Festival, adding to the cost. Finally, the Festival has sixty per cent more seats than the Avon. It is therefore necessary to do twice as many performances of a musical at the Avon in order to realize the same financial profit. But unless there is a huge presale, it is often easier to fill the Avon in the early weeks of the season, until word-of-mouth builds up. And it is increasingly difficult to find straight plays popular enough to fill the Avon. One can do *The Importance of Being Earnest* and *Private Lives* only so many times.

The idea of doing two musicals at the Avon has been tried and proven successful, notably in 1999 with *Dracula* and *West Side Story*. Both were relatively small-scale and had recognizable literary antecedents. There is some concern about undertaking a show that has no literary connections. So far the Festival has avoided *Grease* and *Fame.* But there is also a wariness about musicals that are too esoteric. Stephen Sondheim is an intellectual favourite but might prove to be box-office poison. Nevertheless, his name keeps cropping up. *Sweeney Todd* and *A Little Night Music* both have good tunes and solid books, and *Into the Woods* has family appeal. All three have a role that might provide a splendid showcase for the talents of Louise Pitre, whose rise to stardom in *Mamma Mia* should make her a real draw. She has expressed interest in working at Stratford, but will she be tied up on Broadway for the next year or two?

One advantage of doing two musicals at the Avon would be that a strong musical company could be cross-cast. This idea was advocated by Brian Macdonald and worked reasonably well in 1995 with *The Boy Friend* and *The Gondoliers*. But a musical company that is completely or even semi-independent of the main acting company can present problems of morale and division of authority. In any case two

267

Sondheim musicals would be too much, but Kurt Weill's *Threepenny Opera* might be revived for the first time since 1972. It has good roles for both Dale and Pitre and also Paul Gross. Wouldn't that be a knock-out?

Other possibilities for the 2002 season include an adaptation of a popular classical novel like the 1999 *Pride and Prejudice* or *The Three Musketeers* in 2000. These colourful costume dramas are considered family entertainment and have proved popular with audiences, although perhaps more with elderly ladies drawing on their fond memories of Ronald Coleman and Leslie Howard than computer-game addicted teenagers. A likely choice is *The Scarlet Pimpernel* in an adaptation penned some years ago by Maggie Smith's late husband Beverley Cross, with Jeannette Lambermont to direct and the cast to be drawn from the company: Donald Carrier as Sir Percy and Michelle Giroux as Marguerite, for example. Here is a show that can be substituted at the last moment for any one of the star-dependant Festival stage attractions that might fall through at the last minute.

At the Avon there are also a series of scripts that are more or less waiting in the wings. *The Government Inspector* was played with great comic gusto by William Hutt and later Richard McMillan, and there is now a new version by Michel Tremblay titled *The Guy from Quebec*. A vehicle for Michael Therriault, perhaps? Eduardo de Filippo's *Saturday, Sunday, Monday* or *The Art of Comedy* could prove as popular as *Filumena* in 1997, and they offer roles that might lure Monette back onstage. Another show Monette loves is *Auntie Mame.* I have suggested he might once again don a dress as he did in Tremblay's *Hosanna* and take on the title role himself, but a more likely candidate is Lally Cadeau. A role that Monette is seriously interested in playing is the great scientist in Brecht's masterpiece, *Galileo.*

At the Patterson there is the possibility of a revival of *Elizabeth Rex,* but will Brent Carver agree to come back to reprise his role as Ned Lowenscroft? Or is it possible that one of the other young actors in the company could do it? Paul Dunn, for instance. Another favourite is Tennessee Williams' early play *Summer and Smoke* or his later rewrite of the same material under the title *The Eccentricities of a Nightingale.* This would give an opportunity for Seana McKenna to illuminate another Williams heroine following up on her stunning portrayal of Hannah Jenks in *The Night of the Iguana.* There is also the possibility of a new script if any of the works commissioned from one of several Canadian playwrights actually gets written.

Such were some of Monette's musings in the fall of 2000. Once back in Stratford at the end of January 2001, Monette went into meetings with his literary and production staff and a short list of plays was drawn up. Production manager Douglas Lemcke consulted with his department heads in construction, costume, lighting, make-up, and props and with Libby Anderson in casting to cost the various shows. In some cases this is relatively easy because there exists a previous budget for, let us say, *Richard III,* last produced in 1988. Although costs have risen, the production concept will likely be similar to the earlier productions because the designer usually opts to sets this play in its own period (the late fifteenth century).

Other plays are less predictable. The 2001 production of *The Merchant of Venice* done on the main stage with virtually no set and in Renaissance clothes could not be based on the 1996 production at the Avon which had a large and complicated set but was done in modern dress. Therefore, this budgeting process is vital. The high estimated cost of a production will sometimes scupper the show. An example is Noel Coward's *Present Laughter*, which was scheduled for the Avon in 2001 until the estimates proved unwieldy and the smaller Coward piece *Private Lives* was substituted in its place. (Interestingly, the underfunded Soulpepper Company in Toronto then decided to do *Present Laughter* as part of its 2001 season.) Brian Bedford's Coward persona was easily shifted from one of the roles the Master wrote for himself to another (and, having played the role before, Bedford avoided having to learn another part). An opportunity was provided for Seana McKenna to take on Amanda, a fabulous role immortalized by a series of edgy comediennes—Gertrude Lawrence, Tallulah Bankhead, and Maggie Smith. McKenna commented, "Of course I should have done it ten years ago but I'm looking at it as a woman who has always been attracted to older men and suddenly decides to have a fling with someone much younger. I do sometimes wonder when I'm going to get to play my own age at Stratford."

When the projected program has been properly budgeted it is taken to the Board which has final approval. Gone are the days when board members rubber-stamped whatever was put in front of them. Several years ago, when she was a board member, the late Muriel Sherrin objected to *The Merchant of Venice* because she thought it was too offensive to the Festival's Jewish subscribers; the production was dropped at her insistence. (Monette's 2001 production, which featured a rigorously

269

honest and realistic performance of Shylock by Paul Soles, avoided protest from the Jewish community but the broadly comic performance of Rami Posner as the Prince of Morocco was seized upon by critic Kate Taylor as an example of racism. This alerted Muslim community leaders, who voiced vigorous objections. Monette, not wanting to share the fate of Salman Rushdie, moved rapidly to modify the actor's performance.) When the 2001 season was being put together, a Board member objected to the new Dan Needles piece *Wingfield on Ice* on the grounds that it was nothing but popular pap. Monette went to bat for it, pointing out that it was easy and inexpensive to produce, sure to sell out, and would appeal to a different group than most of the Festival's offerings, thus broadening Stratford's audience base. After a vigorous debate, Monette's arguments prevailed and *Wingfield on Ice* proved as popular as its predecessors.

The planning for the 2002 season was completely disrupted by the news that not only were the rights for *South Pacific* unavailable but also that the rights for many of the major musicals have been tied up by international promoters like Cameron Macintosh and the Mirvishes. Moreover, Tams-Witmark, the international agency that controls the copyright on these works, has upped the royalty percentage, effectively adding another million dollars to the cost of producing one of these works. The Festival has looked on its musical production as the cash cow whose endless stream of silvery milk floats all the less profitable shows of the season. Thus the implications of this new development for the Festival's financial well-being are profound.

However, in the case of *My Fair Lady*, the rights are split between the Lerner Loewe estate which controls productions in London and New York, and CBS which issued the original cast recording and which controls productions in all other territories. As a result, Stratford obtained permission to stage the show at the same time that there is a major revival running in London. Monette decided to go with *My Fair Lady*, in the big house, even though the increased royalties and the elaborate costumes would add over a million to the projected budget for the season. The 1988 production was possibly the most successful musical the Festival has ever done, and *My Fair Lady* is currently a huge hit in London where Trevor Nunn has revived it at the Royal National Theatre. It provides an excellent vehicle for Cynthia Dale and has two other wonderful roles. A search began for a starry actor to play Higgins, ranging from Alan Bates, who visited the Festival in 1967 when he played a highly engaging Richard III, to Eric McCormack, star of the TV sitcom *Will and Grace*, who played a number of minor roles at Stratford in the late 1980s and has recently played the lead in *The Music Man* on Broadway. Both actors have the crisp diction, comic sensibility, and magnetism to handle the role and both are keen to do stage work. Other names are bandied about: Victor Garber, Robert Sean Leonard, Michael York. The comic verve of both James Blendick and Peter Donaldson in the 2001 *Twelfth Night* suggest that either one would make a splendid Doolittle.

The high cost of the musical seems to have effectively eliminated *The Scarlet Pimpernel* with its elaborate Regency costumes and complicated settings, including a working guillotine. Instead, a search was begun to find a small-scale show to play in the Festival Theatre: *Hedda Gabbler,* perhaps, if a well-known actress could be engaged to play it. Seana McKenna has already done it and it really should be done by an actress in her mid-20s. Would there be any chance of attracting someone like Cate Blanchett, for instance? The other play that still seemed to be a possibility at the Festival was Molière's *Don Juan*. But by the time of the 2001 openings at the beginning of June, Monette had learned that neither Brent Carver nor Colm Feore would be available for a full season in 2002. Paul Gross is also unavailable. What about Tom McCamus?

Monette sets out to win and woo this popular actor who left Stratford at the end of the 1997 season. He decides to offer McCamus Richard III. In order to avoid invidious comparisons with the original Guthrie production, it is decided to do the play to open the newly renovated Avon. The connection with 1953 will be underlined by opening on the exact anniversary date, July 13. The play will be directed by Martha Henry, whose fine production of *Richard II* displayed her skill with Shakespeare's histories. Henry and McCamus have a long-time association strengthened by their joint participation in *Long Day's Journey Into Night*.

Anxious to find another suitable vehicle for McCamus, Monette jumps on the idea of *Don Juan* with McCamus's long-time buddy Stephen Ouimette playing the comic servant Sganarelle. These two actors were a brilliant team in *Waiting for Godot*. Molière's blend of philosophical observation and shrewd social comment seems

271

ideally suited to their talents. Having connected with Ouimette, Monette enters into discussions with him which lead to the notion of McCamus playing Macheath in *The Threepenny Opera*, with Ouimette functioning as director. Ouimette has directed a number of smaller scale productions but has preferred until now to exercise his formidable skills as an actor. An example of his comic acumen and the precise calculations that go into producing laughter is illustrated by a story told by the stage manager of a production of *The Comedy of Errors* in 1994 in which Ouimette and McCamus played the Dromio twins. At the end of the play, Adriana goes off to give birth and the two servants are left on stage. Richard Rose, the director, had the bright idea that as the play revolves around two pairs of twins, this final birth should bring forth another set of twins. The technical rehearsal was running late when it came to setting the final cues. Ouimette took charge. "Tom and I are downstage centre. We hear the first cry. We do a take. Then we hear the second cry. We do a double take. Blackout." It gave the show a fine finish and cued enthusiastic applause night after night.

Along with these two strong shows, contrast will be provided at the Avon by de Filippo's comedy *Saturday, Sunday, Monday*. It seems likely that Lally Cadeau will do it again, but Monette's participation is more problematic. William Carden, who staged *Who's Afraid of Virginia Woolf?*, is willing to direct. Having failed to persuade Susan H. Schulman the new York-based director of *Fiddler on the Roof* to return to direct the mainstage musical, Monette will take on *My Fair Lady* himself, in addition to *All's Well That Ends Well* and the initial production in the new Fourth Space.

At the Patterson, plans are proceeding for a two-part *Henry VI* to be directed by Michael Pennington. The experienced British director has long expressed an interest in working at Stratford, and this time the dates coincide. He has done the show before and has worked successfully with North American actors. In contrast, the other Patterson shows will be modern. Tennessee Williams' *The Eccentricities of a Nightingale* will feature Seana McKenna and be directed by her husband Miles Potter. Canadian writer Michael Ondaatje's *Coming Through Slaughter* revolves around the career of the great New Orleans jazz trumpeter Billy Bolden. (Louis Armstrong was fond of saying that Billy Bolden taught him everything he knew, until someone checked the dates and discovered that the year Bolden died, Armstrong was only four years old.) Premiered over a decade ago at Toronto's

Horseshoe Tavern, this richly poetic script should make good use of director Richard Rose's capacity for imagistic invention and his sharp ear for heightened contemporary idiom.

The success of Monette's young actors in 2001 has encouraged him to do *Romeo and Juliet* on the Festival stage, a play that never fails to draw an audience and has a strong appeal to young people. It will feature Graham Abbey and Claire Julien as the doomed lovers, while Jonathan Goad will follow up his headlong impetuosity as Hotspur in *Henry IV, Part I* with an undoubtedly freewheeling and vigorous Mercutio. Monette decides to invite Michael Langham to direct the new version of *Romeo*, one of his greatest early successes at the Festival. Langham accepts, then phones from England to report that his wife Helen Burns is ailing and he must look after her. This opens up the possibility of engaging Leon Rubin, who worked with the Young Company at the Third Stage directing *A Comedy of Errors* and *Waiting for Godot* in 1984 and who has since had a successful career directing both Shakespeare and Dickens at the RSC as well as historical pageants in Thailand. Rubin flies in from Bangkok and agrees to take on all of *Henry VI* instead of *Romeo.* This is a more difficult piece to stage and cast; Rubin watches one half of six different shows and, working closely with Monette, chooses a cast made up entirely of actors in the current company before he leaves town thirty-six hours later. Monette's decision to bring in outside directors in this anniversary season is a deliberate effort to provide a fresh stimulus to challenge his young actors. Having concentrated for the past eight seasons on developing a stable of Canadian directors, he feels it is time to "shake things up a bit." He is resigned to the fact that whether he features Canadians or imported directors he will be criticized for not doing the opposite.

But the big coup in directorial terms for 2002 is landing Jonathan Miller. The celebrated British director has agreed to direct a late-opening show starring Christopher Plummer. Initially they proposed a production of Ben Jonson's *Volpone* at the Avon, but after considerable soul-searching they decided to go for the gold and give us Plummer as King Lear on the Festival stage. The cream of Stratford's acting company will be available for this production, but probably some outside actors will be brought in. One possibility to be explored is an invitation to Tony-winning actor Richard Easton. His highly acclaimed performance in Tom Stoppard's *The Invention*

273

of Love on Broadway will not tie him up; the show has already closed. Easton was a member of the original 1953 company and would be an ideal choice to play Gloucester. This *King Lear* will be a Stratford production, but if it is well received there is a distinct possibility it could travel to London or New York.

By the end of June 2001 the season for 2002 has pretty well come together, although there is a sudden panic when it seems likely that the Mirvishes might import the London production of *My Fair Lady* to play at the Canon Theatre (the former Pantages) in Toronto. (They later decide to do Andrew Lloyd Webber's *The Beautiful Game* instead.) Then William Carden discovers that he cannot direct the de Filippo because of a previous commitment. Monette decides the Italian comedy is not a strong enough draw to fill the Avon and that the season really needs a family show. The favourite replacement is a scaled-down version of *The Scarlet Pimpernel* or *The Prisoner of Zenda*. Either show will provide a good vehicle for Peter Donaldson, who has emerged as one of the strongest players in the 2001 season. In the end Donaldson agrees to Sir Percy in *Pimpernel* and Peachum in *The Beggar's Opera*, a nicely contrasting pair of roles, and will also be in the cast of *The Mandrake*, Monette's inaugural production at the new Fourth Space. This means that James Blendick will almost certainly be Doolittle in *My Fair Lady*.

In early August a leak to the press is picked up by reporters who take delight in speculating on the casting for Higgins in *My Fair Lady*. It is rumoured that Colm Feore will agree to play the role in the first half of the season, partly because his wife Donna will choreograph. But his acceptance is conditional on the Festival meeting several demands, one of which is that the role be taken over by a player of equal stature to his own. This leads to the wooing of Paul Gross, whose picture appears on the front page of the *Toronto Star* as a potential Higgins for the second half of the season. The extensive publicity, usually reserved for foreign movie stars, is a boon for both actors and for the Festival itself. And for Cynthia Dale too, who gets into the act when she is interviewed by Richard Ouzounian and suggests that Monette himself may play Higgins after Feore's departure. Pressure for Monette to return to the boards appears to be escalating.

Slowly, slowly through the summer the pieces are falling into place. Monette remains extremely anxious about the participation of Plummer. He and Miller have committed themselves but some spectacular offer may lure them away anytime in the next twelve months. The process of cross-casting begins. This is complicated and involves establishing which shows play against each other. For example, *Richard III* will play at the Avon at the same time that *Romeo and Juliet* plays at the Festival and *Coming Through Slaughter* plays at the Patterson. Any actor who is in one of these shows cannot be cast in either of the other two. Most actors will play three roles; the working out of the minor casting is diabolically complicated.

Then came the shocking events of September 11 in New York and Washington, and it was decided that the season had to be drastically cut back. With the prospect of war, recession and decreased American patronage, several plays will have to be abandoned.

Monette will spend many hours a day scheming, juggling, cajoling, stroking. The Board has passed his projected season but the dance goes on, and will do throughout the summer and into the fall and probably the early winter. Offers will be made to actors and directors, some soon, some not until late in the season and invariably some offers will be turned down, frequently by a member of the company Monette was sure he could count on. Every week brings fresh surprises, new brainwaves, mini-crises, unforeseen catastrophes, sudden capitulations. That's the fun of it.

WAITING FOR GODOT · 1968

Director: *William Hutt*

Designer: *Brian Jackson*

WAITING FOR GODOT · 1996/98

Director: *Brian Bedford*

Designer: *Ming Cho Lee*

WAITING FOR GODOT

The most critically acclaimed play of the twentieth century in the English language. (Though it was originally written in French.) This is an actors' play, brilliantly theatrical, drawing on the performance skills of vaudevillians and clowns. It is a poem, rhythmic, cyclical, full of proliferating images, hoary wheezes, jagged japes, and recurring internal symmetries. It is both heartbreaking and hilarious, a bittersweet burlesque, a nostalgic nosegay of ancient quips and worn-out quibbles.

1996: Stephen Ouimette as Estragon, Tom McCamus as Vladimir

1996: Tom McCamus and
Stephen Ouimette

*B*oth of Stratford's major productions have been directed
by consummate actors,
William Hutt and Brian Bedford, the
most accomplished and inventive
comedians in the Festival's fifty-year
history. Both of their productions
were soaked in the brine of seasoned
clownery. They instinctively understand the timing and precision
required to bring off the outrageous
jest, the spontaneous riposte, the
antic shenanigans, the slightly
melancholy afterglow that follows a
truly preposterous bit of buffoonery.
Both productions offered sparse,
isolated figures in an empty space as
the text demands. Bedford's designer
Ming Cho Lee had the inspired idea
of setting the play in an abandoned
theatre; its crimson curtains and
tarnished gilt justified the theatricality of the actors who introduced
snatches of old routines, crowned by
Tom McCamus' song at the top of
the second act.

1968: Powys Thomas as Vladimir,
Eric Donkin as Estragon

Both Hutt and Bedford were blessed with skilled actors. In 1968, Hutt made use of two performers new to Stratford, following his natural bent for encouraging young talent. James Blendick and Eric Donkin, each of whom would become a major fixture at the Festival. Blendick proved to be a natural Pozzo with his vibrant baritone, the weight both physical and magisterial of his presence, his implacable authority. He would reprise the role 28 years later in Bedford's production, adding a sonorous maturity to his earlier interpretation and proving that this play and its characters stand outside time.

The two protagonists, Vladimir and Estragon, are individuated and yet complementary: non-identical twins, ego and id, heads and tails. In Hutt's production, Powys Thomas was an imposing and extravagant Vladimir, but it was the delicacy of Eric Donkin's Estragon, peevish, cowardly, then suddenly vicious, that provided the quicksilver changes that propelled the drama through its labyrinthine turns and twists.

Bedford was blessed with the team of Tom McCamus and Stephen Ouimette. Close friends since their schooldays who share a pervasive and freewheeling sense of fun that spills over into everything they do, they brought a natural affinity to these inter-connecting roles. (Interestingly enough, as apprentice actors they were both protégés of Hutt, who gave them major opportunities when he was artistic director at Theatre London in the 1970s.)

Again it was McCamus as Vladimir who was extroverted, provocative, and challenging, Ouimette's Estragon who took it on the chin, plunged into self-pity, then suddenly hit out with a stinging retort. The byplay between these two sensitive and imaginative actors allowed them to shift gears from performance to performance, re-inventing the play each night but never letting it push out of shape.

The fourth role, Lucky, is a tour de force, with its nonsensical but curiously moving monologue. In 1968, Hutt boldly cast a mime, Adrian Pecknold, in the role, who devised a wonderful physical counterpoint to match his wild rant. Bedford's choice, Tim MacDonald, was more centred, providing the necessary vocal timbre to complete the quartet.

The theatre of the absurd has come and gone, yet this play remains a monument to its vision, which in the middle of the twentieth century freed drama from its superficial concern with the surfaces of life. Beckett's heirs include Pinter and Stoppard, Albee, Shepard, and Mamet. Significantly, Beckett is the only name these major writers all cite as an influence and the only one for whom they all profess unreserved admiration.

1996: Tom McCamus as Vladimir, James Blendick as Pozzo, Tim MacDonald as Lucky, Stephen Ouimette as Estragon

WHOSE SHOW IS IT ANYWAY?

ON THE VERY FIRST OPENING NIGHT IN 1953 the applause was deafening, rapturous, endless. The bows went on and on. Finally, Alec Guinness took charge of the situation. Stepping out alone on the Festival stage, he held up his hand for silence and said, "I want to pay tribute to the only man who could make this possible." Dramatic pause. "William Shakespeare." The crowd went wild.

Fifty years later, Stratford is still dominated by Shakespeare, although his name has been dropped from the Festival's title. Every year, programming starts with the choice of at least three of the plays in the canon and the season is built around them. But over the five decades of Stratford's existence the perception of Shakespeare has changed radically. For most theatregoers in the 1950s, *All's Well That Ends Well* and *Timon of Athens* were virtually unknown, and even *Two Gentlemen of Verona*, *Othello*, and *Antony and Cleopatra* were rarities. Nowadays enthusiasts have seen all of these, and many of us have seen some of them many times. I love *Twelfth Night* and know almost every word of it (I have played in it and directed it twice). But I feel that I don't want to see it again unless it is wonderfully realized, just as I don't care to hear a pedestrian performance of Mozart's *Eine Kleine Nachtmusik*.

Over-familiarity with Shakespeare is not confined to the audience at Stratford. The Royal Shakespeare Company and the Royal National Theatre of Great Britain are experiencing the same phenomenon. Charles Spencer, reviewing the 1998 RSC season in *The Daily Telegraph*, wrote, "Is the RSC bored with Shakespeare?... once again the Shakespeare productions range from the inadequate to the disgraceful." Michael Billington in *The Guardian* observed, "[RSC] productions exist only because of the mechanical demands of the system: the factory has to be kept ticking over."

Is the Festival in a similar rut? Over a twenty-year period, the six most popular Shakespeare plays have been given five productions each at Stratford. All of these plays are comedies, with the single exception of *Macbeth*, possibly the most studied literary text in our high schools. But these plays still sell. Shakespeare may have diminishing box office clout in his native Britain, but in Canada his plays continue to sell better than any other productions except the main stage musicals, however much the critics carp and cavil.

Canadian regional theatres (probably following the example of their American counterparts) have stopped producing Shakespeare as the essential "classical" component in their subscription seasons. On the other hand, there are over 100 Shakespeare festivals of varying size operating in North America. The Bard is known to an ever-widening public even if the cognoscenti have become jaded. While the critics crave novelty and innovation, the larger public seems to want something they know about. They expect Stratford to keep on serving up Shakespeare. His works will continue to be the central element at the Festival in any foreseeable future. The problem is how to make them fresh, exciting, and stimulating for both the grandees and the groundlings.

The world of cinema suggests possibilities. The success of Kenneth Branagh's Shakespearean films, from his gritty, sweat-stained *Henry V* to his gracefully lyrical *Much Ado About Nothing*, Baz Luhrman's funky contemporary *Romeo and Juliet* starring Claire Daines and Leonardo di Caprio, and the swashbuckling *Shakespeare in Love*, studded with Stoppard's memorable aphorisms, indicate that Shakespeare is alive and well and his audience is growing. But this public looks for a fresh take on his work and the movies seem to be well ahead of the legitimate theatre in providing it. They have the technical capacity to move through time and space and the financial resources to line up star power.

Shakespeare alone cannot keep a theatre vital and engaging to an audience; there is another very important component: actors who are bright, inventive, and boldly adventurous, even if they are not recognizable international stars. A company like Stratford cannot hope to meet the financial demands of a Gwyneth Paltrow (though she did play Rosalind for a few sold-out weeks in Williamstown, Massachusetts two seasons ago) or a Kevin Spacey (though Keanu Reeves played *Hamlet* in Winnipeg; it sold out in advance and Reeves evidently gave a very credible performance). Paul Gross's *Hamlet* in 2000 was a similar risk-taking experiment (though Gross has had considerable stage experience in addition to his TV stardom) and it paid similar box-office dividends.

There are some stars who long to take a crack at the big Shakespearean roles, but

281

these parts require actors who have vocal technique as well as personal charisma. Many film actors lack the vocal chops, as Stratford discovered early on when James Mason was invited to play Oedipus and Angelo. Many of Stratford's finest productions have featured actors who were not film stars (or at least not yet). Colm Feore, Tom McCamus, and Stephen Ouimette are three such actors who come to mind, though none has appeared at Stratford for several seasons.

Feore is that rare thing, a leading man who is lucid, energetic, sharp-witted, and sexy. In his golden decade he played a surprisingly sympathetic Petruchio, a deliciously calculating Iago, a roistering, rollicking Pirate King, and an extravagant, biting Cyrano, as well as Hamlet, Richard III, Romeo, Mercutio, Cassius, Leontes, and a gaggle of young Restoration and Elizabethan gallants. Ouimette is that equally rare animal, an original comic who is able to draw on a deep well of emotion. He was a troubled, introspective Hamlet, a wonderfully silly Sir Andrew Aguecheek, a gauche, boastful Mozart in *Amadeus*, and an anguished, self-deprecating Estragon in *Waiting for Godot*. McCamus is closer to a leading man in appearance, his sensitive face and boyishly thoughtful air undercut by a wild streak of comic irreverence. His performance as the bruised but tenacious Edmund in *Long Day's Journey into Night*, his bright-eyed, rueful King Arthur in *Camelot*, and his manic, extravagant Vladimir in *Waiting for Godot* give an indication of his range and flexibility. These actors have served valiantly on the Stratford's stages, but have arrived at a point in their careers where they are not willing to commit themselves year after year. Now too old to reprise Romeo and Hamlet, too young for Lear or Prospero, they find other outlets in shorter runs or in the more lucrative world of film.

Brent Carver has also made a major impact at Stratford, playing such varied roles as Hamlet, Edmund Tyrone, the Pirate King, and the Master of Ceremonies in *Cabaret* with style and verve, before his acclaimed appearances as Tevye in *Fiddler on the Roof* and the actor Ned Lowenscroft in *Elizabeth Rex* in the 2000 season. Slight and ethereal with the kind of boyish good looks that call to mind Leslie Howard or Leonardo di Caprio and a voice of great sweetness that he uses to evoke a vast range of subtle nuance, Carver always commands the interest and sympathy of an audience, whether he is playing a doomed hero or a shameless extrovert. Although he has been assiduously wooed almost every year for both musical and dramatic roles, he usually prefers to play the field in Toronto and New York. These four actors have made a huge contribution to the Festival but not a lifelong commitment. Probably this will be the pattern in the future.

Stratford is the poorer without these players, but others will replace them because they must if the Festival is to go on. In 2001, Peter Donaldson returned to the fold. Never an obvious leading man, Donaldson has developed strength, assurance, and a deft sense of comedy. His Petruchio in 1997 was a model of sanity and patient forbearance. Some of the same phlegmatic quality informs his masterfully underplayed and edgily witty George in *Who's Afraid of Virginia Woolf?*, which contrasts vividly with the colossal insensitivity and self-regard of his Malvolio and the bored, easygoing opportunism of his Trigorin in *The Seagull*. Also highly distinctive is the work of Richard McMillan, who left the showy role of Scar in *The Lion King* in Toronto to give us a splendidly self-important and befuddled Hector Mackilwraith in *Tempest-Tost* and an impressively imposing and astute Worcester in *Henry IV*. The 2001 season also offers an example of a surprise star-turn from an unexpected quarter. Paul Soles, an actor in his 70s never before seen at Stratford, called to step into the shoes of Al Waxman following his sudden death in December 2000, turns in an honest, finely honed, and highly moving performance as Shylock.

"Stars, they come and go," the song has it, but Stratford has depended through the years on a phalanx of core actors, some of them now gone, who have stayed the course and given a huge portion of their lives to it. Several names come to mind: Edward Atienza, Wayne Best, Mervyn Blake, Domini Blythe, Barbara Bryne, Douglas Chamberlain, Patricia Collins, Patrick Crean, Keith Dinicol, Eric Donkin, Pat Galloway, Lewis Gordon, Amelia Hall, Max Helpmann, Roland Hewgill, Bernard Hopkins, Eric House, Barry MacGregor, Marti Maraden, William Needles, Nicholas Pennell, Leon Pownall, Mary Savidge, Alan Scarfe, Joseph Shaw, Powys Thomas, Brian Tree, Tony van Bridge, Kenneth Welsh, Susan Wright. They have not always played great roles but they have provided a matrix, a community of artists that makes a high standard of performance possible.

These players have gained in stature and technique through experience and at the same time illuminated the plays in which they have appeared. Each has natural assets and acquired skills, preferences and prejudices, individual practices, habits, and quirks. It is on these talents with all their idiosyncrasies that the Festival's most memorable productions have been built. It is not possible to profile them all, but a

283

handful of rapidly sketched portraits of major long-term players may indicate their pivotal importance to Stratford.

Douglas Campbell has been a powerful force since he first stepped out on stage as the boastful, seedy hanger-on Parolles in *All's Well That Ends Well* in 1953. He has played all the big tragic roles save Hamlet, most memorably his sonorous masked Oedipus in Guthrie's 1955 production. But it is as Shakespeare's clowns that he has made his greatest mark: Pistol, Sir Toby Belch, Touchstone, and his fourth Falstaff in both parts of *Henry IV* in 2001. This wily, self-seeking old rascal, manipulative, fun-loving, larger than life, exposing in the end the pathetic vulnerability of a libertine in old age, makes use of all Campbell's resources. He has played a wide range of other comic roles with admirable dexterity, including the ambitious, lovestruck peasant Lopakhin in *The Cherry Orchard,* the gullible, good-hearted Orgon in *Tartuffe*, and the preposterous, prancing Don Alhambra in *The Gondoliers.*

Campbell is himself larger than life, a walking, orating compendium of twentieth-century theatre, linked through his parents-in-law Sibyl Thorndike and Lewis Casson to the grand old traditions of the British stage and through his rocker son Torquil to the pop music of the twenty-first century. Campbell can quote Shakespeare by the ream, choreograph a sword fight or a morris dance, direct any play the Bard has penned, prompting young actors without hesitation and without book. Stratford would be a poorer place without his ongoing presence and participation, though he has been known to say that the Festival should be allowed to die quietly. It is this maverick side of Campbell, the grandiloquent socialist and red-blooded vegetarian, that gives edge and a quality of surprise to his work, even after fifty years.

Following in Campbell's footsteps, onstage if not off, is James Blendick, whose sinister presence as Pozzo in *Waiting for Godot* contrasted with the sprightly comic invention of his Toby Belch in *Twelfth Night*. He has played a number of heavies, including a tough-talking Big Daddy in *Cat on a Hot Tin Roof,* an ingenuously stubborn Lopakhin in *The Cherry Orchard*, a fatuous Sir Epicure Mammon in *The Alchemist*, and a slyly opportunistic Falstaff in *The Merry Wives of Windsor*, capped by the charming, eloquent, self-important lawyer and politician Matthew Brady in *Inherit the Wind* in 2001.

Martha Henry began her forty-year association with the Festival in 1962 as Lady Macduff. The intense young woman who combined integrity and grace, passion and intelligence played many of Shakespeare's young heroines in the next decade: a winning but rather vacant Cressida, a wise and rueful Viola, a brave and clear-eyed Cordelia, a sexy and willful Titania, as well as the clever and elegant Elmire in *Tartuffe* and the wicked Milady de Winter in *The Three Musketeers*. She was one of the brightest fixtures in the firmament of Robin Phillips, who helped her explore new emotional depths as she portrayed two of Shakespeare's most complex heroines: Isabella in *Measure for Measure* and Helena in *All's Well that Ends Well* alongside Elizabeth Proctor in *The Crucible,* Hecuba in Edward Bond's *The Woman* and Olga in *The Three Sisters.* Unlike many actresses whose charm and fragility make them admirably suited to the youthful heroines but who cannot encompass the greater vocal and emotional demands of mature roles, Martha Henry made the transition and emerged with an extended range in both capacities.

Proud and principled, Martha Henry left Stratford with the other members of the Gang of Four in 1980, declaring she would not come back until an apology had been made. In the next fourteen years she would work with Phillips, make several films, begin to direct, and become artistic director of the Grand Theatre in London. She returned to Stratford with a stunningly vivid and moving performance as Mary Tyrone in *Long Day's Journey into Night* in 1994, followed up by an equally moving depiction of the knowing, half-mad wife in *The Stillborn Lover*, and the grandiose drug-addled Princess in *Sweet Bird of Youth*. In the 1998 season she portrayed the scheming matchmaker Frosine in *The Miser*, and a sharp, vehement Beatrice in *Much Ado About Nothing*. In 2001 she took on the roles of the cantankerous, wise-cracking Martha in *Who's Afraid of Virginia Woolf?* and the vain egotistical actress Arkadina in *The Seagull*, rounding out her gallery of Chekhov heroines. To this staggering range of roles must be added her directorial projects: a clear, economical, skillfully staged *Richard II* and her triumphant interpretation of *Elizabeth Rex*.

William Hutt and Douglas Rain, both members of the original company in 1953, quickly emerged as major players. Hutt was extravagantly grand with a natural bent for comedy, and his Jacques, Pandarus, and Sparkish were wonderfully original creations topped by Khlestakov in *The Government Inspector* in 1967, the apotheosis of vanity and pretension. Hutt would achieve richly inventive comic performances as Sir Epicure Mammon, Volpone, Tartuffe, Argan, and even Lady Bracknell, an inspired bit of casting from Robin Phillips, who insisted that Hutt probe his emotional understanding even of comic roles. His Fool in Phillips' *King Lear* evoked great pathos and laid the foundation for his mature performances of Lear and Prospero, which wonderfully employed his unique comic gifts to give edge and humanity to these troubled tyrants.

Hutt has also directed many productions, beginning with *Waiting For Godot* in 1968 and including *The Tempest* in 1976, in which he played his first Prospero. He has been a deeply caring mentor to many youthful actors from Pamela Brook to Michael Therriault and he is now recognized as both the Grand Old Man and the Eminence Rouge, often consulted by Monette on matters of repertoire and casting. Recently he expressed his appreciation of his two most respected directors. "Robin compels you to do your best. Richard *allows* you to do your best. The freedom is tremendous."

Douglas Rain is a very different kind of actor: precise, private and somewhat flinty. At his least effective in roles that require innate charisma, he is nevertheless a master of timing and has given brilliantly comic performances as Malvolio, Dromio of Syracuse, Monsieur Jourdain, Bottom, Orgon, Polonius, and Humpty Dumpty. But it is his intensely introverted portraits that were most memorable as he depicted the proud decline of Cardinal Wolsey, the overbearing misjudgement of King John, the tortured lust of the repressed Angelo, the sharp-tongued integrity of Gloucester, the spiky rigour of the betrayed Shylock, the dry down-home wisdom of the Stage Manager in *Our Town*, the unbudging conviction of Sir Thomas More in *A Man for All Seasons*. Never much open to experiment or collaboration Rain has become increasingly remote and solitary. He has been absent from the Festival for several seasons and indeed seems in danger of disappearing into his own idiosyncrasy.

Seana McKenna and Lucy Peacock appeared on the Stratford scene at about the same time and quickly made their mark, Lucy for her refined wit and natural charm, Seana for her blazing intelligence and quicksilver emotional responses. Both women rapidly found themselves playing leading roles. Lucy has been a gentle, bewildered Ophelia, a searching clear-eyed Nora in Ingmar Bergman's updating of Ibsen's *The Doll's House*, a determined and forceful Helena in *All's Well That Ends Well*, a regally sensuous Titania, and a forthright vulnerable Rosalind. The combination of inner strength and outward openness makes her a highly sympathetic and attractive presence in all these roles. Her innate breeding and athletic grace (she is an expert horsewoman) give her work a combination of suppleness and aristocratic distinction that perfectly suits Shakespeare's young heroines, especially in "trouser" roles. Her natural beauty transcends stylishness and reinforces her air of innate spontaneity. Always game for whatever theatrical adventure offers itself, she seems completely at ease. "Maybe I should be ambitious to work in London or the movies, but I've been given every opportunity I could dream of right here. Why go looking for what you've already got?"

Seana McKenna moved from a bright and winning Diana in *All's Well That Ends Well* to offer an impetuous Juliet, a pert Kate Hardcastle, a sharp-tongued, adventurous Viola, and a volatile, knowing Portia. If Martha Henry is the *prima attrice assoluta* of Stratford, these two actresses are now the leading ladies of the company. Lucy Peacock is still playing roles like Portia and Rosalind with sparkling humour, but her wise and confident Elmire in *Tartuffe* in 2000 gave an indication of what her mature work could be. Seana McKenna has moved on to give us a wickedly malicious Lady Sneerwell, a high-minded, courageous Hannah in *Night of the Iguana,* a deeply damaged and powerfully vindictive Medea, a razor-tongued, impossibly inconsistent Amanda in *Private Lives,* and a brave, confused invalid in *Good Mother.*

Brian Bedford came to the Festival in Robin Phillips' first season and played a hugely self-satisfied Malvolio and a chill, calculating Angelo in *Measure for Measure.* He admirably partnered Maggie Smith in *Private Lives* and *The Guardsman* and was a gleefully treacherous Richard III, a sardonic Jacques, and a Benedick who was at once-self-absorbed and self-doubting. He remained after Phillips' departure and went on to create a despicably slimy Tartuffe, a jovial, self-satisfied Bottom, a crabbed, cantankerous Shylock, a deliciously effete Lord Foppington, a perplexed, self-deceiving Arnolphe in *The School for Wives,* and a befuddled, infatuated Sir Peter Teazle in *The School for Scandal.*

Bedford's directorial debut was the Festival's first production of the brutal early tragedy *Titus Andronicus* in 1978, which he followed with productions of *Coriolanus, Othello,* and Racine's *Phaedra.* A highly gifted comedian, he once told Monette, "I can't direct comedy, and you can't direct tragedy." He proved himself wrong with his exquisitely modulated bittersweet production of *Waiting for Godot* in 1996. In 2001 he took Monette's production of *The School for Scandal* and redirected it on a proscenium stage in Chicago that played to enthusiastic houses. Astute and highly disciplined, Bedford is able to establish an instant rapport with an audience. He has skillfully used Stratford as a testing ground for his talents, playing roles he originated there in various American cities from Los Angeles to New York.

This list is inevitably incomplete but is intended to illustrate the central importance of actors in the life of the Festival. All of these players maintain homes in Stratford or the surrounding countryside and their presence influences the planning and daily life of the organization. They meet in the green-room, the bars, the supermarkets, the streets, at small private parties, and large social functions. They have their fans, their friends, and sometimes their feuds. They have given, in Monette's words, "of their lives and their art" to the Festival, and he believes that the Festival in return has an obligation to them. He builds his repertory around them as did his predecessors, choosing plays to showcase their talents and avoiding scripts that cannot be cast from the available actors. If you don't have a Cleopatra or a Falstaff, you don't do the plays they dominate.

But you also need an ongoing stream of young actors to play Hamlet, Viola, Romeo, Eliza Doolittle, Joseph Surface, Hedda Gabler, Cyrano. We have seen these roles played by people who were patently too old. If they are wonderfully skilled, we suspend our disbelief, but grudgingly. "Young actors right out of school think they know it all, but the fact is they don't know what they don't know. Maybe after ten years here they'll come to realize this," comments Colm Feore. But young actors bring their own assets: energy, innocence, boldness, a willingness to question and experiment. And they have a physical appeal that often they themselves don't fully understand.

In the mid-1990s there was a danger that Stratford would continue to be dominated by its senior actors who seemed determined to go on forever. The key production was Monette's "geriatric" *Much Ado About Nothing* in 1998, which went to New York. Casting Martha Henry as Beatrice and Brian Bedford as Benedick seemed like a bright idea and brought certain benefits. These mature, highly skilled performers fenced with delicate skill, while William Hutt stole one scene out from under them with his brilliant evocation of Leonato as a tipsy old bon vivant. But the show was lambasted by the *New York Times* critic who panned Stratford for showing tired old warhorses instead of something new and vital. Peter Donaldson has said, "I thought then if they're going to go on casting senior people in those roles, I'm out of here.

This is my time as a mature actor and I have to make the most of it. I came back when they offered me good roles I'm the right age to play." Seana McKenna echoed this sentiment: "Of course I couldn't pass up the chance to play Amanda even though she should be in her thirties. But I wonder am I going to be playing Ranevskaya and Cleopatra in my sixties?"

Perhaps not coincidentally, Monette set up his Conservatory the next year and its graduates were given a chance to strut their stuff in the 2001 season. Leading the parade is Graham Abbey, who had given an impetuous, agile D'Artagnan in *The Three Musketeers* and a languid, implacably self-centred Algernon in *The Importance of Being Earnest* in the 2000 season. Then came his forceful, hard-driving, and charismatic Prince Hal in *Henry IV*, *Falstaff*, and *Henry V*. Originally a student of political science, Abbey has put this early training to good use. "I didn't foresee I was going to be a king instead of prime minister," he jokes with a grin at once assured and self-deprecating, a combination that suggests his potential not just as a leading man but as a star.

Other young actors who have demonstrated their abilities in recent seasons are Paul Dunn, Jonathan Goad, Michael Therriault, and Nicolas Van Burek. Dunn followed up his debut as the young Glenn Gould with a sensitive boy actor in *Elizabeth Rex*, a deadpan comic performance as Launcelot Gobbo in *The Merchant of Venice*, and an intriguing combination of innocence and knowingness as the Boy in *Henry V*. Goad has given us a rash, intemperate Hotspur in *Henry IV*, a hilarious rustic *in Falstaff* and a smoothly charming cad in *Tempest-Tost*. Therriault gained notice as the spoiled, vindictive brat Mordred in *Camelot*, followed by an energetic, nervy young lover in *The Miser*, a spirited Ariel in *The Tempest*, a down-trodden but determined Mottel in *Fiddler on the Roof*, and an extravagantly foolish Sir Andrew Aguecheek in *Twelfth Night*. Van Burek first appeared at Stratford as the troubled, introverted teen-ager in *Equus* and followed this up with a coolly rational Malcolm in *Macbeth*, a sincere, concerned Peter in *The Diary of Anne Frank*, an outspoken Gratiano in *The Merchant of Venice*, and a passionate Sebastian in *Twelfth Night*.

These lively young bucks are matched by spirited damsels. Claire Julien's sweet simplicity as Miranda in *The Tempest* contrasted with her decidedly more sophisticated and quick-tongued Cecily in *The Importance of Being Earnest* and her ditsy, tipsy Honey in *Who's Afraid of Virginia Woolf?* Tara Rosling, making her debut in the

289

Whose Show Is It Anyway?

2001 season weighed in as both a sharp-tongued, perceptive Viola in *Twelfth Night* and a touchingly pathetic Pearl Vambrace in *Tempest-Tost*. Michelle Giroux has shown a particular aptitude for willful, witty, and elegant young women in her portrayals of Lady Teazle in *The School for Scandal*, Gwendolyn in *The Importance of Being Earnest*, and Olivia in *Twelfth Night*. "The chance to work with other young actors and at the same incredibly skilled and experienced players is fantastic," she says. "You absorb so much and at the same time you're out there doing it on that incredible stage. It's work and it's a dream and it's a whole life."

All of these young players have had the advantage of Conservatory training and are a testament to its value. They have been given not only experience but exposure in Stratford's recent publicity campaigns. They owe much to the mentorship of the directors they have worked with, in particular Monette himself, and he takes great care to select directors with whom his actors are comfortable or at least compatible. These relationships are defined mainly in private conversations between artistic director and actors. But there can be difficulties. A visiting actor may agree to do a role and then find a week into rehearsal that he cannot work with a certain director. On occasion this has meant that a director will be replaced or the artistic director will go in and supervise rehearsals, but these extreme measures are rare.

There are, however, situations where a director and an actor are engaged in a prolonged and pitched battle. It may seem that the director should be the victor, but it is the actor who goes out on stage every night and gives the performance. Many a director has revisited his show two or three months into a run and been astonished to find it substantially altered. Whether the results are an improvement is not always easy for him to judge. It is not given to every artist to possess a high degree of objectivity about his work.

Good actors want to work with good directors who will provide fresh stimulus, make unforeseen demands, set wider challenges. One of the reasons actors decide to leave after a certain number of seasons is that they feel they have become too secure, that their work is stale, flat, and unprofitable, not financially but in terms of artistic growth. The dynamic between actor and director is constantly changing and, as in a marriage, sometimes the relationship sours or enters the doldrums and the conviction grows that it is time to sever the connection. This can be painful. But as Douglas Campbell observes, "the actor's profession calls for commitment, a sense of adventure

Romancing the Bard

and a willingness to move on. It is not about security or comfort."

The actor's commitment to any institution must be balanced against his commitment to his own art and talent. And so any company has an evolving centre, a core that continues but constantly changes and renews itself. Direction and script are important to theatre, but in the end it is the acting that matters most. You can have a theatre without design, without music, without direction, even without a text, but you cannot have a theatre without actors. When all is said and done, Stratford belongs to the actors. It cannot be any other way.

Nicolas Van Burek as Sebastian,
Michelle Giroux as Olivia

Tara Rosling as Viola, Sean Arbuckle as Orsino

This exquisitely intricate fable provides the pattern for the great comedies of manners and social observation that have evolved throughout the four centuries since it was first penned by Shakespeare. It provides a paradigm where Molière meets Chekhov and Wilde joins hands with Anouilh and de Filippo. Not surprisingly, *Twelfth Night* has been the most often produced of Shakespeare's comedies at the Stratford Festival. Antoni Cimolino's 2001 production offers not only some welcome originality but also grace, comic invention, and happy symmetries.

Director: **Antoni Cimolino**

Designers: **Peter Hartwell, Francesca Callow**

The opening sequence with Orsino drunk and violent in his wild protestation of love is set against the ordeal of Viola cast up on an alien shore and sets a tone of barely governed passion that will sharply underscore the lyrical and verbal dexterity in the scenes that follow. The production's evocation of early twentieth-century Greece offers a juxtaposition of provincial elegance and controlling morality. In this rather rigid milieu the action begins to unfold and the stage is set for the riot of misrule that accelerates as the characters act out their amorous or ambitious fantasies.

The chief delight of this production is in the delicate balance of folly and wisdom, age and youth, madness and sanity. At the heart is the wise fool Feste, perfectly embodied in William Hutt, whose seemingly effortless sallies never fail to provoke laughter and

293

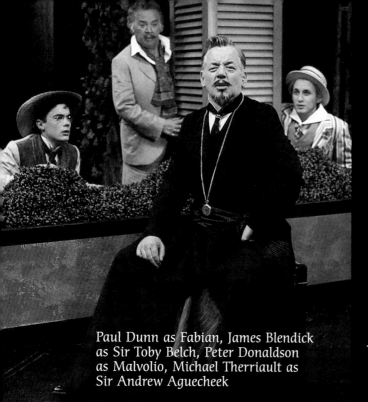

Paul Dunn as Fabian, James Blendick as Sir Toby Belch, Peter Donaldson as Malvolio, Michael Therriault as Sir Andrew Aguecheek

whose bittersweet songs provide a sharp comment on the transience of love and life.

The young lovers are vigorous, impetuous, engaged: Tara Rosling is a fearlessly questing Viola, following her instincts she knows not where; Michelle Giroux a quick, extravagant Olivia, ready for whatever adventure presents itself. She responds to the sudden assault of Nicolas Van Burek's headstrong Sebastian just as Viola cannot resist the intemperate passion of Sean Arbuckle's Orsino.

Set against this is the easy-going, fun-loving, surprisingly graceful spirit of James Blendick's irrepressible Sir Toby and Domini Blythe's capable, inventive, endlessly amused Maria. These amiable, mature pranksters have a deeply felt understanding. They run the show, leading the vain, gullible Sir Andrew of Michael Therriault and the pompous, over-inflated Malvolio of Peter Donaldson to embrace ruin and disgrace with such willful alacrity that we cannot feel sorry for them.

The production is well served by Peter Hartwell's austerely simple set and Francesca Callow's colourful costumes, but most of all by Berthold Carrière's melodic settings of the songs and atmospheric background music that impart both flavour and poignancy to the action as it unfolds. But the chief glory of the production is in the ensemble work of the actors as it brings together veterans and newcomers: the honed skills of mature players setting off the exuberance and energy of youth in an exhilarating mix that augurs well for the future of Shakespeare on the Festival stage and reaffirms our faith in the sheer delight of Shakespeare's comedy.

William Hutt as Feste

Acknowledgements

I am indebted to my friend John Uren for putting the idea of this book into my head and to my good friend Richard Monette for supplying a vast amount of information and much encouragement.

The book is based in part on a great number of conversations and interviews with actors, directors and technical people, some of which took place years ago, some conducted much more recently. The people of the Stratford Festival have been generous in giving me their time and unpacking their memories.

My former colleague Ronald Bryden read the first draft and made some valuable comments and suggestions. My friend Ann Stuart also vetted the text, giving me fresh insights and correcting many inaccuracies.

My editor Ramsay Derry was a sensitive and intelligent counselor and greatly helped me to give the work a more coherent shape while rigorously rooting out inconsistencies and irrelevancies. The copy editor Martin Boyne improved my grammar and punctuation. The opinions expressed are my own. I must also take responsibility for any errors that remain.

I am grateful to Executive Director Antoni Cimolino and to Jane Edmonds and her assistant Ellen Charendoff at the Festival Archives for giving me access to the photographs and to Canadian Actors' Equity for giving me permission to use them. Nora Polley kindly helped me to get in touch with the actors.

Designer V. John Lee assembled the images with insight and ingenuity, creating a book that is a splendid visual tribute to the actors, directors, and designers who have brought Stratford's productions to such vigorous life over the years.

The quotation by Robertson Davies on page 226 is taken from a lecture delivered at Stratford in 1983 and is reprinted by kind permission of Pendragon Ink.

I have drawn on a number of previous books about the Stratford Festival, including scholarly and journalistic histories and personal reminiscences.

Tyrone Guthrie, Robertson Davies and Grant Macdonald, *Renown at Stratford*. Clarke, Irwin & Company Limited, 1953

Tyrone Guthrie, Robertson Davies and Grant Macdonald, *Twice Have the Trumpets Sounded*. Clarke, Irwin & Company Limited, 1954

Robertson Davies, Tyrone Guthrie, Tanya Moiseiwitsch and Boyd Neel, *Thrice the Brinded Cat Hath Mew'd*. Clarke, Irwin & Company Limited, 1955

Herbert Whittaker, *The Stratford Festival 1953-1957*. Clarke, Irwin & Company Limited, 1957

Tyrone Guthrie, *A Life in the Theatre*. Hamish Hamilton, 1960

Joan Ganong, *Backstage at Stratford*. Longmans Canada Limited, 1962

Nicholas Monsarrat, *To Stratford with Love*. McClelland and Stewart Limited, 1963

Peter Raby, ed., *The Stratford Scene, 1958-1968*. Clarke, Irwin & Company Limited, 1968

Grace Lydiatt Shaw, *Stratford Under Cover*. NC Press, 1977

Maurice Good, *Every Inch a Lear, a Rehearsal Journal*. Sono Nisi Press, 1982

Martin Knelman, *A Stratford Tempest*. McClelland and Stewart Limited, 1982

Floyd S. Chalmers, *Both Sides of the Street*. Macmillan of Canada, 1983

Alec Guinness, *Blessings in Disguise*. Hamish Hamilton, 1985

John Pettigrew and Jamie Portman, *Stratford: the First Thirty Years*. Macmillan of Canada, 1985

Tom Patterson and Allan Gould, *First Stage*. McClelland and Stewart Limited, 1987

Diane Mew, ed., *Life Before Stratford: The Memoirs of Amelia Hall*. Dundurn Press, 1989

J. Allan B. Somerset, *The Stratford Festival Story*. Greenwood Press, 1991

Herbert Whittaker, *Whittaker's Theatricals*. Simon and Pierre, 1993

Mavor Moore, *Reinventing Myself*. Stoddart, 1994

Barbara Reid and Thelma Morrison, *A Star Danced*. The Beacon Herald, Stratford, 1994

Fred Euringer, *A Fly on the Curtain*. Oberon Press, 2000

Photographic Credits

The Stratford Festival has been fortunate to have its productions covered by some of the finest photographers in the country, who have created a splendid pictorial record of its work. Photographs in this book are the work of the following artists:

p. 1-2 *The Taming of the Shrew* 1962	Peter Smith & Co.
p. 7 *Colours in the Dark* 1967	Douglas Spillane
p. 14,16 *Richard III* 1953	Peter Smith & Co.
p. 20, 21, 23 *All's Well That Ends Well* 1953	Peter Smith & Co.
p. 35, 36, *Oedipus Rex* 1954/55	Peter Smith & Co.
p. 37 *Oedipus Rex*, 1955	Donald McKague
p. 38, 39 *Medea* 2000	Michael Cooper
p. 51, 52, 53, 55 *Alice Through the Looking Glass* 1994/96	Cylla von Tiedemann
p. 67 Christopher Plummer as Henry V	Peter Smith & Co.
p. 68, 69 *Henry V* 1956	Herb Nott & Co. Ltd.
p. 77, 78, *Tartuffe* 1968	Douglas Spillane
p. 78, 79 *Tartuffe* 2000,	Cylla von Tiedemann
p. 81 *Tartuffe* 1968	Douglas Spillane
p. 82, 83, 84, 85, *The Cherry Orchard* 1965	Peter Smith & Co.
p. 95, 96 *Glenn* 1999	Michael Cooper
p. 105, 106, 107, *The Threepenny Opera* 1972.	Robert C. Ragsdale
p. 108 *The Mikado* 1982	Robert C. Ragsdale
p. 111, 113 *My Fair Lady* 1988	Michael Cooper
p. 122, 123, 125 *Measure for Measure* 1975	Robert C. Ragsdale
p. 133, 134 *Private Lives* 1978	Zoe Dominic
p. 134, 135 *Private Lives* 2001	V. Tony Hauser
p. 142, 144 *Hamlet* 1976	Robert C. Ragsdale
p. 143 *Hamlet* 1957	Robert C. Ragsdale
p. 144 *Hamlet* 1986	Robert C. Ragsdale
p. 145, 146 *Hamlet* 2000	Cylla von Tiedemann
p. 147, 149 *King Lear* 1979	Robert C. Ragsdale
p. 148 *King Lear* 1964	Peter Smith & Co.
p. 150 *King Lear* 1996	Cylla von Tiedemann
p. 162, 163, 164 *A Midsummer Night's Dream* 1993	Cylla von Tiedemann
p. 174, 175, 1/6, *Timon of Athens* 1963/64	Peter Smith & Co.
p. 188, 189, 191 *Long Day's Journey into Night* 1994/95	Cylla von Tiedemann
p. 203, 204, 205, 206 *Love's Labour's Lost* 1961	Peter Smith & Co.
p. 207, 208, 209 *As You Like It* 1977/78	Michael Cooper
p. 210, 211, 212 *The Taming of the Shrew* 1988	Michael Cooper
p. 221, 223, *Camelot* 1997	Cylla von Tiedemann
p. 224, 225 *Pericles* 1973/74	Robert C. Ragsdale
p. 235, 236, 237 *Romeo and Juliet* 1960	Peter Smith & Co.
p. 1987 *Romeo and Juliet* 1987	Michael Cooper
p. 249, 250, 251, 252 *Colours in the Dark* 1967	Douglas Spillane
p. 261, 262, 263 *Elizabeth Rex* 2000	V. Tony Hauser
p. 276, 277, 279 *Waiting for Godot* 1996/98	Cylla von Tiedemann
p. 277 *Waiting for Godot* 1968	Douglas Spillane
p. 292, 294, 296 *Twelfth Night* 2001	Michael Cooper

299

Index of Theatrical Works

Index of Proper Names

300

303

Index of Proper Names